GUS FOSTER

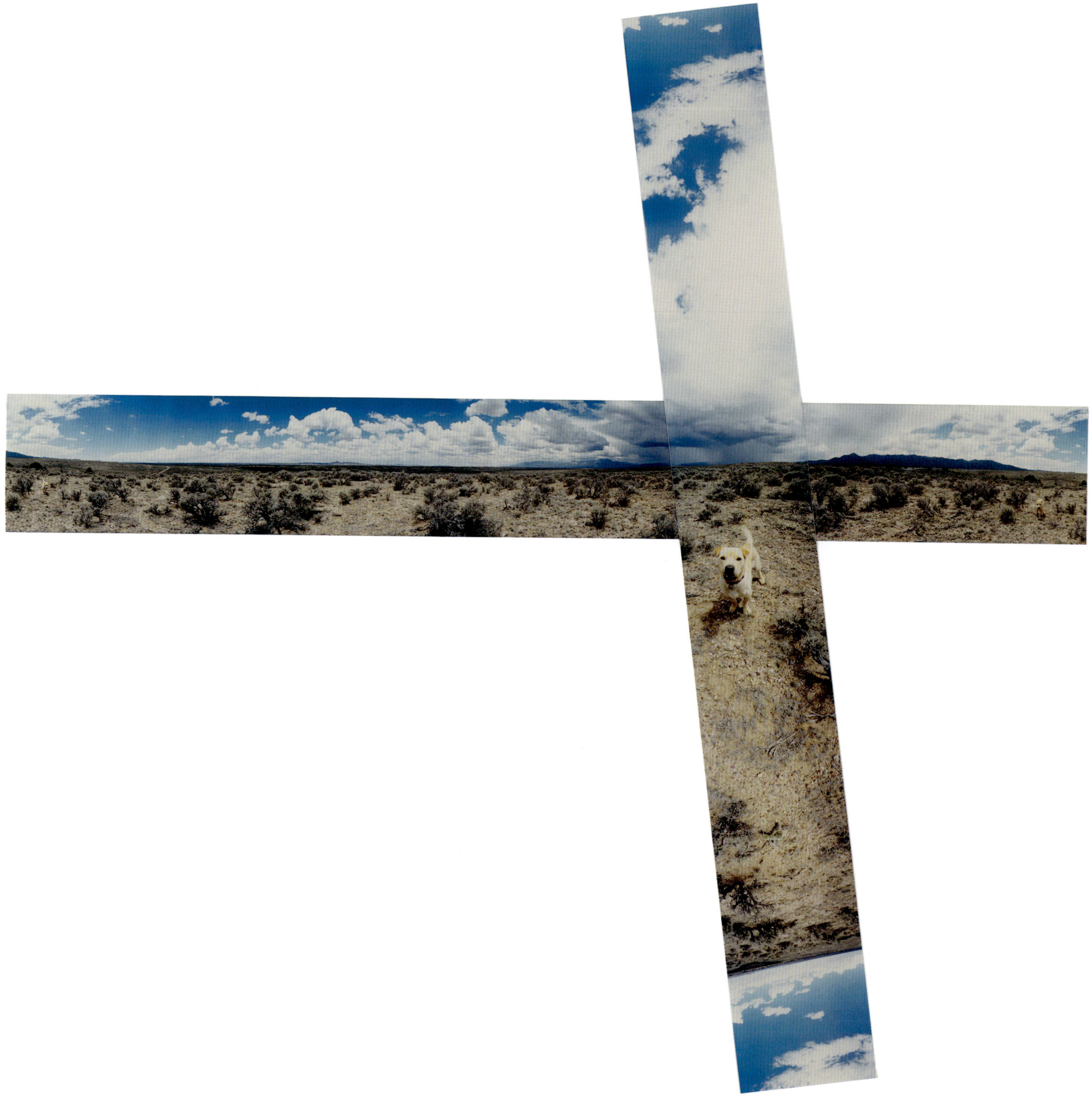

GUS FOSTER | AMERICAN PANORAMAS

ESSAYS BY JAMES L. ENYEART, EDWARD T. HALL, AND EVAN M. MAURER

FOREWORD BY LARRY BELL

MUSEUM OF NEW MEXICO PRESS

SANTA FE

Director: Anna Gallegos
Editorial director: Lisa Pacheco
Art and production director: David Skolkin
Designed by Michael Motley
Composition: Set in Sharp Sans by Sharp Type, NYC
and Trajan by Carol Twombly for Adobe
Manufactured in China
10 9 8 7 6 5 4 3 2 1

Library of Congress Control Number: 2020936681

ISBN 978-0-89013-659-1

Museum of New Mexico Press
PO Box 2087
Santa Fe, New Mexico 87504
mnmpress.org

Frontispiece: *Cyrano: Time Cross, Taos County, New Mexico*, 2004, 392° x 392°
Cover: *Eagle Peak Ridge, Yellowstone National Park, Wyoming*, 1997, 377°

CONTENTS

FOREWORD

LARRY BELL

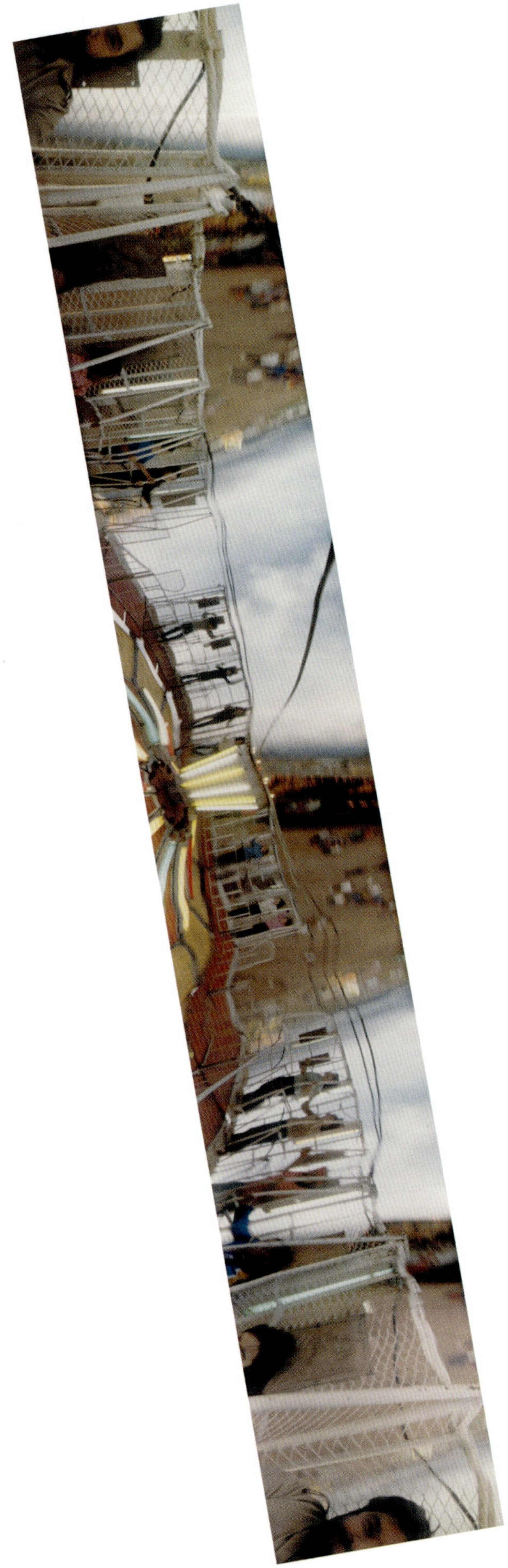

When Gus asked me to write the foreword for this collection of pictures, he sent me a series of memoirs that described various moments of his adventures with panoramic photography. When I look at the pictures, I am totally overwhelmed by the strength of the images and the majesty of the scenes, which convey a love of nature and challenge. In reading the memoirs, I am impressed with the patience that must be sensuous to him, or he would not be climbing 14,000-foot mountains and enduring temperatures of minus 6 degrees Fahrenheit. I hate to be cold! I also have a short fuse for long hikes.

Having spent more than forty years living next door to Gus and knowing his experience with his art form, I am absolutely impressed with his creative drive and inventive style. We are artists of different sensibilities. I have little patience with my media, while Gus is constantly challenged with media-related realities. His cameras are either ancient or brand-new contraptions that suit his creative sensibilities. I recall his tribulations having a special camera built for his panoramic images. The frustration during the twelve years the camera was developed was enormous, and I'm sure he was not expecting the company that made the film for this camera to go out of business and end the useful life of his camera. That twelve-year venture must have been horrendously frustrating.

Fortunately, Gus has a great sense of humor, and his images show it: a panoramic image of a desert landscape with a huge dark cloud covering the entry of the full moon as a dot of light in the center; the silliness of a ride on a roller coaster with the cameraman appearing twice in the center with a sillier grin of pleasure on his face. While much of his work concerns poetic landscapes, he has also developed a series of images that bring time into the picture. These images require the viewer to look carefully at the details of the photo: on one side the image might show an orca leaping out of the water with a trainer on his nose, while the other side shows that the giant creature is no longer in the air. From one side to the other the camera has returned to the original starting point in less than a second. So Gus is able to stretch or compress time within his images.

There is a charismatic voodoo to these pictures, especially the distorted ones. One sees realistic shapes and architecture, but they are woven into a phantasmagorical knot of reality. The images have an "ol' fashion" psychedelic look, as if his camera was born during the hippie days and somehow fell into the hands of someone who knew how to use it in many visual languages.

We all thank you, Gus, for this most interesting visual treatise of your awesome skill.

RELATIVITY RIDE, TAOS COUNTY, NEW MEXICO | 1983 | 360°

A TRAVELER'S NOTEBOOK: RECONSTRUCTING FEELINGS

JAMES L. ENYEART

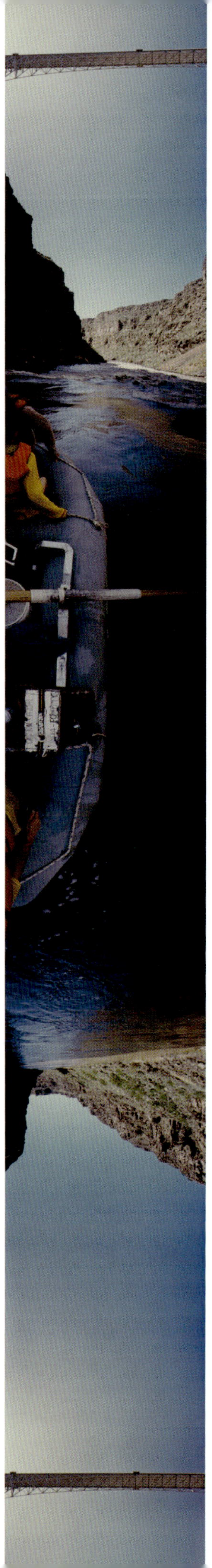

A lifetime of travel places Gus Foster in a succession of artists who have gained insight and inspiration from the exotic and unfamiliar.[1] In the nineteenth century the designation "traveler" was reserved for the idle rich, explorers, or social anarchists such as gypsies, artists, and entertainers. Shared goals—seeking knowledge, expanding opportunity, learning new skills, satisfying curiosity, and most importantly, digging a deeper well of emotional experiences that would mold, explain, and define their personal selves—bonded this unlikely group of travelers. The invention of photography, in the middle of the century, brought the world to everyone's doorstep virtually overnight and also helped stimulate a desire on many people's part to experience foreign lands and cultures firsthand. Photography fueled a new industry in the form of tourism. As transportation simultaneously improved, shortening time and lessening the difficulty required to cover great distances, the concept of being a traveler in the original sense began to lose its distinction of privilege or eccentricity. Traveling because it was possible, rather than as a personal obsession, changed the very nature of travel itself.

Today, people travel regularly to their destinations of choice regardless of distance. Travel itself has created a new vocabulary—commuting, tourism, vacations, and visits. "Visiting" a foreign country for some is an experience similar to visiting Disneyland. Travelers rush to acquire impressions of the unusual and the dramatic; these impressions enhance their sense of worldliness and add to their accumulation of new places, events, and sights, the "rewards" of travel. These modern-day travelers might have become travel minded but are not, for the most part, travelers with an interest in the same philosophical and subjective qualities as the nineteenth-century irrefutable traveler who sought an expanded vision of self.

The exceptions, here in the twenty-first century, are artists such as Gus Foster who express the original traveler's commitment to exploring the potential of new places. These artists reveal a deeper sense of self-awareness and share their insights in the artistic work they produce. As travelers—and the list includes many of the world's image makers—such artists extend the nature of personal experience into the realm of aesthetic experience. The hardship and sacrifice that inevitably accompany the production of works of art know no bounds, but creating art satisfies personal obsession and also gives something of value to the public. Ironically, an artist's selfishness of purpose hides a selflessness that binds art to the public.

Gus Foster first manifested this traveler's motive as an artist in 1972. While driving around California he photographed through his car window, using his camera as a notebook, a record of where he had been. It was for him, as he described to me, "a process which lent itself to self-examination and a means of reconstructing the feelings and experiences of my travels." This experience, photographing through the moving car's window, greatly influenced his later use of panoramic cameras and his exploration of the panoramic technology's inherent philosophic characteristic, time itself.

UNDER THE GORGE BRIDGE, TAOS COUNTY, NEW MEXICO | 1983 | 388°

In 1975 Foster experimented with making films through the moving car's window, films that did not require editing. These films combined the still image as a notebook concept with the moving image's ability to add a sense of time. With these experimental films he discovered his love for the comprehensive, complex element of time intrinsic to photography, an element that was made even more apparent by the moving image of 16mm film and that he later rediscovered in the nature of the panorama photograph. Foster recalls what he felt while making one of his films: "I would drive sixty miles in sixty minutes and make one continuous shot—something in that experience of viewing the world through a car window evoked in me a meditative feeling. One such film was titled *Death Valley Sunrise*. This film began in the hour of predawn blackness, proceeded through twilight over a mountainous ridge on the horizon to the east, to the completion of sunrise—all the while recording the sound of the moving car."

During this time Foster purchased his first panoramic camera, at the suggestion of a friend. He subsequently acquired more and more sophisticated equipment, cameras that can produce negatives of continuous exposure as the camera lens rotates 360 degrees or more. Foster believes that his car window experiments led him to an awareness of the potential of the panoramic photograph and also led him to adopt it as his medium of choice.

Foster and many other photographers are quick to discuss and acclaim the merits of their equipment; they acknowledge the rigorous requirements for making images in especially difficult situations, such as Foster's scaling of mountain peaks. But this essay concentrates on the images, rather than on equipment, process, and technology, with the intent of imparting a deeper understanding of the photographs as idea. All too often visual content in photography is obscured by a fascination with its technology. I do not discount the importance of mastering the uncooperative mechanics of panoramic cameras. But once the vision is in place, an artist's choice of materials and technique are but the price of admission for aesthetic discovery. We may admire the craftsmanship behind process, but we are not confronted with it in our role as viewers. What we see in the final work requires more than admiration. Works of art demand of viewers understanding, empathy, and a willingness to be emotionally and intellectually guided by the artist's ability to reconstruct feelings.

A 1991 project of Foster's revealed the depth of his traveler's approach to making photographs and disclosed the sophistication he brought to making panoramic images. Inspired by the early nineteenth-century woodblock prints of the Tokaido Road by Ando Hiroshige, Foster retraced the route of the fifty-three stations, described by the artist, that dotted the landscape between Tokyo and Kyoto from the eighth century on. He saw in Hiroshige another traveler who memorialized fleeting emotional responses to the beauty of a linear, panoramic landscape (the 300-mile length of the Tokaido Road) and who also used travel to reveal the elements of his aesthetic desire. In a 1993 artist's statement, Foster wrote of the parallels between his scroll-like photographs and the westernized realism in Hiroshige prints: "People are as fascinated by kite flying today as they were then, the rain that fell on paper parasols then falls on today's umbrellas, people that gathered at the shrines for festivals then attend the same rites today. Now the memento is a group photograph at the temple gates. The monumental work made by an artist 160 years ago still speaks today; it was his effort and the panoramic account of life in his time that led to my own journey and an account by a traveler in the late twentieth century."

Foster left Los Angeles in 1975 to move to Taos, New Mexico, where he and the artist Larry Bell bought a studio together. When Foster reflects on the artists he admires, like Hiroshige, who have had some ambient effect on his visual thinking, he includes Larry Bell, Robert Rauschenberg, and Edward Ruscha for their command of their materials and ideas. He also includes photographers Lee Friedlander, Garry Winogrand, Jacques-Henri Lartigue, and Henri Cartier-Bresson, who for him represent time, time as life itself, where the appearance of reality is defined by photography.

In Taos Foster narrowed his interests to the panoramic photograph and began exploring its inherent potential for rendering elements of time, leaving tracings of circumstances in which time past and time present were simultaneously represented at the beginning and the end of an image. Shadows of people and objects revealed the passage of time in an otherwise still and contemplative tableau. He liked the elements of the panoramic process that paralleled his earlier films. A ten-inch-wide roll of film, six feet long, made a negative of a 360-degree panorama, which was comparable to filming a continuous image for sixty minutes at sixty miles per hour. Foster saw and felt a 360-degree turn of time. In the space of its rotation, events and positions of objects had changed and time had its own way with the world and with the making of an image.

In his photographs, Foster's interest in the unpredictable evidence of time's many faces is held in a kind of aesthetic suspension. He combines the variable that he cannot control, time, with his highly visual instinct for pleasurable images. His personal feelings, his reactions to the reality of the moment, imbue the subject matter of his photographs. For the viewer Foster's photographs are silent testaments to the commingling of the eternal nature of time and the very temporal nature of our observation over which it has dominion. Foster reconstructs feelings that merge from the intellect and the emotions simultaneously in stasis. The result is the Zen-like beauty of Foster's panoramas, a beauty that engulfs viewers without explanation, in ways different from most other panoramic images by photographers who focus only on the uniqueness of the technology.

Once in New Mexico, Foster turned into an outdoor person with yet another obsession to embrace, hiking in wilderness country. As he explains it, he became totally immersed in the outdoors not because it was there but because it was everywhere. He was already a student of the work of photographers who preceded him in the artistic pleasures of the majestic and primordial Southwest landscape, William Henry Jackson and Timothy O'Sullivan among them. He felt the lure of the mountains just as they had, because hidden among the snow-capped peaks were visions and vistas not yet seen by the human eye.

Between 1978 and 1981 Foster's approach to selecting and photographing various mountain peaks in the Pecos from both their bases and summits reflected no particular pattern. He made his choices randomly according to where he thought he would like to test himself and his equipment, where the reward might be especially pleasing. Then in 1982 a friend invited him to join him on a hike to the summit of Handies Peak in the San Juan Mountains of Colorado. This 14,000-foot peak turned out to be an oracle of sorts for him. It was, as he told me, "like looking at infinity from all points on the compass—all the world became a single emotion." In these words Foster veritably describes his panoramic photographs of the Rocky Mountain Range from Canada to Mexico. After Handies Peak, Foster returned to the Pecos Wilderness in New Mexico, where he became addicted to "the image," that is, making panoramas that could re-create his epiphanous experience at Handies Peak. A pattern to his choices of images began to emerge as he obsessively set out to climb most of the peaks of the Pecos Wilderness. So, while in his early forties, Foster finally found in nature an experience that exactly matched his intuition for what the panoramic image should contain. For him, the mountain peaks became a single emotion, and the elements of time and observation became a single image.

The extraordinary nineteenth-century photographers Vittorio Sella, Samuel Bourne, and the Bisson Freres studio set the standard for making large-format photographs in the mountains of Europe and India, but it is not their legacy that can be called upon when trying to find images comparable to Foster's, or a comparable passion for photographing at the summit. Certainly the difficulty quotient is present in these nineteenth-century pioneers' works considering they prepared and made large glass-plate negatives in the field. And their keen eyes and aesthetic choices are faultless. But their drummers are too distant and the look of their images too restrained. It is, rather, from the work of a twentieth-century photographer, scientist, mountaineer, artist, and traveler that an artistic endeavor relative to the Rocky Mountain images of Foster is found.

Bradford Washburn (1910–2007), who by age twenty-seven in 1937 was the preeminent mountaineer and photographer of the Alaska Range, also became this country's leading aerial photographer of Mt. Everest in the Himalayas and Alaska's Mt. McKinley. His aerial photographs of mountain ranges from the Alps to New Hampshire's Presidential Range remain the very maps used by climbers to make ascents and plan climbing routes the world over. Washburn continued actively photographing and mapping the world's highest peaks well into his seventies. His achievements are legendary in the scientific world. His photographs, however, were about more than the exacting science and perfectionism required to produce large-format images from the air.

The Museum of Modern Art, the George Eastman House, and the Center for Creative Photography, among many other museums, have included Washburn's photographs in their collections and exhibitions for decades. His work, a forerunner to Foster's, is about the joy and love of high places and about sharing the drama of those singular moments where time is suspended. He, like Foster, was a traveler in the original sense for over half a century, letting no mountain peak of respectable challenge escape his eye or his passion for creating a work of art that does justice to the experience of having been there.

Washburn's and Foster's lives share similarities other than their commitment to photographing mountain ranges. Washburn chose to refine large-format aerial photography while Foster chose the grand panoramic format. Both photographers pushed their tools beyond the expected range of possibility. Both photographers' backgrounds include museum experience. Washburn was director of the Boston Museum of Science for most of his career, and Foster was Curator of Prints and Drawings at the Minneapolis Institute of Art early in his. Their scholarly and educational experiences deepened their understanding of the merits of research and planning in the execution of their photography, helping to lessen the likelihood of failure and the possibility of a fatal accident.

The value of identifying Washburn's work as a significant prototype to Foster's imagery lies in the fact that every good idea needs to be continuously reinvented or it dies. It matters little that these two photographers did not know one another's work. It matters greatly that the world knows that they exist and have taken very different but related paths to unimaginable parts of the world.

Foster refers to himself today as the adopted son of the Rockies and admits that the Rockies are all he needs the rest of his life. At age seventy-nine he will not be climbing Mt. McKinley, but the Rocky Mountain Range remains his metaphor for the panoramic image. Foster describes the Continental Divide as the place where he walked along the spine of the United States. He constructed a pattern from this metaphor by observing that at the top of any given peak in the American Rockies he can see for about one hundred miles. So each new peak he photographed was approximately one hundred miles away. Although such a pattern might seem arbitrary, the photographed peaks can be connected by dots on a map, revealing their own pattern in the making.

With Foster's newest panoramic metaphor and its earlier manifestation on the Tokaido Road, time is once again the leading issue. The geological time that created and placed the Rocky Mountain peaks in their configuration is for Foster becoming real time, stretching into its own measure, forcing a longer view of the elements of time in our lives. Here in this book is the broadest possible view, a true panoramic vision, of what it is like to see time turn back upon itself.

Note

1. This essay originally appeared in *The American Rockies: Photographs by Gus Foster* (Albuquerque, NM: Albuquerque Museum, 1999), published in conjunction with the exhibition of the same title at the Albuquerque Museum, May 16–August 22, 1999. It has been lightly edited for this book.

VISUAL MYSTERIES AND BEAUTIFUL JOURNEYS: THE PANORAMIC PHOTOGRAPHS OF GUS FOSTER

EVAN M. MAURER

The most beautiful thing we can experience is the mysterious.

– Albert Einstein

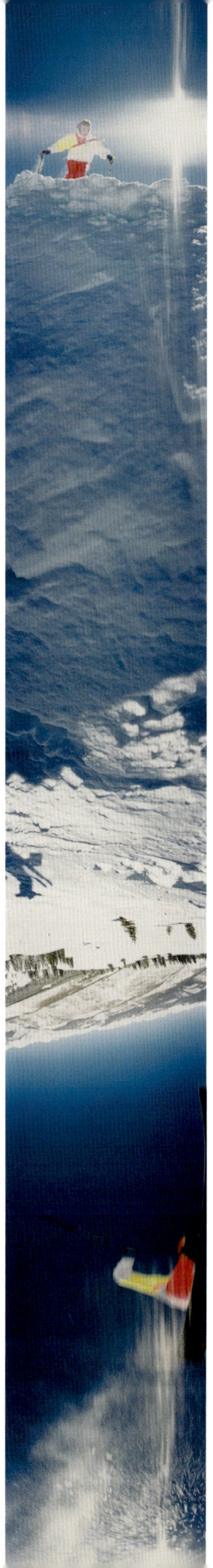

Photography must be acknowledged as the most mysterious of the arts. With gears, springs, and finely ground glass lenses, the camera captures an image using light projected onto a sheet of blank paper. Through an alchemical process, the image appears and the world can be held in your hand.

There are many ways to make a photograph, but they all produce what we can see in front of our eyes. Gus Foster takes that even further by showing us more than we can possibly see as his panoramic camera turns in a circle; at one glance, you can see everything around you—to infinity from any point on the compass.

As Gus told me, "It's like having eyes in the back of your head." The 360-degree image before you demands a greater suspension of disbelief to make this visual illusion work. As you approach one of Foster's panoramic landscapes, you assume that the image is like all other photographic images—a flat facsimile of what is before you.

Then, as you move nearer and can examine the photo more closely, you are hit with a visual and metaphysical conundrum. The tree on the left margin is the same tree on the right margin. You have stepped into a time warp in which you forfeit your ordinary conception of the "reality" of the image. You are no longer looking at what is in front of you but also what is behind you. At this point, you are asked to stand in the middle of the landscape and believe that the edges of the image actually wrap around you. As the viewer you are in the metaphysical realm, where 180 degrees is what you see in reality but only half of what is revealed in the photograph; to accomplish the illusion of space, the viewer must become an essential element that completes the work of art.

It was Foster's antiquarian interests that initially led him to experiment with an early-twentieth-century panoramic camera, the Cirkut, invented in 1902. These cameras had been used to create the famous long-format panoramas of large groups of people, from army regiments to civilian group portraits. But for Foster, the most intriguing and fascinating images were the early landscapes of the mountain West by Carleton Watkins, Timothy O'Sullivan, and W. H. Jackson, documenting the majestic vastness of the Rockies.

In 1979, Foster began mountain climbing but photographed only a few mountains with the Cirkut as it was exceedingly heavy and cumbersome to deal with in alpine terrain. In 1985, Foster started using the Globus-Holway camera, a state-of-the-art invention with the same uses as the Cirkut, but capable of much larger photographs. This newer model, one of only three then in existence (the other two belonging to the inventors, Globus and Holway), could produce images of 360 degrees or more. Foster was fascinated by this perceptual enigma, and he was able to use the camera in ways that went far beyond its initial purpose. As Foster became more familiar with its possibilities, his artistic vision was to create images that could

KJESSEL KJUMPING, EAGLE COUNTY, COLORADO | 1989 | 433°

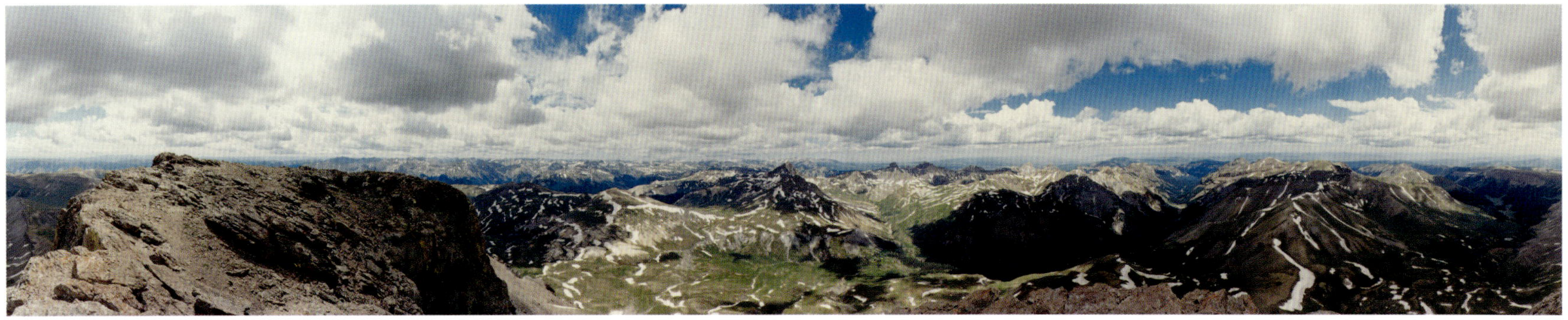

have an extraordinary presence when printed in large scale. First there were prints measuring eight feet long and, later, prints of twelve and even sixteen feet. Their extraordinary physical and emotional presence engages the viewer in a unique dialogue not only with the photo and the natural spaces and forms it represents, but also with issues of time and perspective.

MOUNTAINS | Never a man to do things by halves, Foster began a multi-year project to hike to the summits of seventy-five mountains, including the most spectacular of the Rockies that rose above fourteen thousand feet. There were few trails to these peaks. The camera, tents, equipment, and provisions had to be packed into a base camp; on the day of the climb the camera and tripod were carried to the summit. He essentially did things the way his nineteenth-century predecessors had, a test of physical endurance in the service of art. Starting at age forty, it took Foster many months of training and research to do these trips. He initially had climbing partners who helped haul the gear; then as the trips became more distant, lengthy, and complex, two burros were added, and in the last years a pack goat named William Henry, after William Henry Jackson, the great pioneer photographer of the West. It often took a few days to reach a base camp, then a day to summit, make the shot, and descend, then trek back out to the road to travel to the next location. His most frequent climbing partners were Tom Simons, Roger Badash, and John Chamberlain, with other family and friends joining the group from time to time. The burros (over succeeding

UNCOMPAGHRE PEAK, COLORADO | 1993 | 364°

generations) were Stewball and Maggie, then Maggie and her offspring Sidney, and finally, Chico and Angel. William Henry was the final addition to the crew in 1995.

In certain situations Foster had only a short period of time to set up his complex equipment and take what might be the single chance to make a photo. At such high altitudes, the air is thinner, and each breath, each step, is an effort. As he told me, "It's kind of an internal challenge to go see those places. Simply because, you know, what other fool would try to lug a sixty-five-pound camera to that elevation? It was just nuts."

But it was a sublimely foolish enterprise that yielded spectacular results. In many ways the entire undertaking can be understood as a piece of performance art, one in which we can share in the summit—where, in clear weather, you can see 100 miles to the horizon that surrounds you.

Foster has brought us to the metaphorical "top of the world," a place that has been sacred to ancient cultures around the planet. From the ziggurats of Mesopotamia to the massive pyramids of Egypt and ancient Mexico, humans have desired to rise increasingly farther from the surface of the earth and ascend to a place closer to the heavens, home of their gods and spirits of natural power. Foster's mountain panoramas take us to higher places, in which we are closer to these spirits.

The panoramas Foster was able to make at these altitudes are sharply detailed. The clean air and strong light produce a wealth of visual information: aspects of the stone canyons, huge boulders, crags, and cracks that make up these monuments to the awesome power of nature. In the nineteenth century, these mammoth mountains would have been described as sublime landscapes, creating a visual and emotional experience that carries the human spirit to a higher level of consciousness and inspiration. With his extraordinary efforts, Foster's panoramic photographs of inherently challenging places made him a true aesthetic adventurer. He devoted a good deal of his life to fulfilling his goals as an artist, and we are fortunate to be witnesses to his journey.

TIME | One usually thinks of a photograph as holding a single frozen instant of time, the split second of an exposure, often a hundredth of a second or less. Making panoramic photographs changes the split-second nature of photography. From 1982 to 2004, Foster used a small, newly invented 35mm camera called a Globuscope to make what he called "Time Photographs." This handheld device made a 360-degree revolution in .8 seconds—compared to the nearly 40 seconds for his large camera—and would continue exposing film as long as the trigger was engaged. This resulted in continuous, multiple 360-degree images that recorded the changing events of passing time.

Foster explained, "Most of the time, one looks at a photograph without the necessity of a direction, the need for a beginning or an end—the information is simply there. These photographs, because the element of time is present, need to be seen in the same sequence as the events occurred, from left to right." Time and space are intermeshed, as in *Time to Disappear*, in which the story is told in less than a second. Another example, *Antiques Roadshow Nebraska*, is a panoramic record over a longer period of time, 2.4 seconds, which is further complicated as the camera is moved through space—in a moving vehicle—while completing three circuits. This panorama records the result of two movements: the forward motion of the camera down the road and its simultaneous revolution around a pivot point. In this case, the storytelling is accelerated, as the participants in the tale are moving toward each other at highway speeds. These distorted images engage your imagination as they stretch your perceptions, challenging you to comprehend this new image of time, space, and speed.

Foster felt he was onto a new method of representation but was astonished when, on a visit to the Asian galleries of the Museum of Fine Arts, Boston, he came upon a fourteenth-century Chinese scroll painting that used the same methodology. The twenty-foot-long scroll, a minimally painted black-and-white landscape, included the figure of a monk or poet in a red robe, who appeared repeatedly every three feet as if representing a narrative of the periods of his life. Having thought he'd discovered a new way of telling a story, Foster was abashed to learn that an artist sitting on a mountaintop six hundred years ago had been there first.

FOOD | As Foster's fifteen-year project photographing the American Rockies reached its culmination in the late 1990s, he began to think about other aspects of the American landscape, about the vast acreage devoted to the production of food in the United States, and the fact that the country was often called the breadbasket of the world. About a billion acres of land in this country are currently in agricultural production, somewhere around 44 percent of the American landmass. The big three—corn, wheat, and soybeans—each have a distinctive visual footprint as one moves across the landscape, so Foster began seeking out and photographing individual crops across the lower forty-eight states.

In 1998, he was asked to participate in a national exhibition and symposium contemplating the status and significance of life in the United States as the millennium approached. Foster's contribution was to focus on the look and production of food in this country, and one of the ideas he entertained was what a typical Thanksgiving meal might look like from the viewpoint of where it was grown and the landscape that produced it. Foster explained, "Imagine if you will a menu: oysters, turkey, stuffing, potatoes, wild rice, corn, salad, cranberry sauce, pecan or pumpkin pie, fresh raspberries, etc., and consider where all those items came from." For the next decade, often while on his annual pilgrimage to the Northwoods, he looked for distinctive food landscapes. Foster made an odyssey from coast to coast and from the Canadian border to the Gulf of Mexico to photograph food—sugarcane in Louisiana; cranberries, Holstein cattle, and a pumpkin patch in his native Wisconsin; oysters and Chardonnay in California; Texas wheat; Nebraska corn; Iowa soybeans; and pecan groves in Georgia. Stops at a hot-dog factory in South Dakota and a free-range chicken farm in Minnesota further filled the cornucopia. When possible, Foster placed his camera in the middle of these fields of production so the images would reflect an infinity of food from the nearest plant to the far horizon.

Foster's panoramic images, from the towering Rocky Mountains to vast open farming spaces, literally embodied the poetic images of one of our most enduring patriotic songs, "America the Beautiful," written by the poet Katherine Lee Bates, inspired by her 1895 ascent to the top of Pike's Peak in Colorado:

O beautiful for spacious skies
For amber waves of grain
For purple mountain majesties
Above the fruited plain . . .

Bates's verses extol the boundless spaces that became a critical aspect of America's self-image, and this ideal terrain is captured anew in Gus Foster's panoramic photographs. He is a major figure of the genre, and we are indebted to his powerful new aesthetic perspective for placing us in the center of this world that we inhabit, often without being fully present, and challenging our perceptions of it.

From twenty years into the twenty-first century, when Photoshop, deepfake technology, and cell-phone cameras have changed how we can record our visual culture, Gus Foster's analog adventures and artifacts testify to his curiosity, creativity, and utter tenacity in the pursuit of his artistic vision. Viewers don't need to know the difficult travel and technical innovations behind the images to appreciate their scale and beauty. His panoramas are masterpieces that boldly express the magnificence of the North American continent. Today, you may be able to take a panorama with your cell phone, but like the red-robed monk depicted on the fourteenth-century Chinese scroll painting, Foster was there a long time ago and did it the hard way.

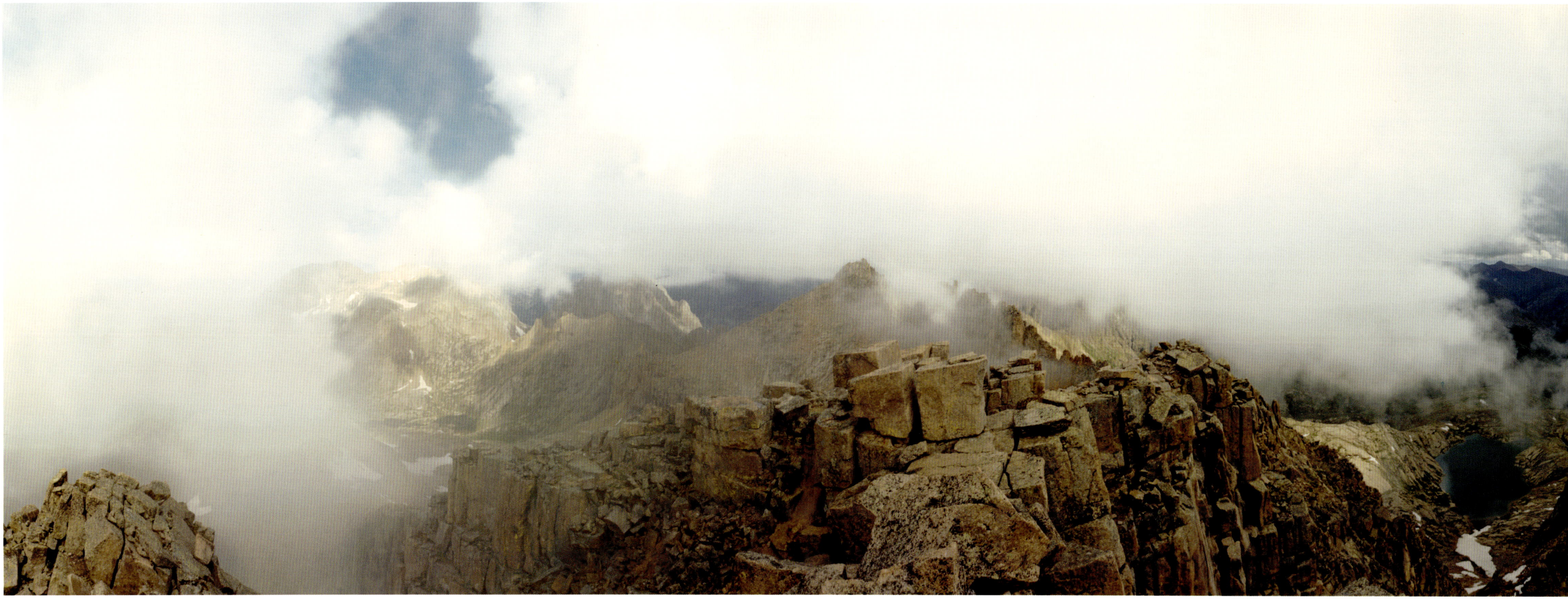

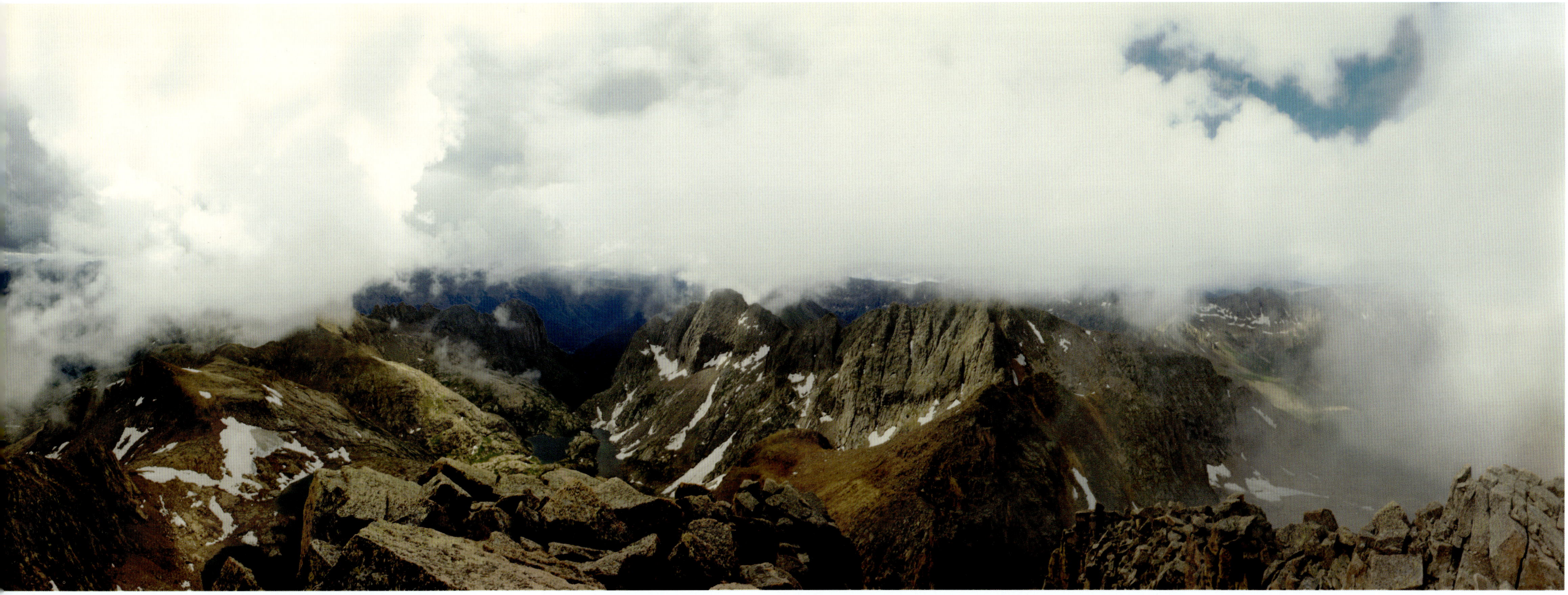

1 | WINDOM PEAK, WEMINUCHE WILDERNESS, COLORADO | 1989 | 378°

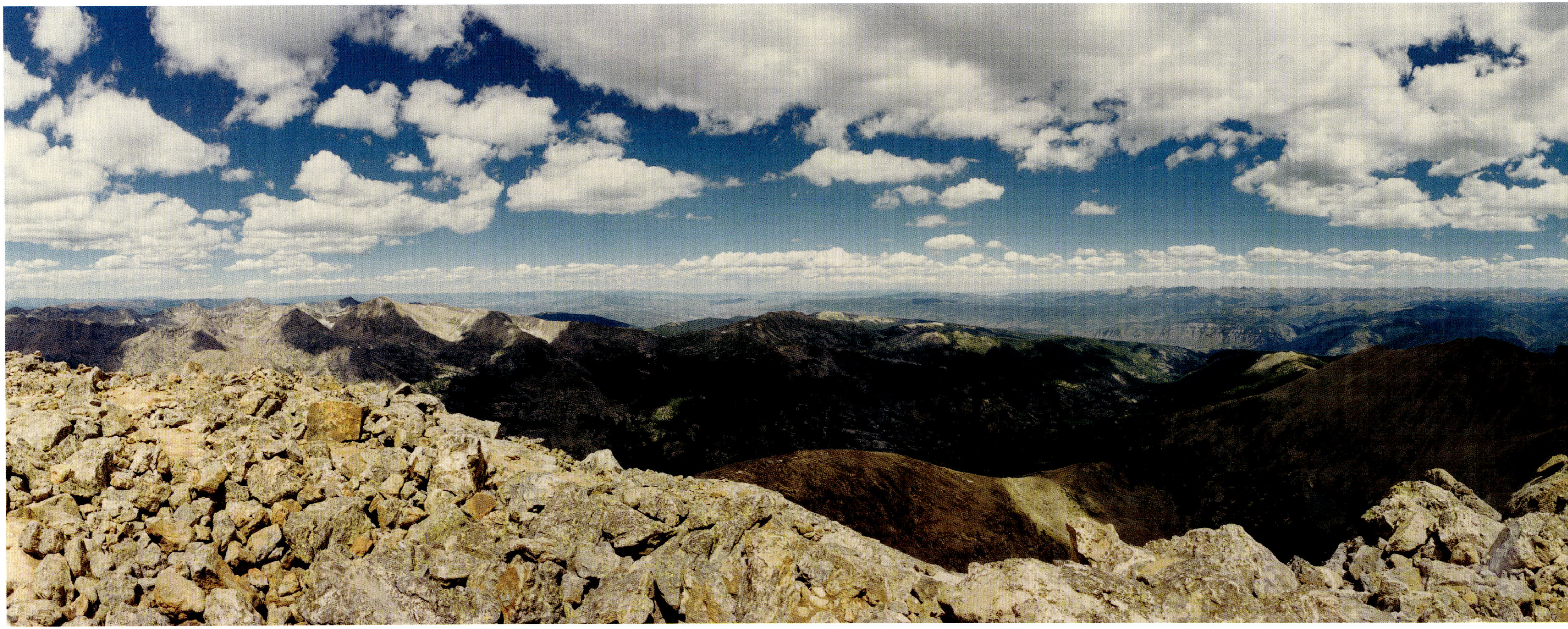

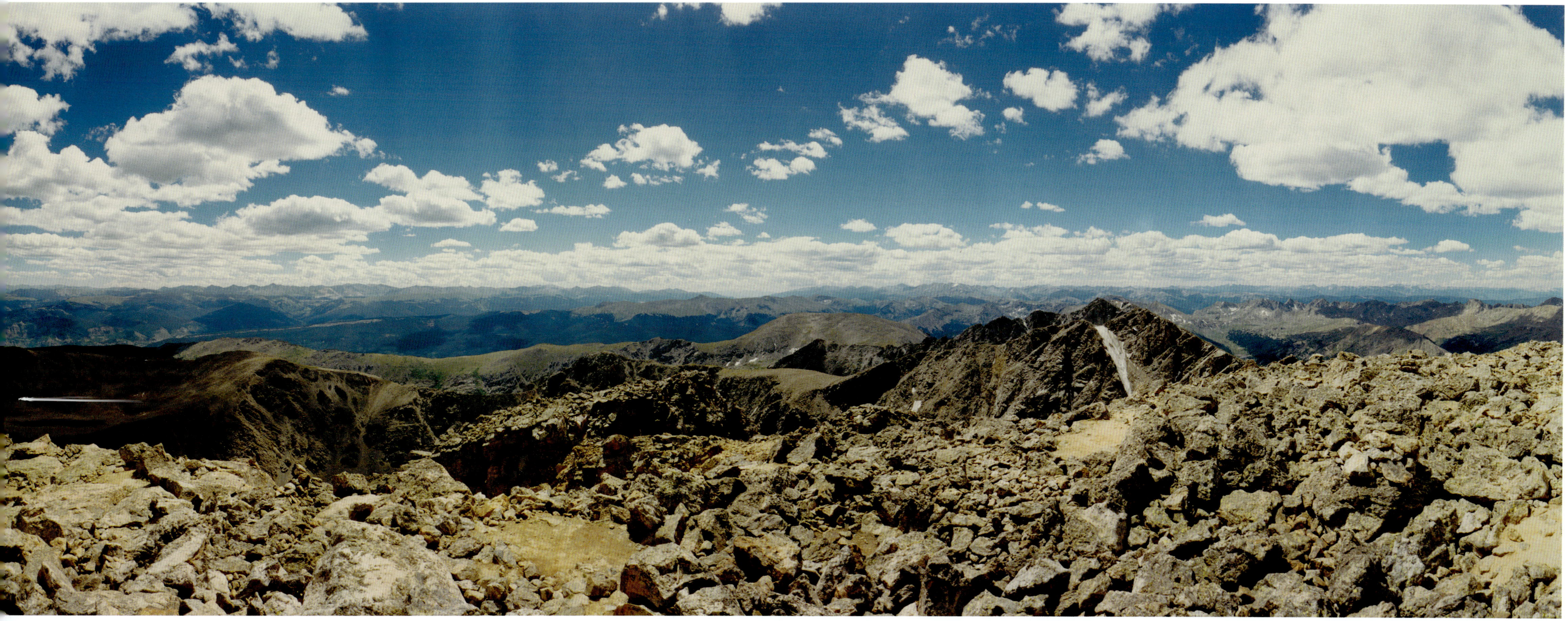

2 | MOUNT OF THE HOLY CROSS, COLLEGIATE PEAKS WILDERNESS, COLORADO | 1988 | 361°

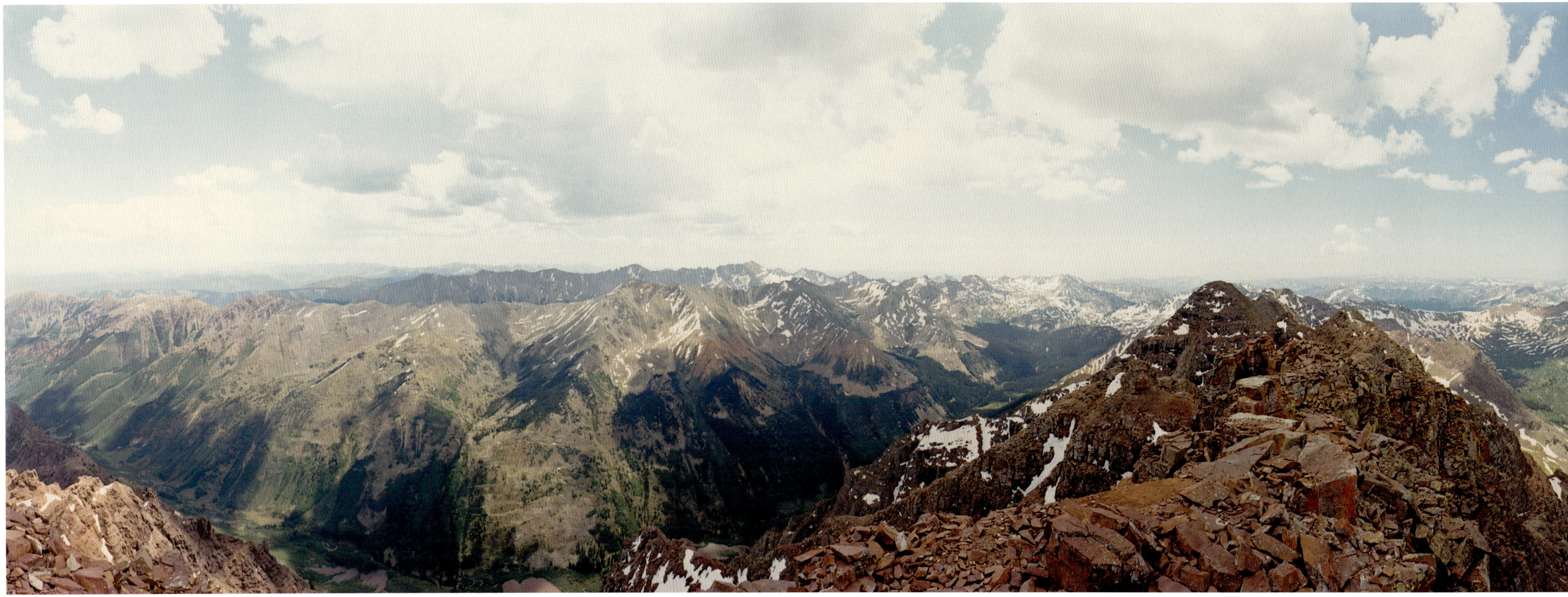

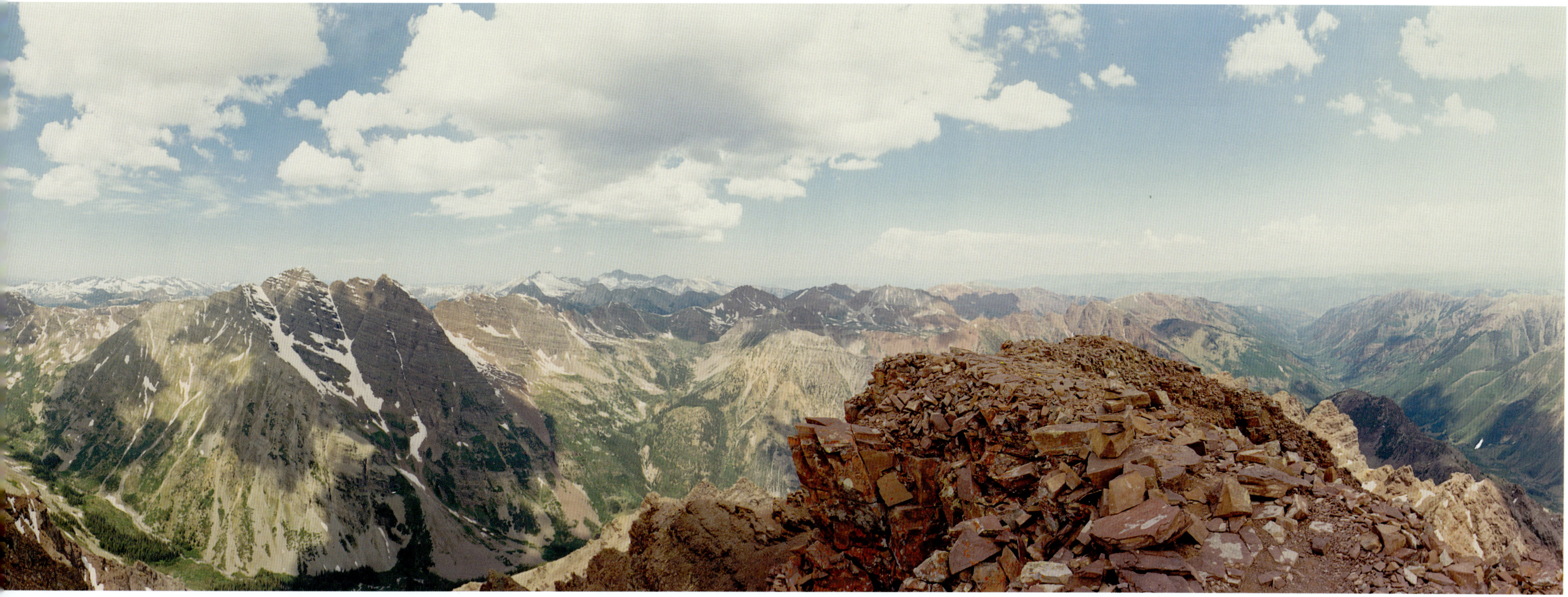

3 | PYRAMID PEAK, MAROON BELLS-SNOWMASS WILDERNESS, COLORADO | 1989 | 381°

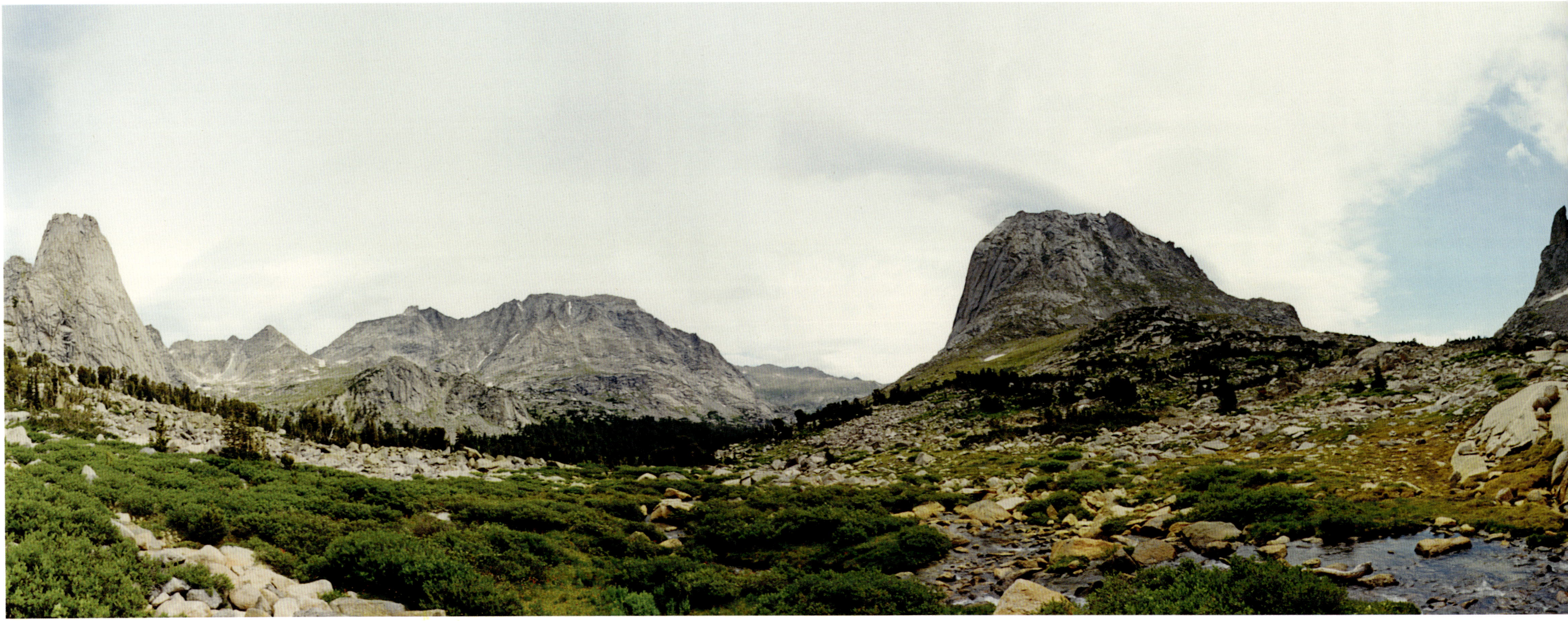

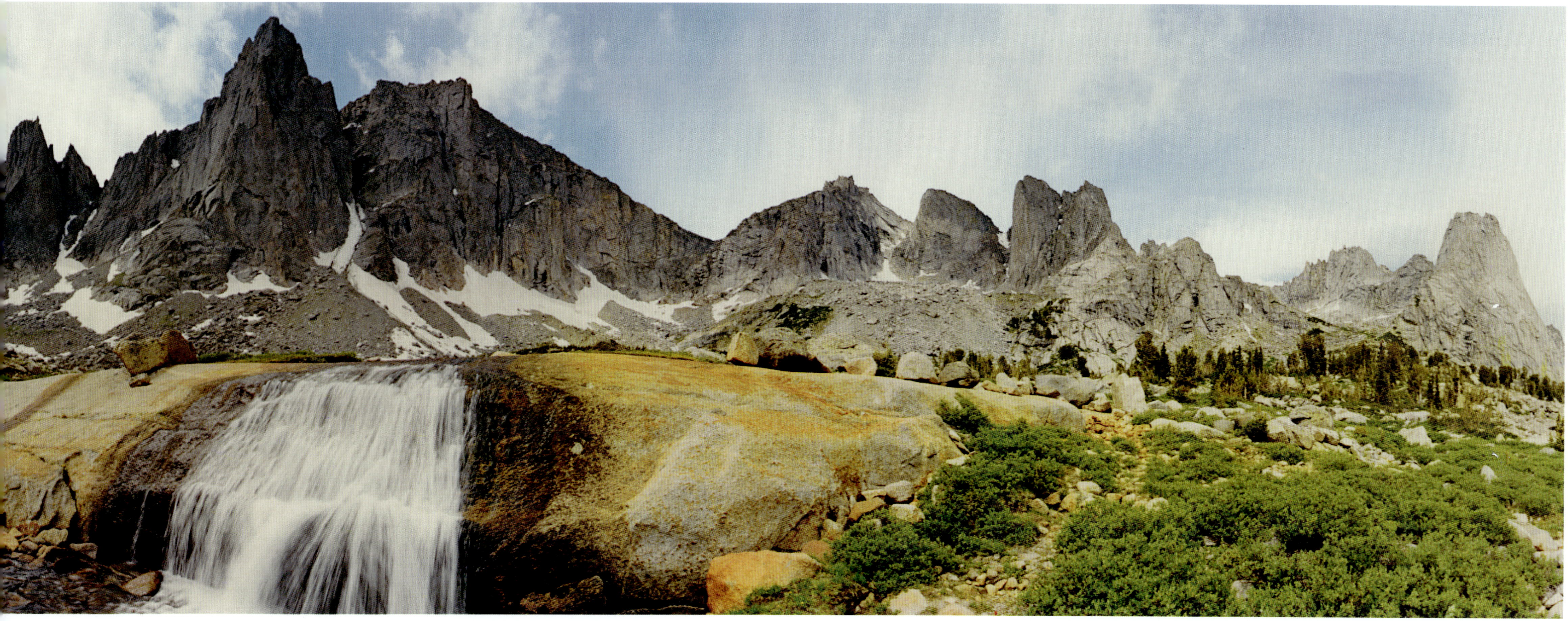

4 | CIRQUE OF TOWERS, BRIDGER WILDERNESS, WYOMING | 1990 | 380°

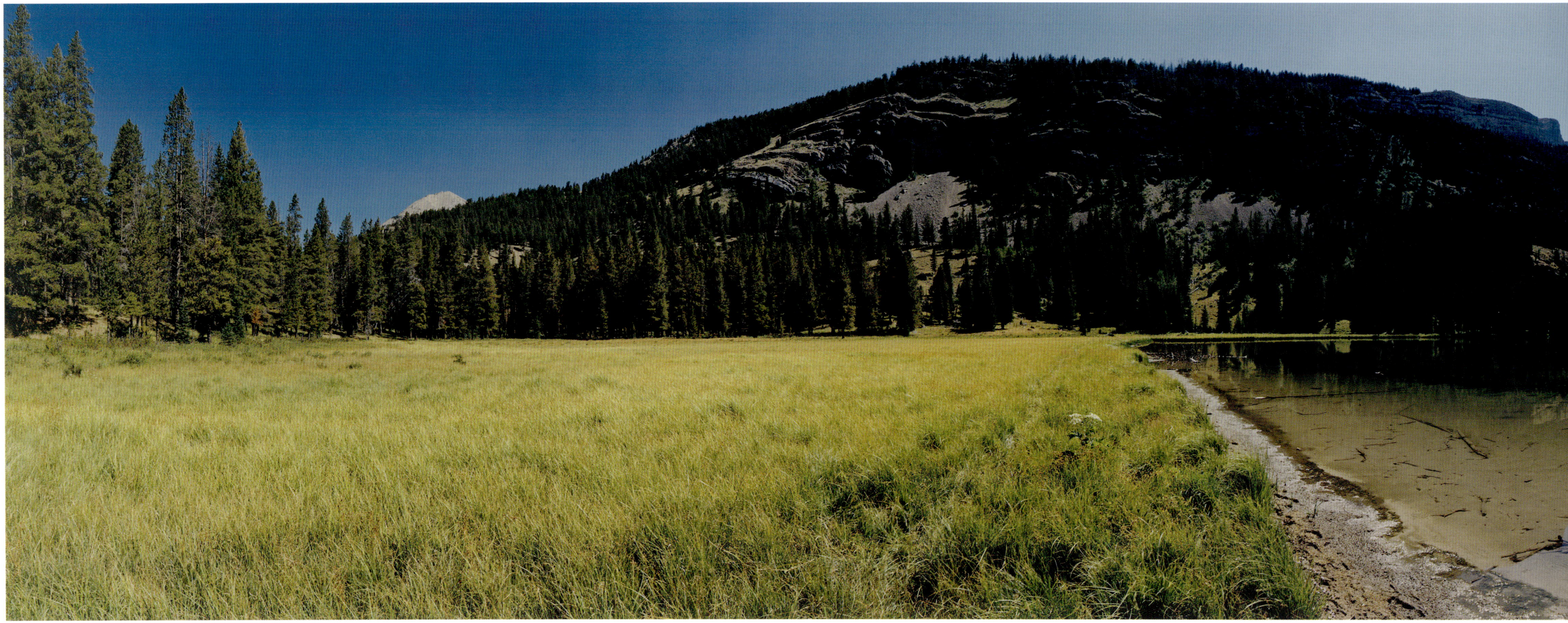

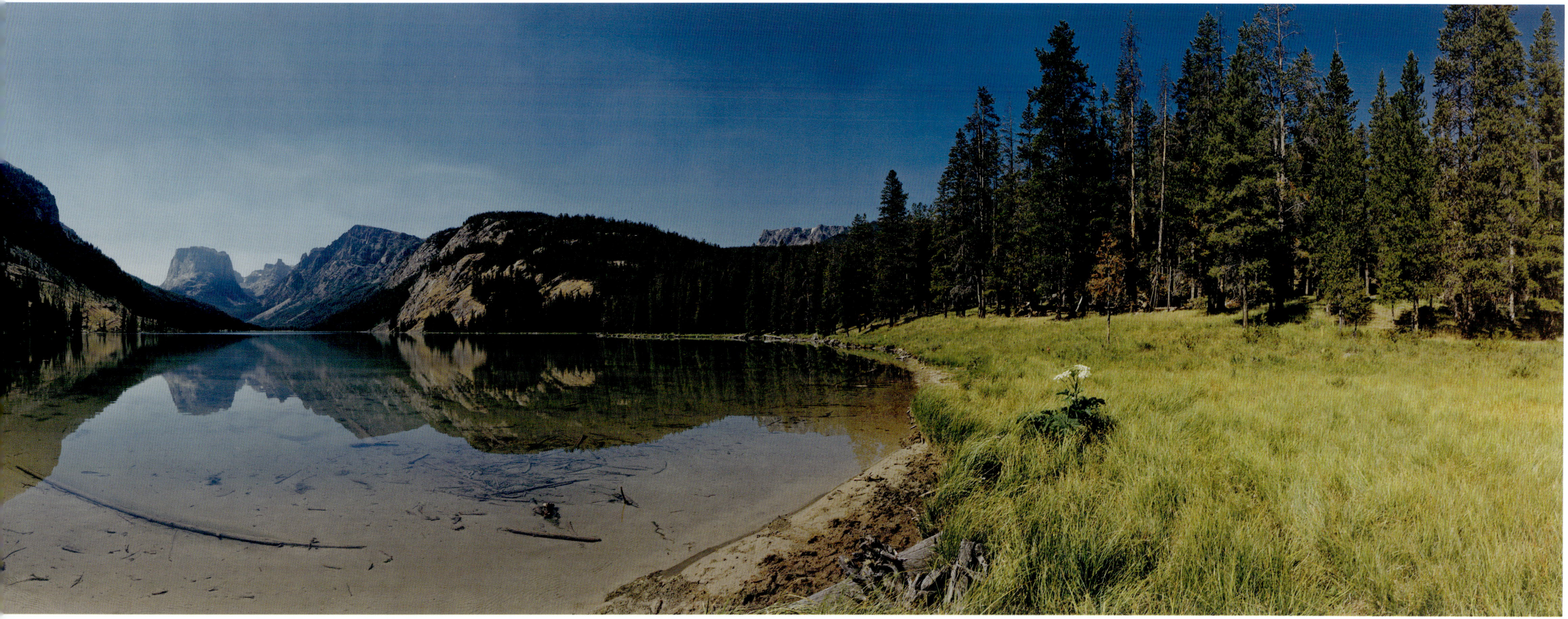

5 | GREEN RIVER LAKES, BRIDGER WILDERNESS, WYOMING | 1994 | 383°

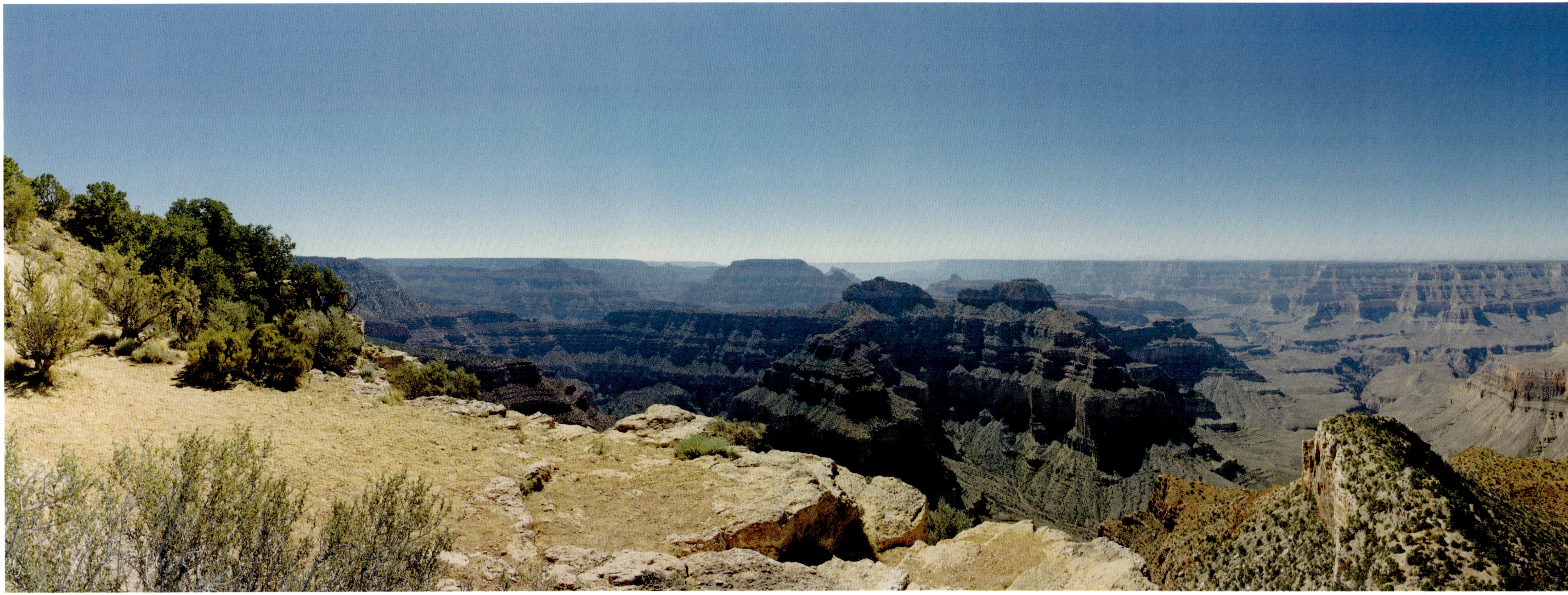

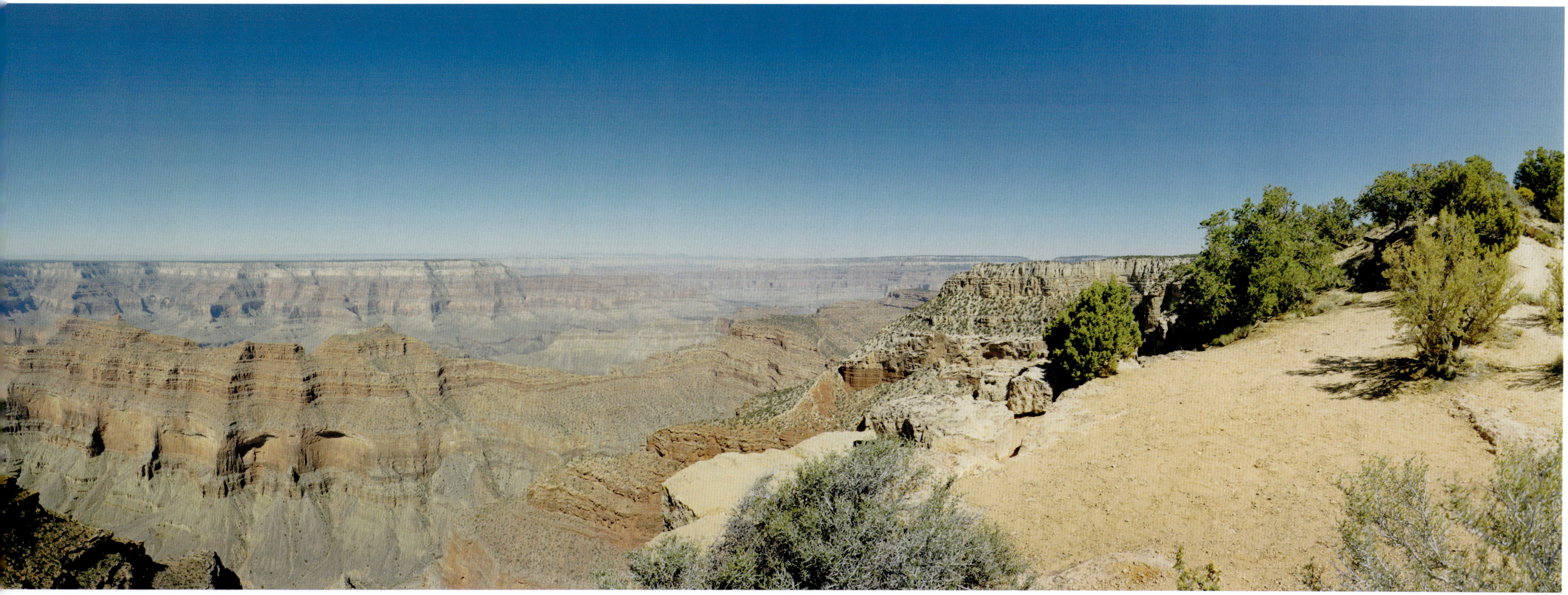

6 | POINT SUBLIME, GRAND CANYON NATIONAL PARK, ARIZONA | 1990 | 360°

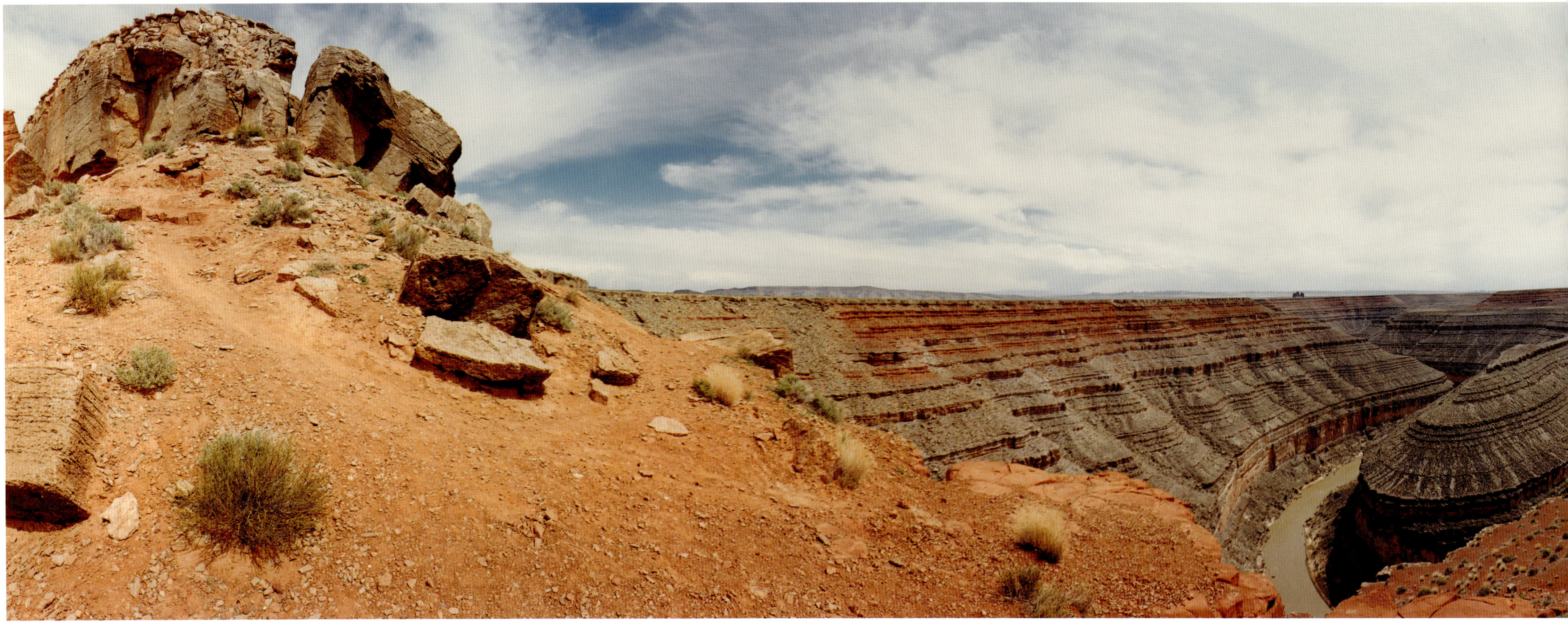

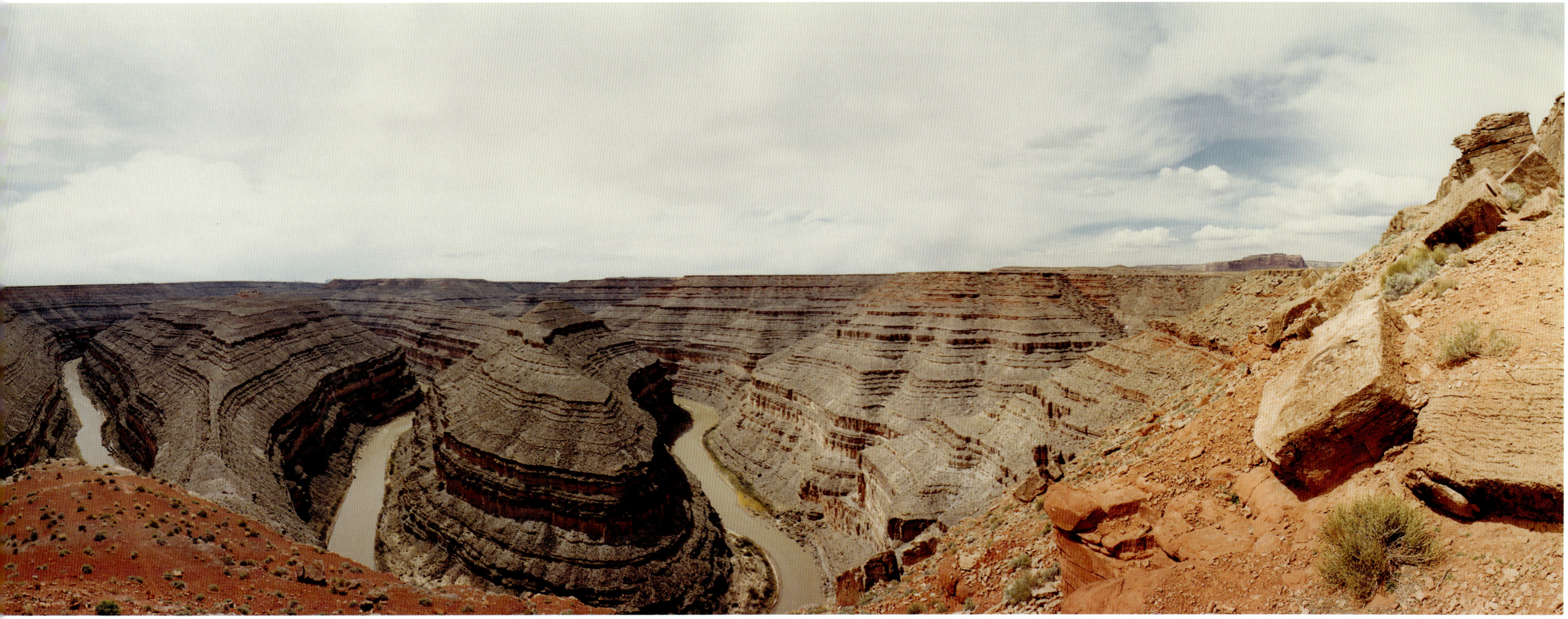

7 | GOOSENECKS OF THE SAN JUAN, SAN JUAN COUNTY, UTAH | 1995 | 365°

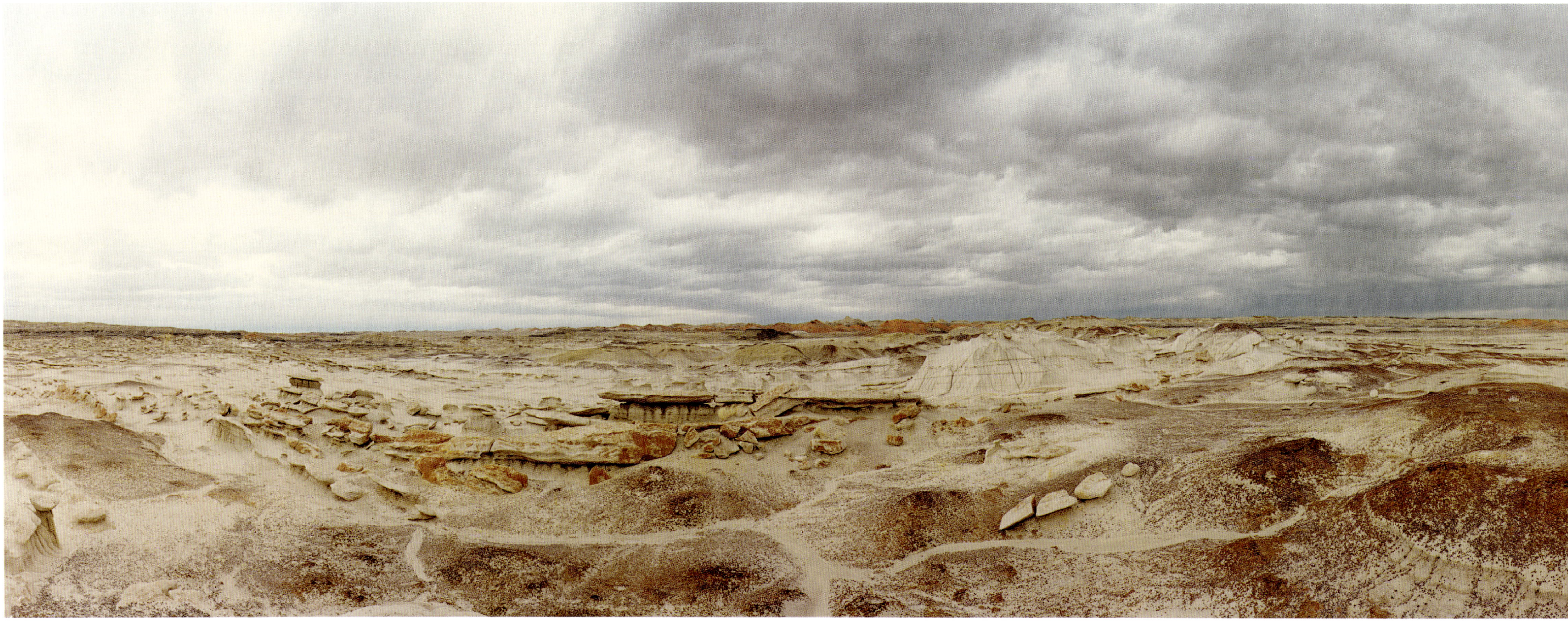

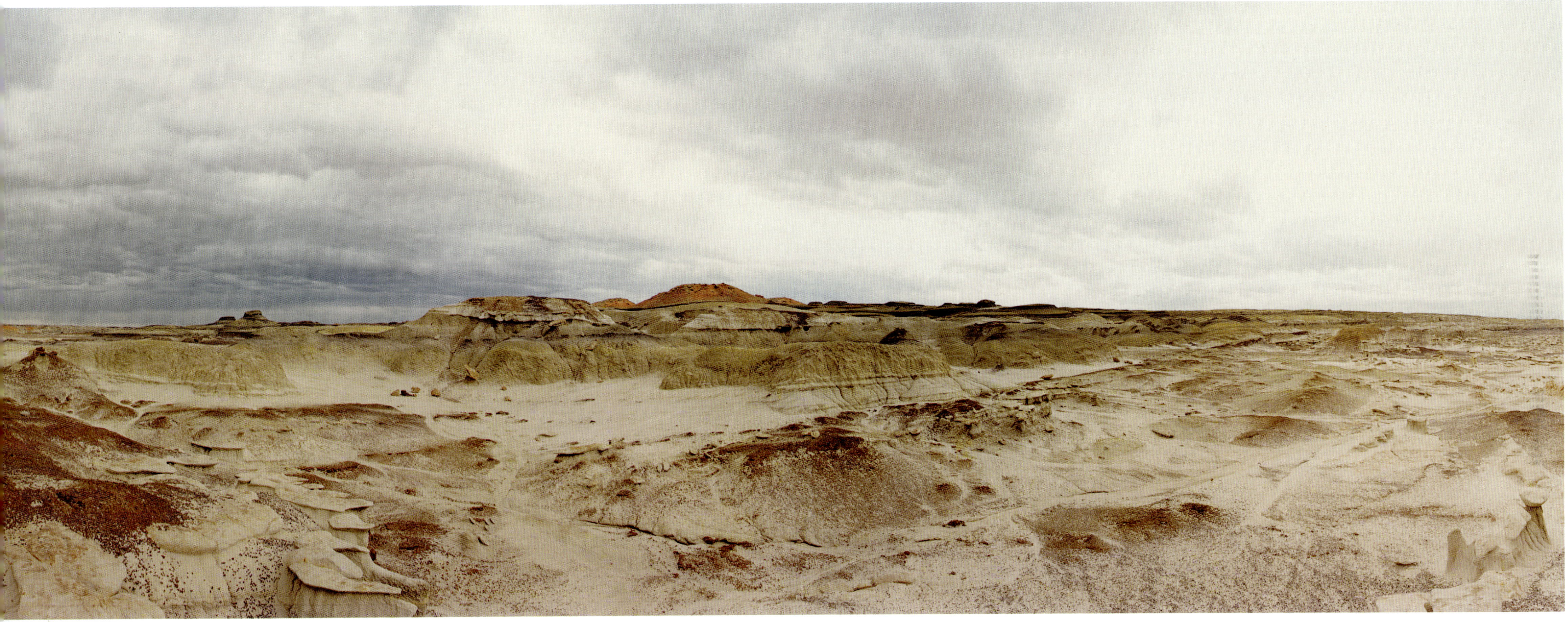

8 | BISTI / DE-NA-ZIN WILDERNESS, NEW MEXICO | 1995 | 368°

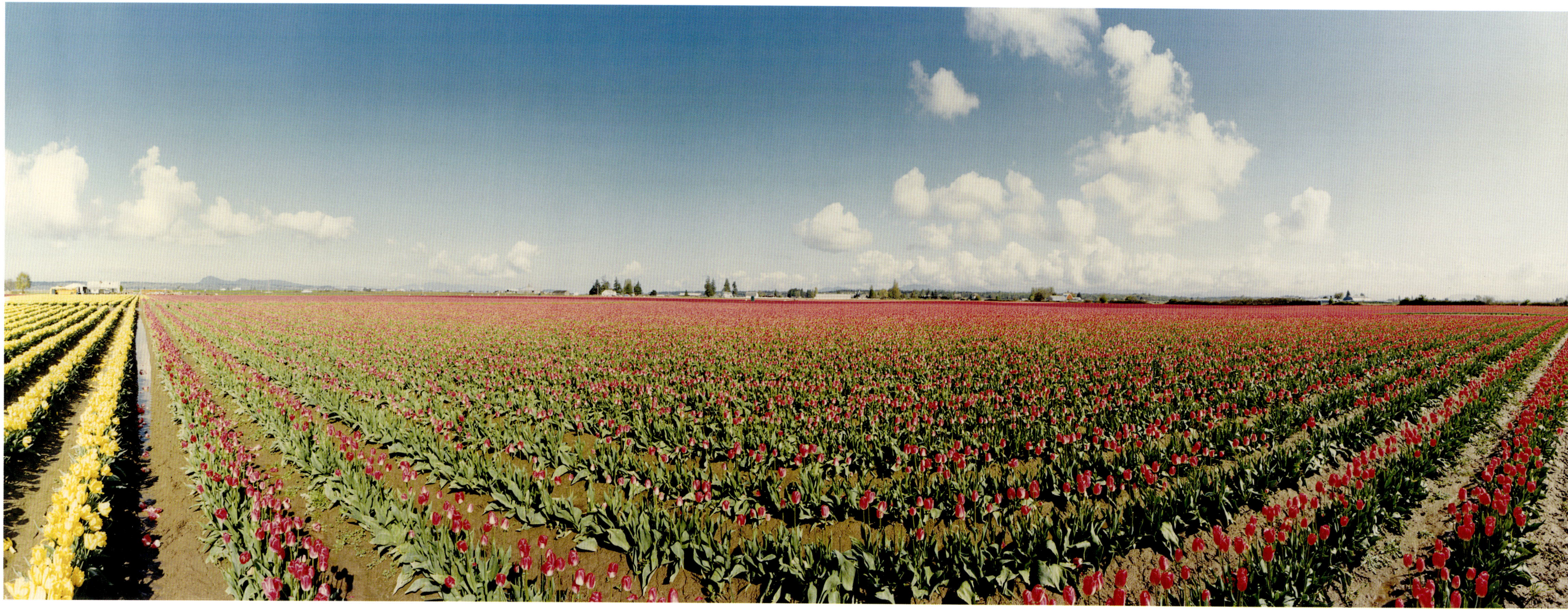

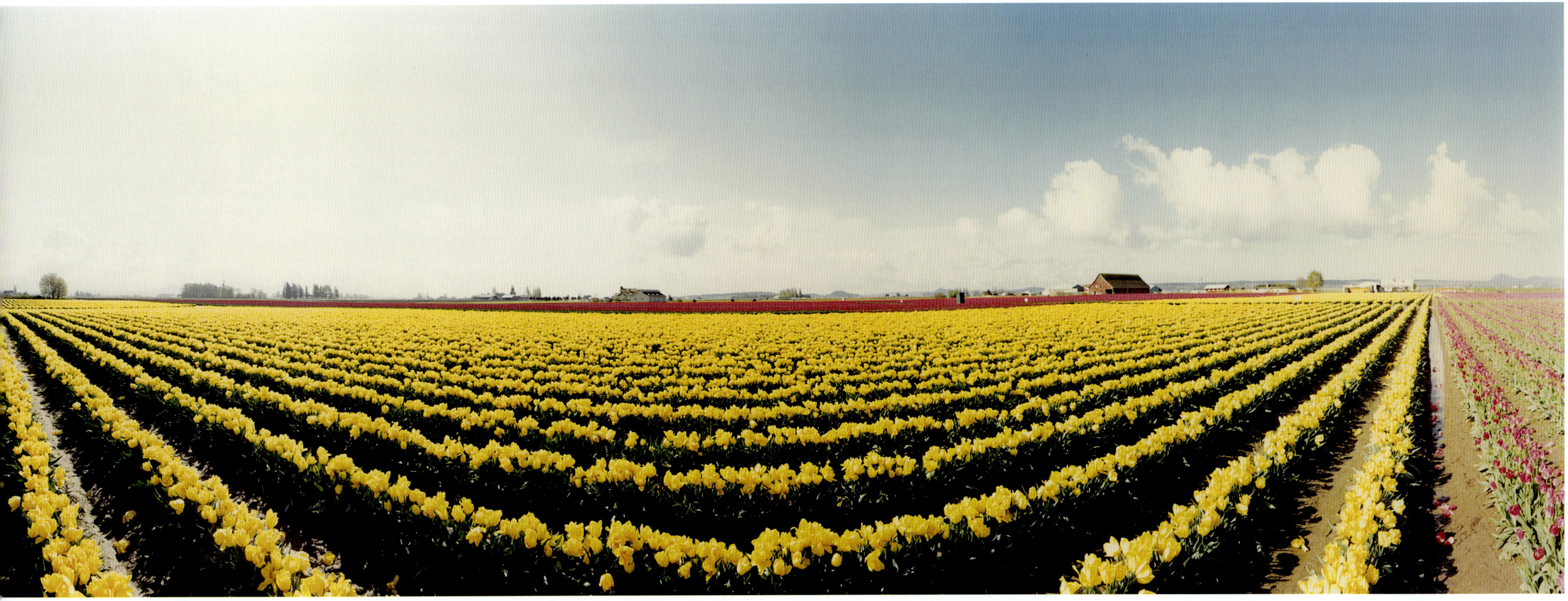

9 | TULIPS, SKAGIT COUNTY, WASHINGTON | 1995 | 393°

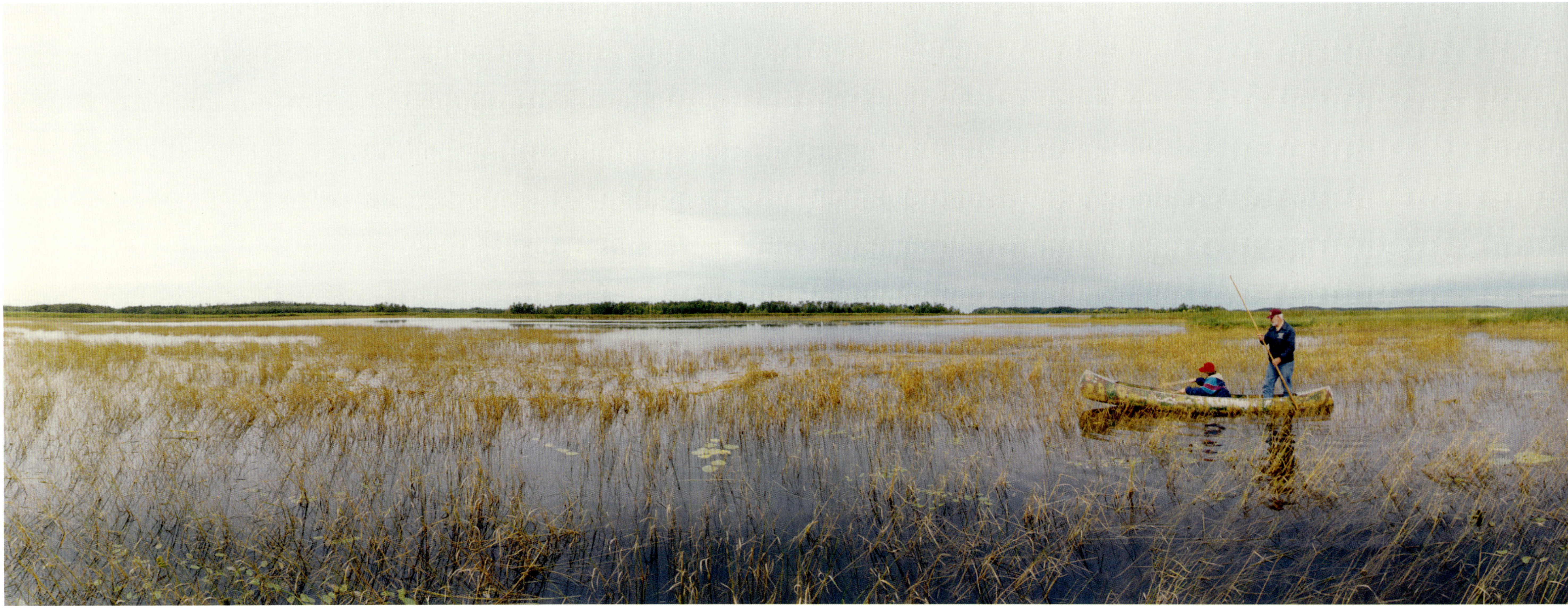

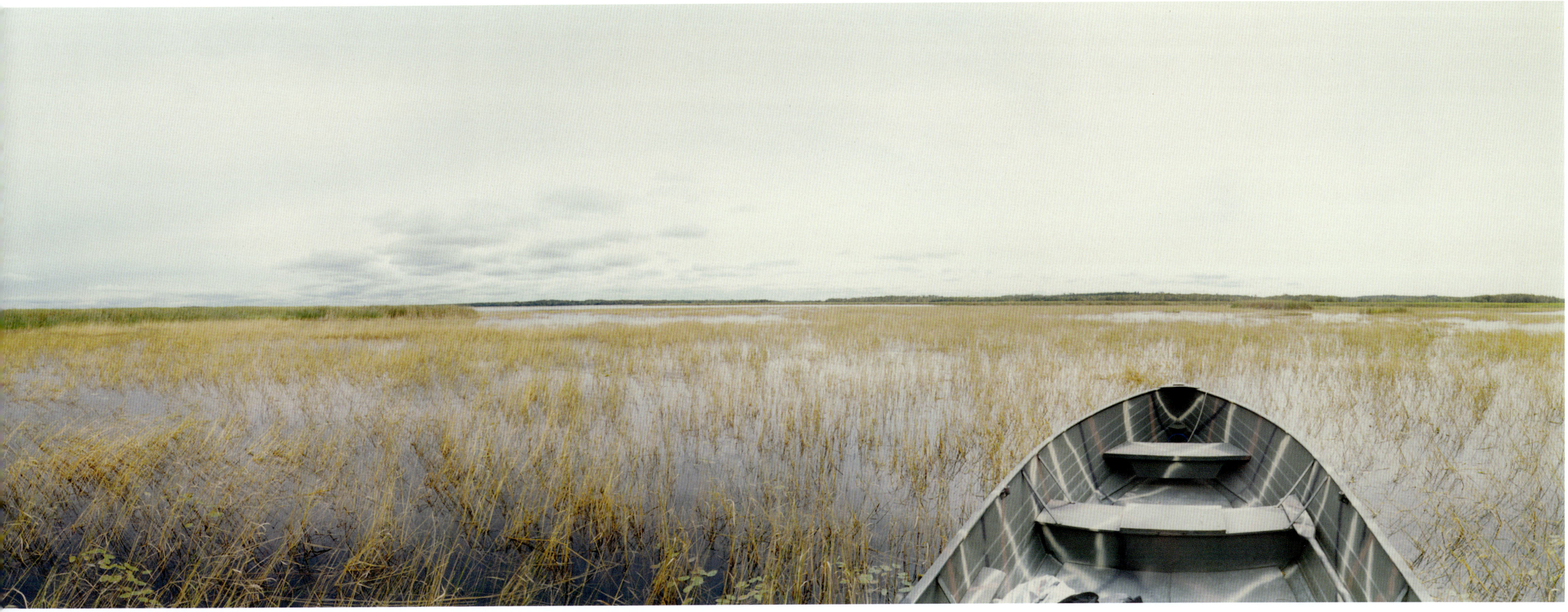

10 | HARVESTING WILD RICE, LEECH LAKE, CASS COUNTY, MINNESOTA | 1999 | 367°

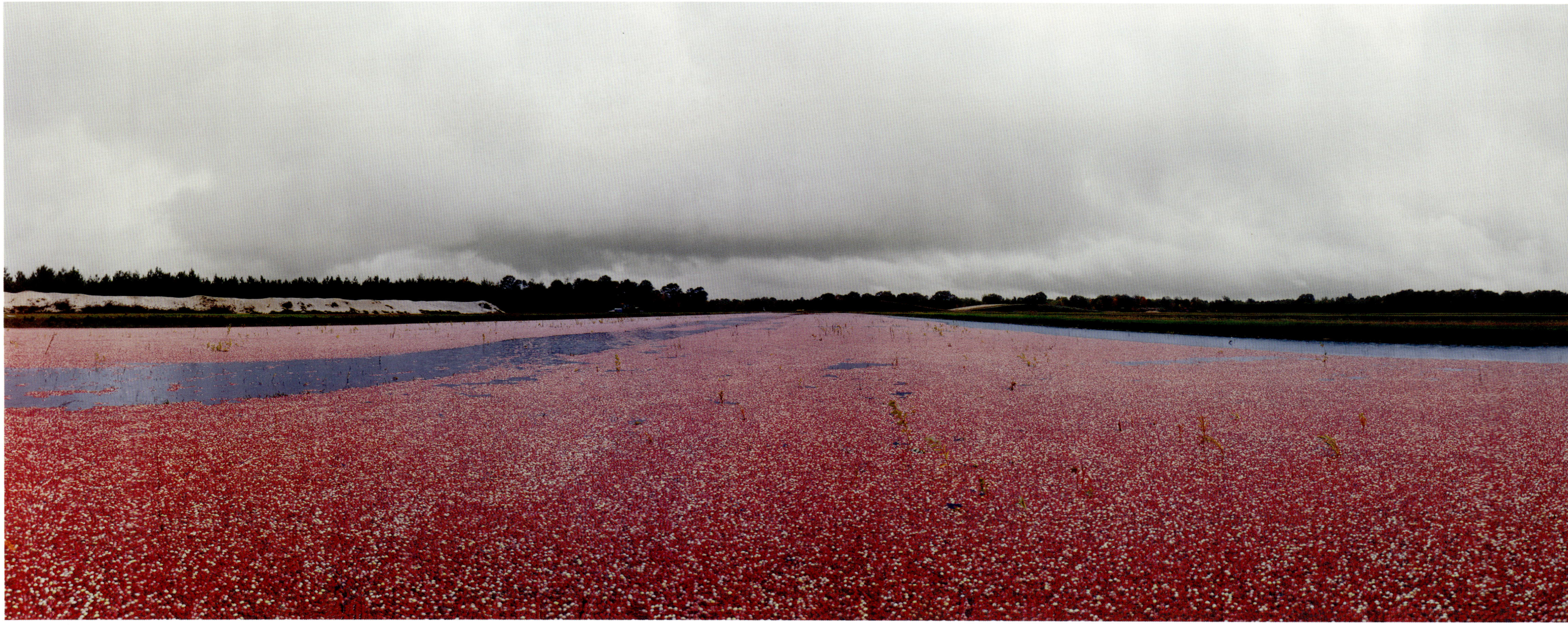

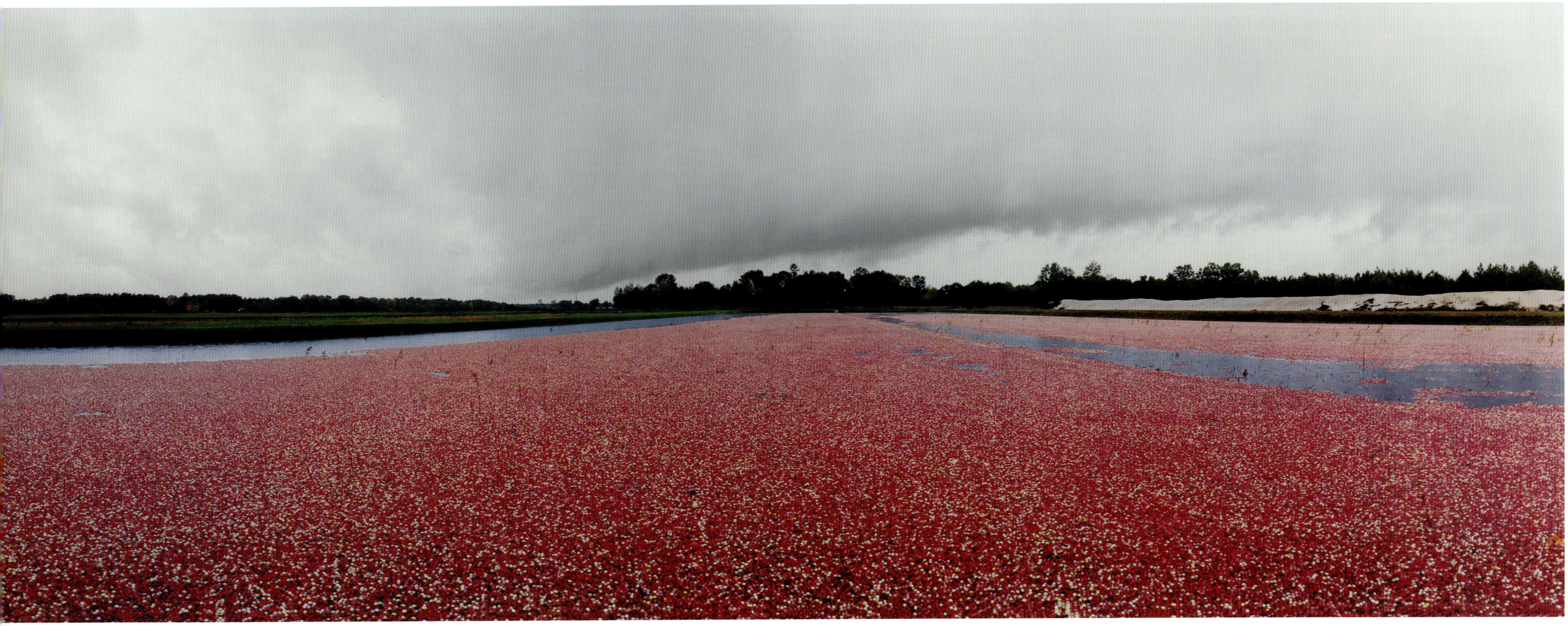

11 | CRANBERRIES, WOOD COUNTY, WISCONSIN | 1998 | 364°

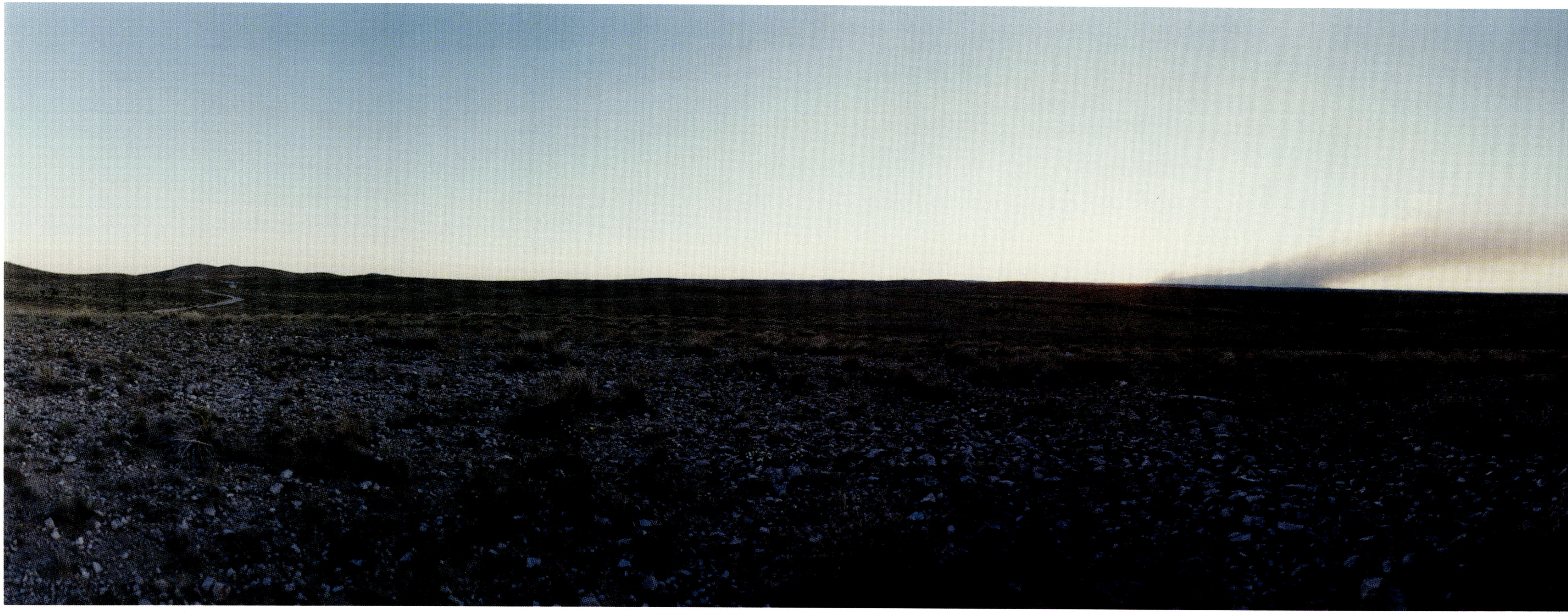

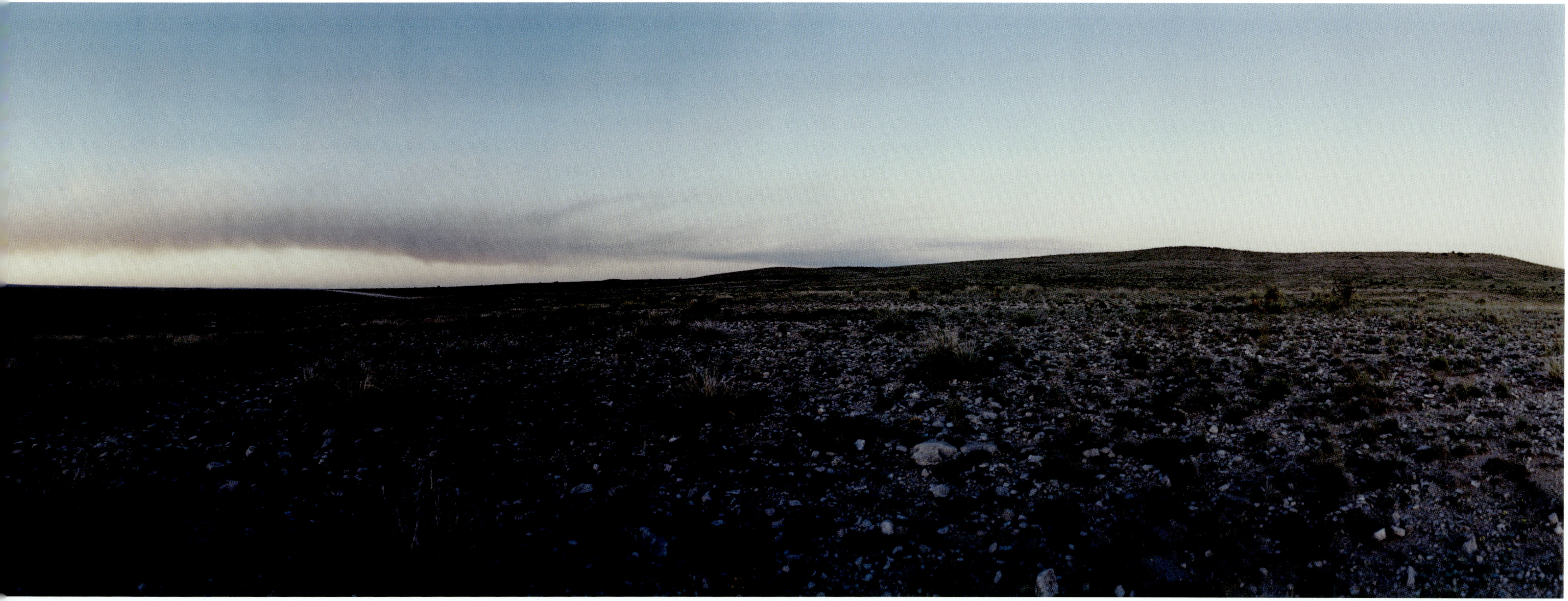

12 | PEPPIN WILDFIRE, CHAVES COUNTY, NEW MEXICO | 2004 | 368°

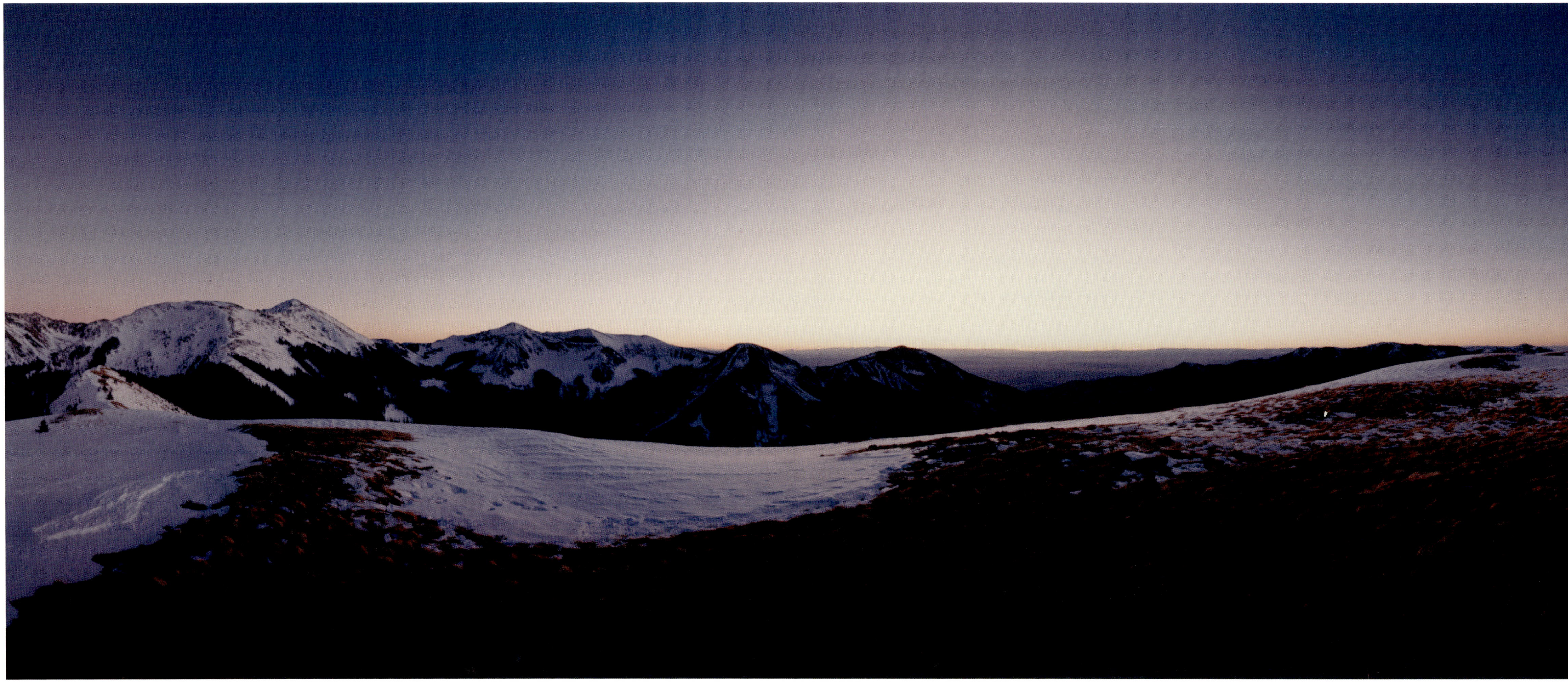

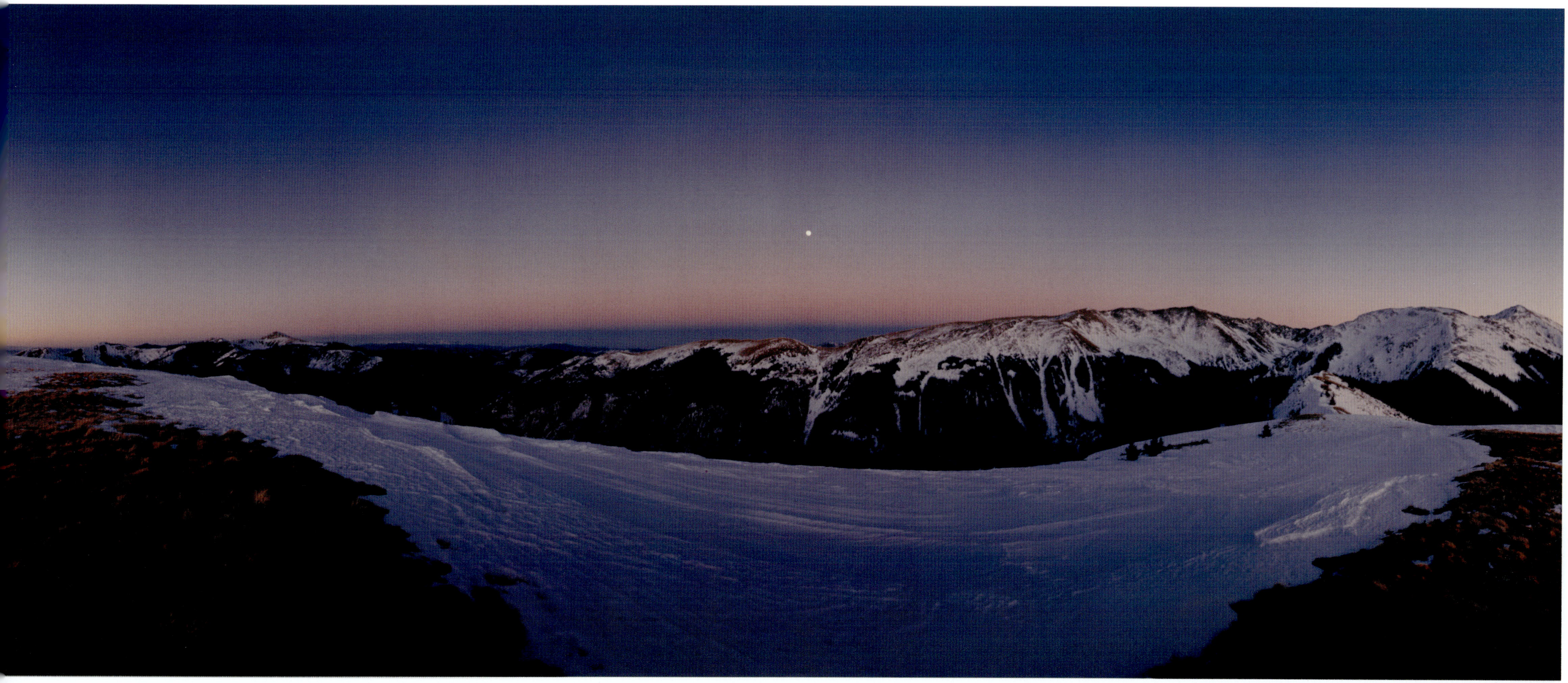

13 | SUNSET, MOONRISE, HIGHLINE RIDGE, TAOS COUNTY, NEW MEXICO | 1986 | 403°

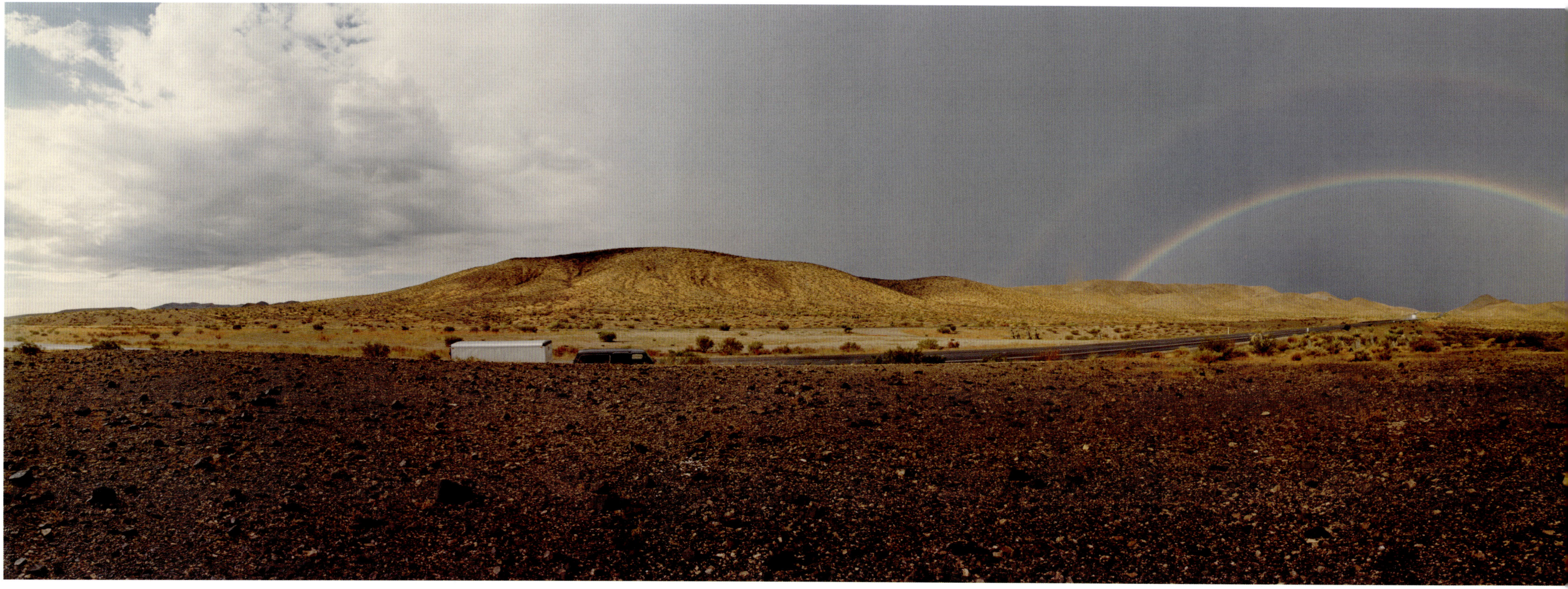

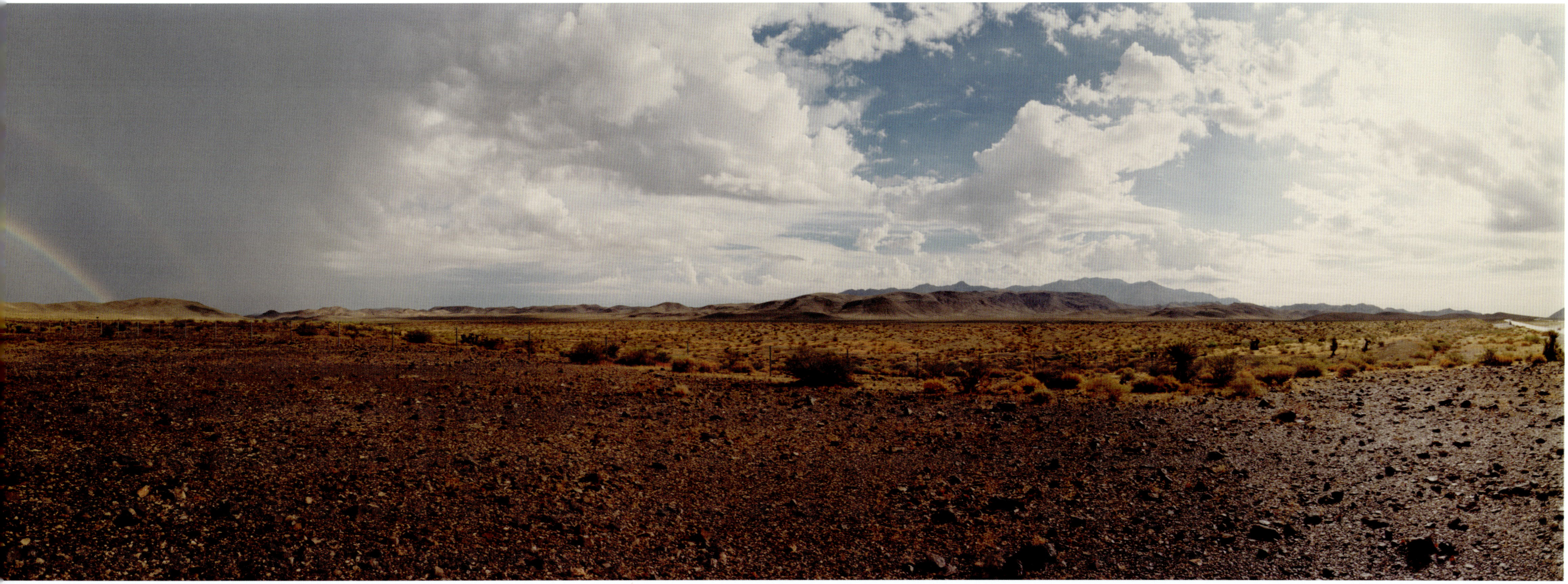

14 | MOJAVE RAINBOW, SAN BERNADINO COUNTY, CALIFORNIA | 1989 | 355°

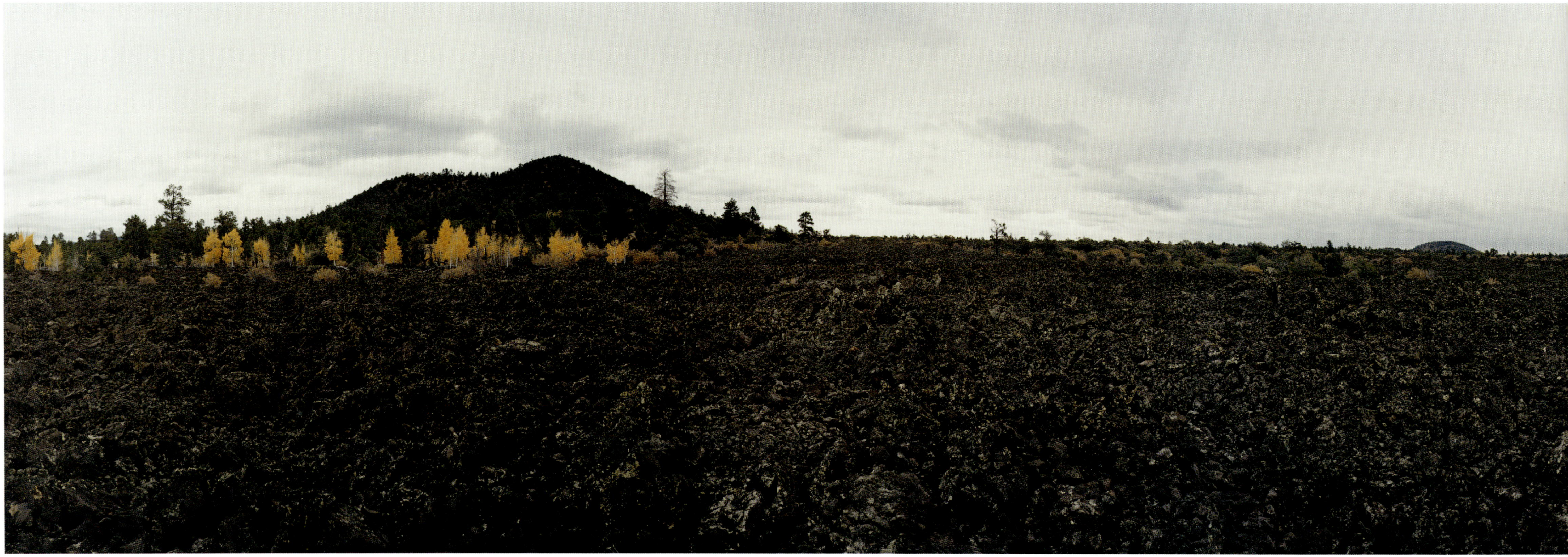

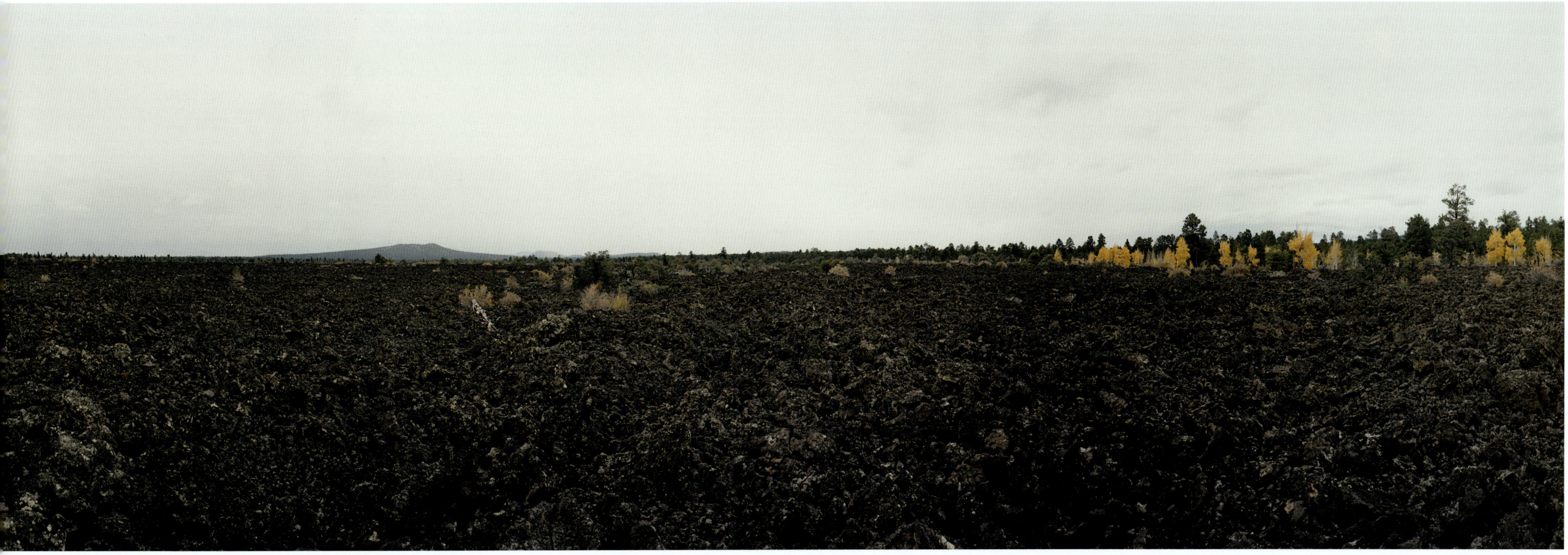

15 | EL MALPAIS WILDERNESS, NEW MEXICO | 1987 | 395°

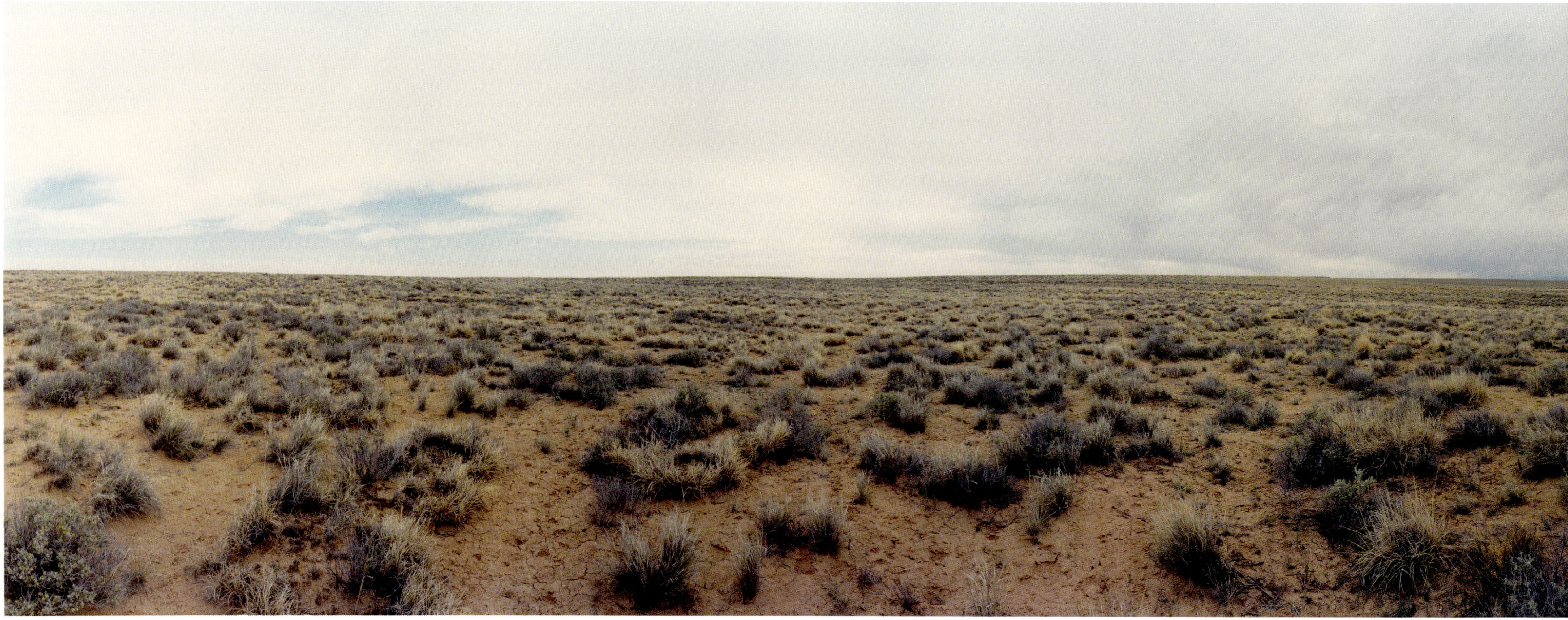

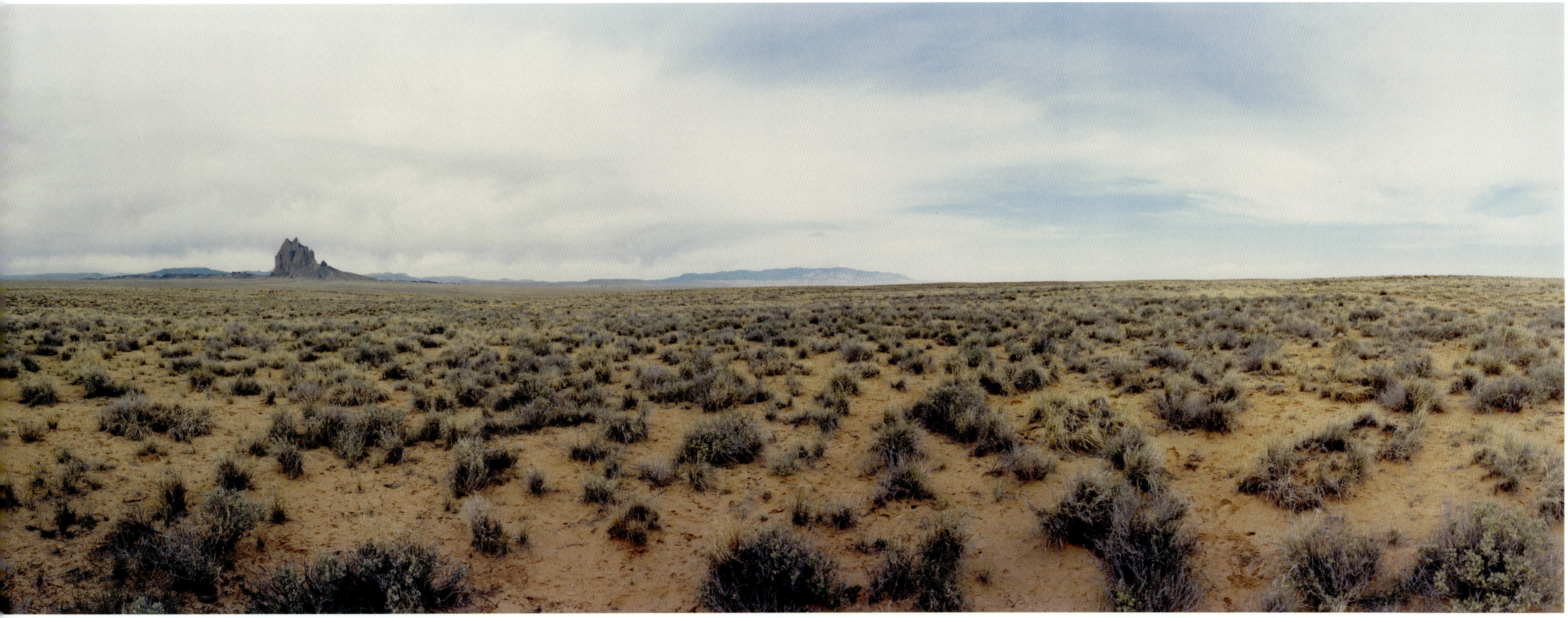

16 | SHIPROCK, NAVAJO RESERVATION, SAN JUAN COUNTY, NEW MEXICO | 1995 | 373°

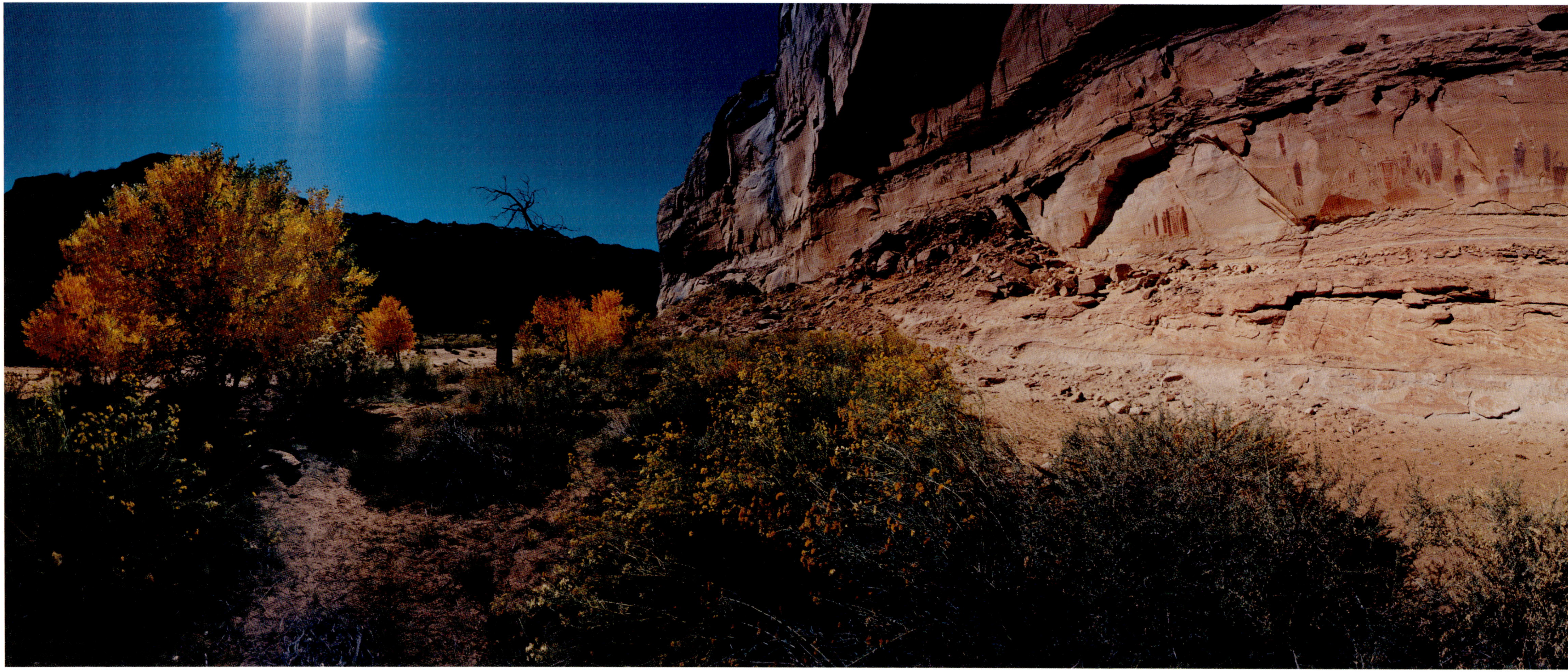

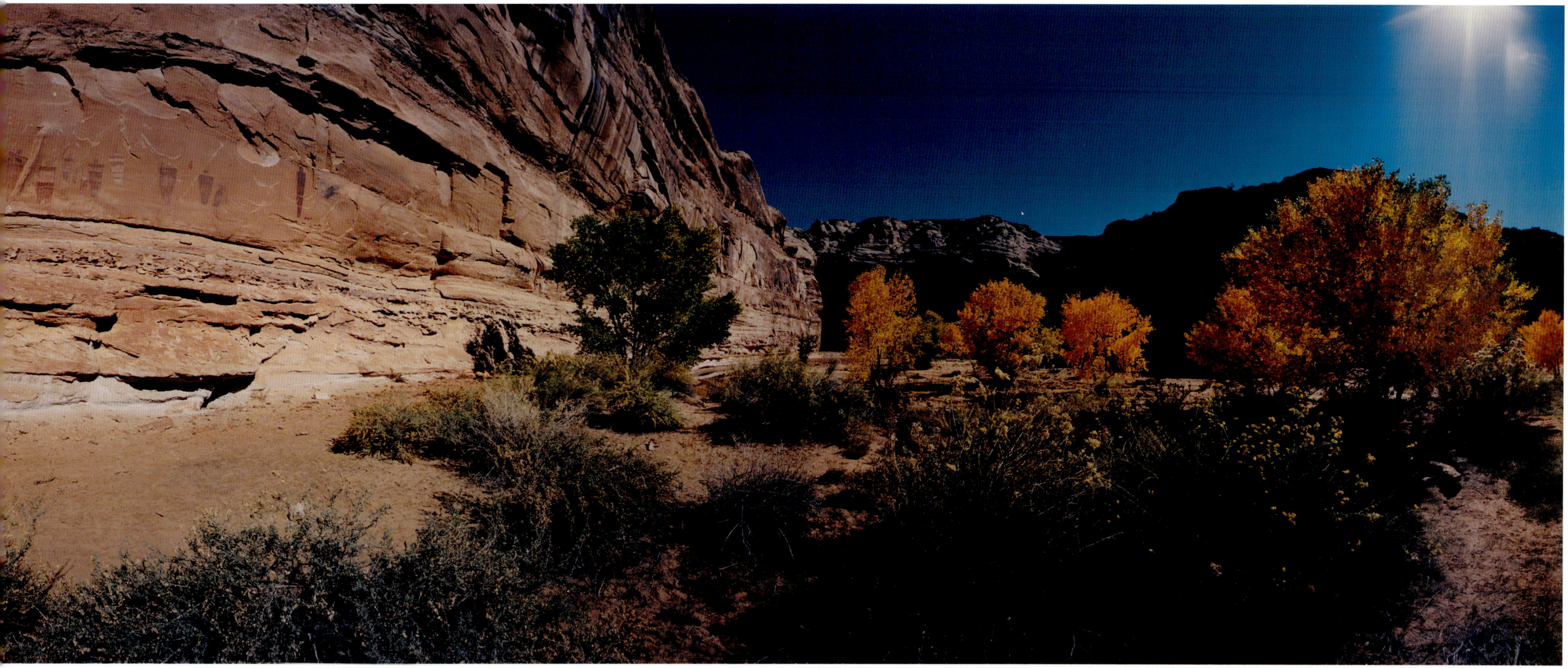

17 | BARRIER CANYON PETROGLYPHS, CANYONLANDS NATIONAL PARK, UTAH | 1986 | 412°

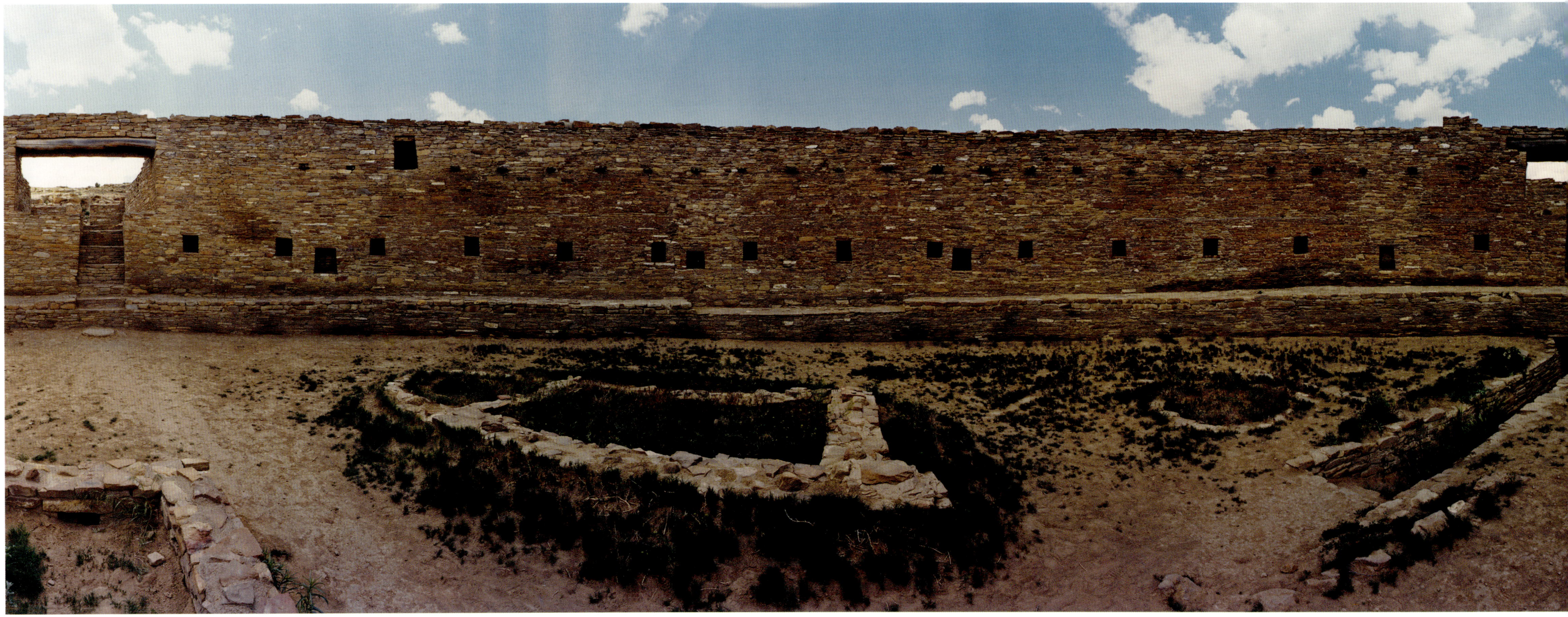

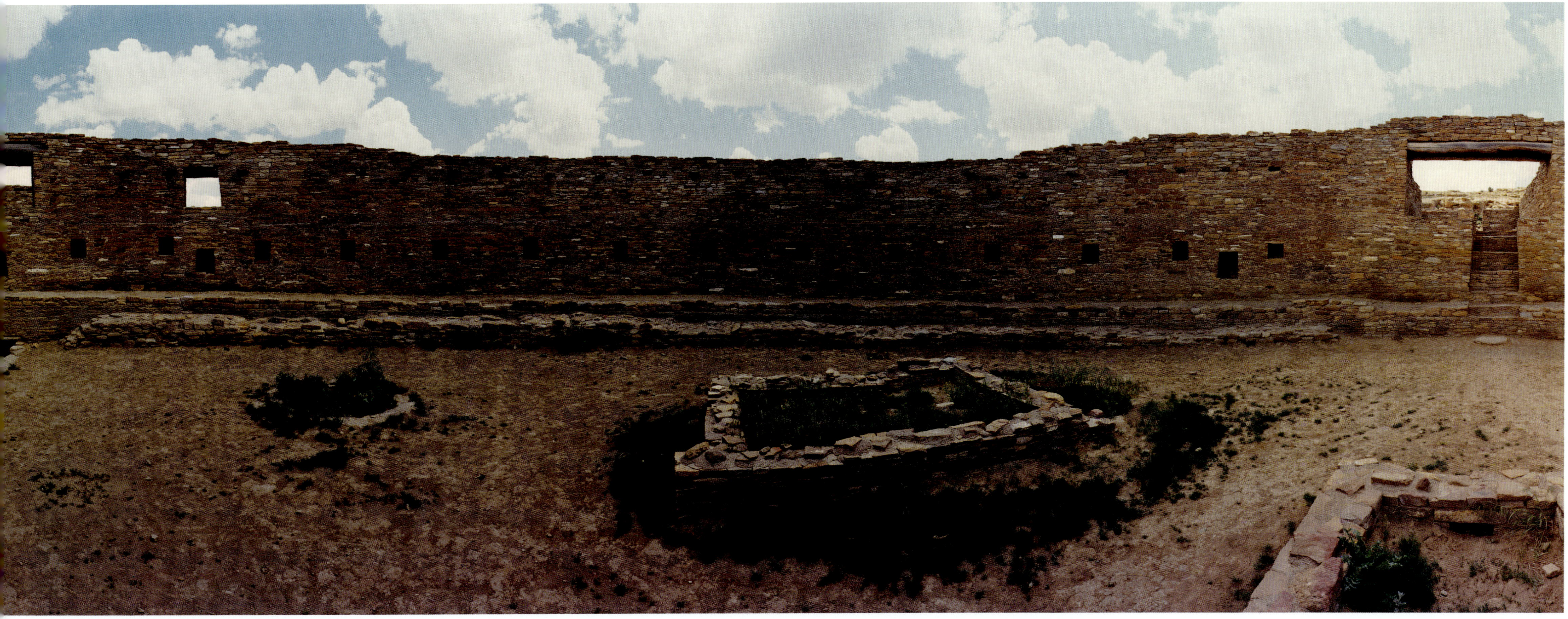

18 | CASA RINCONADA, CHACO CULTURE NATIONAL HISTORIC PARK, NEW MEXICO | 1989 | 404°

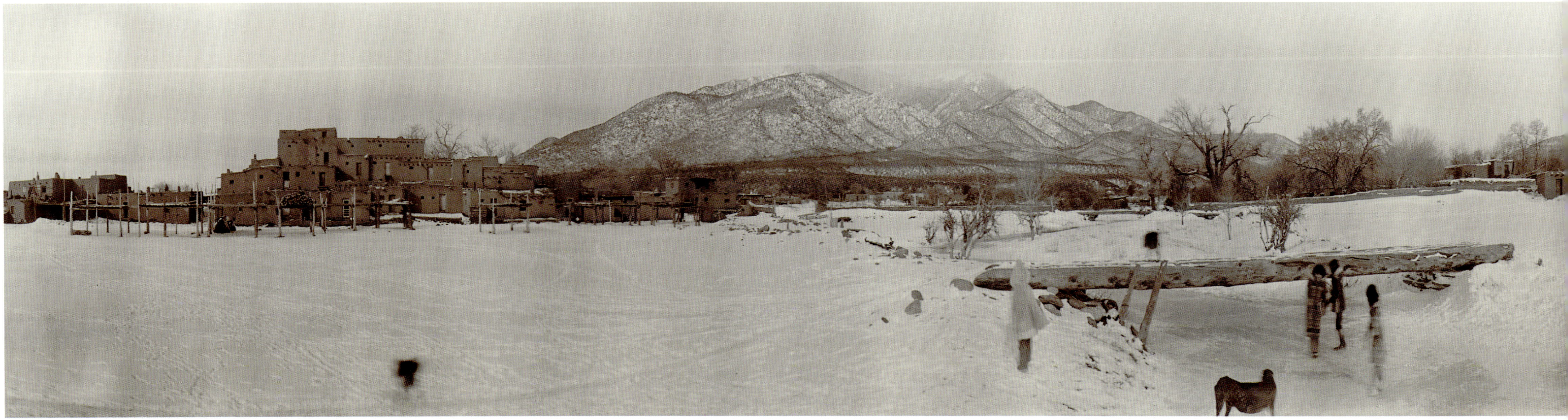

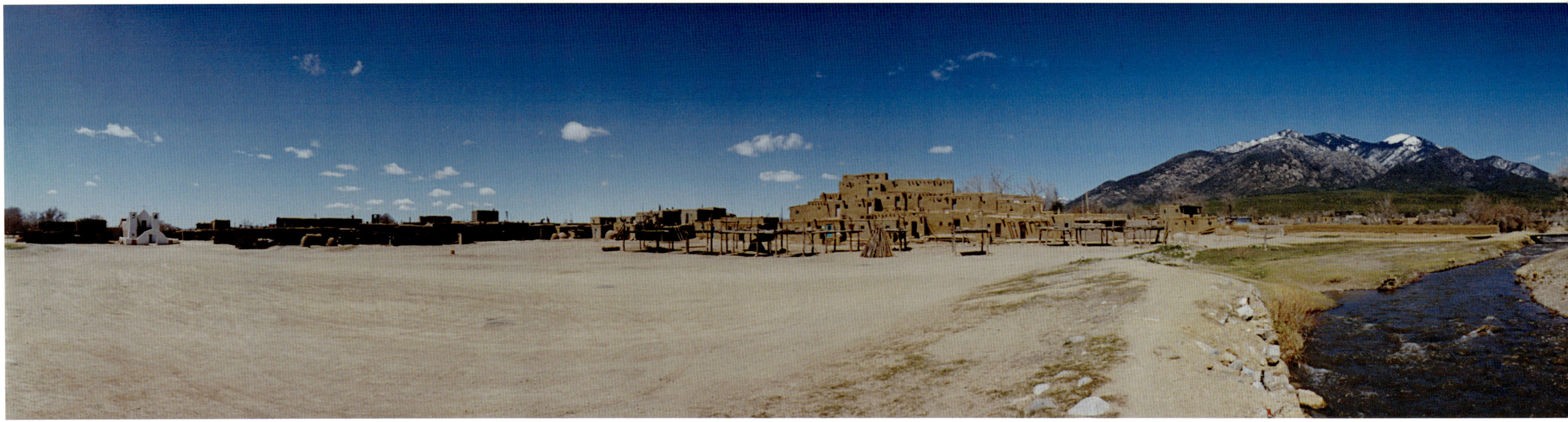

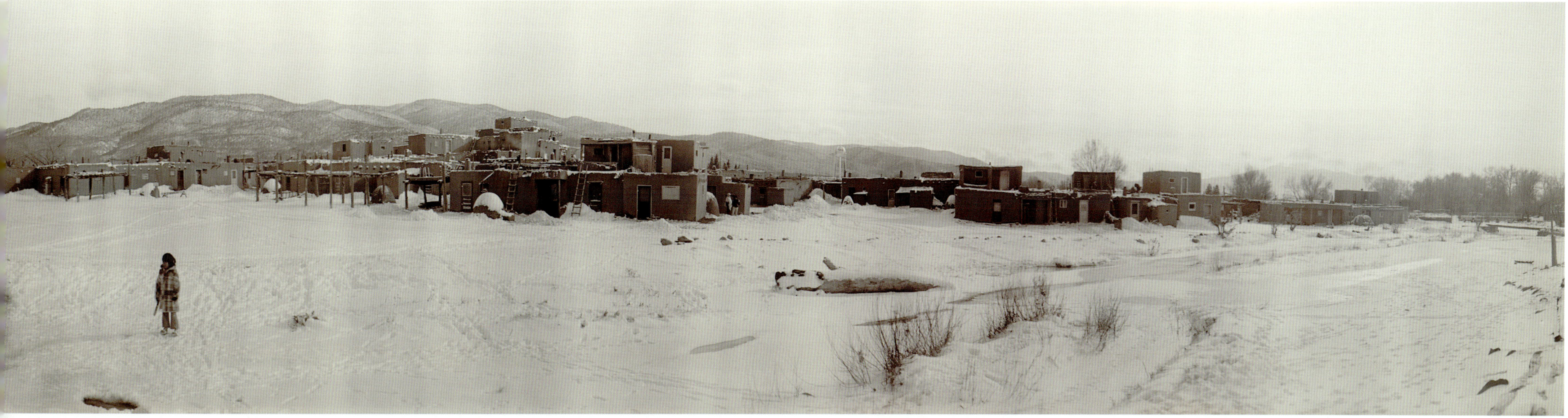

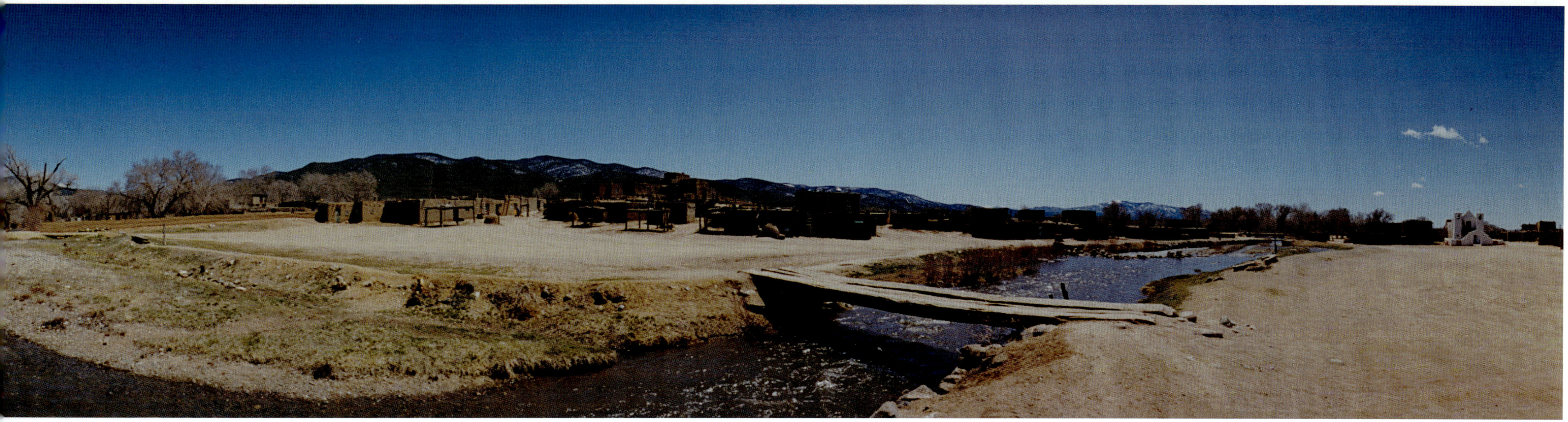

TOP: 19 | TAOS PUEBLO, NEW MEXICO | 1978 | 267° • *BOTTOM*: 20 | TAOS PUEBLO, NEW MEXICO | 1983 | 388°

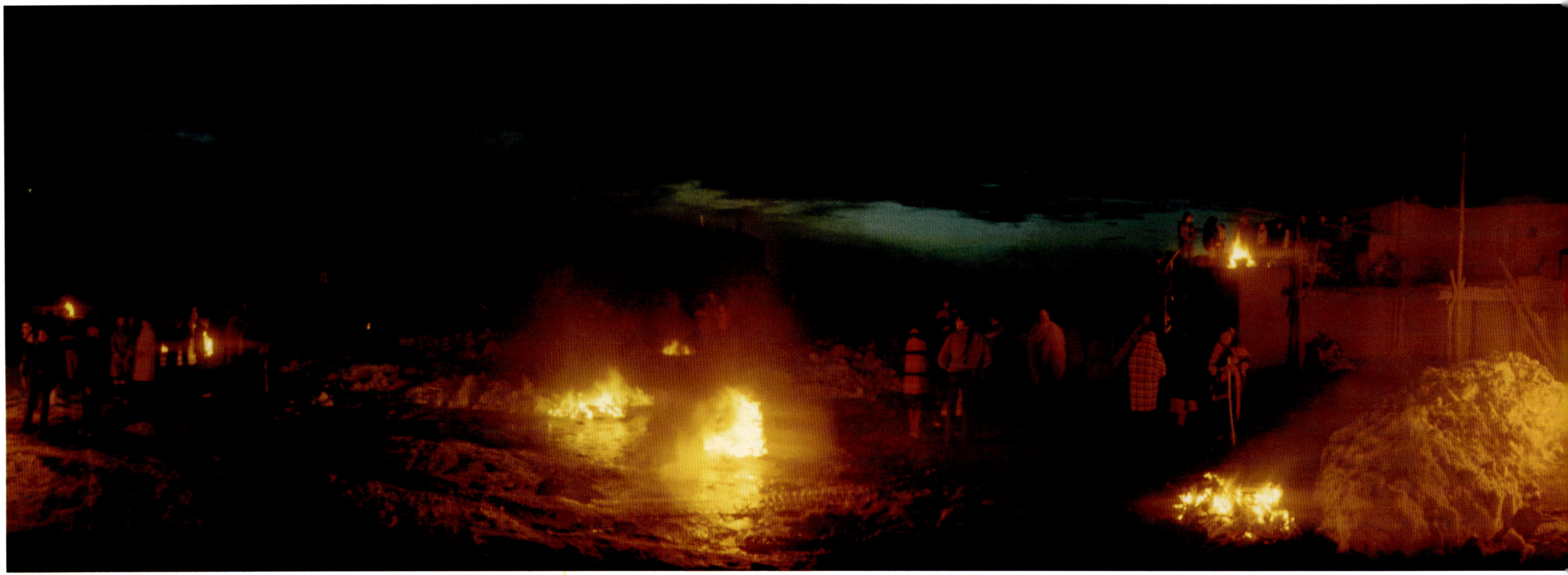

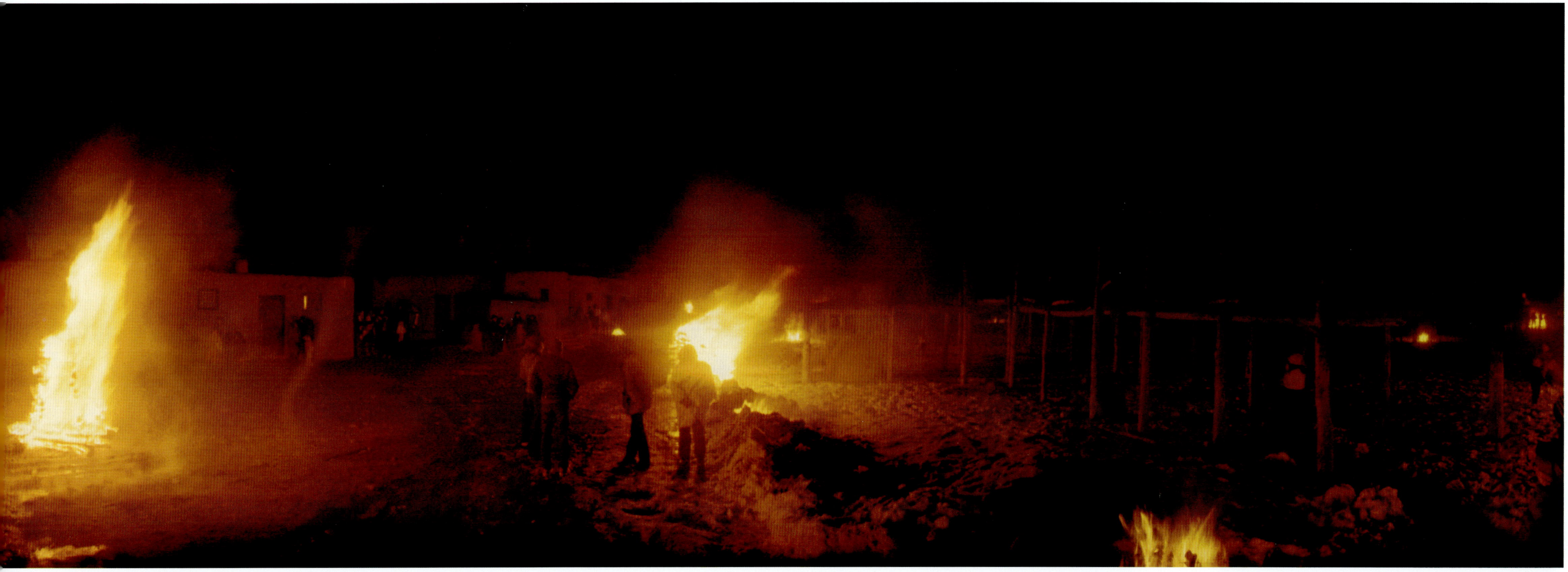

21 | TAOS PUEBLO CHRISTMAS EVE, NEW MEXICO | 1983 | 315°

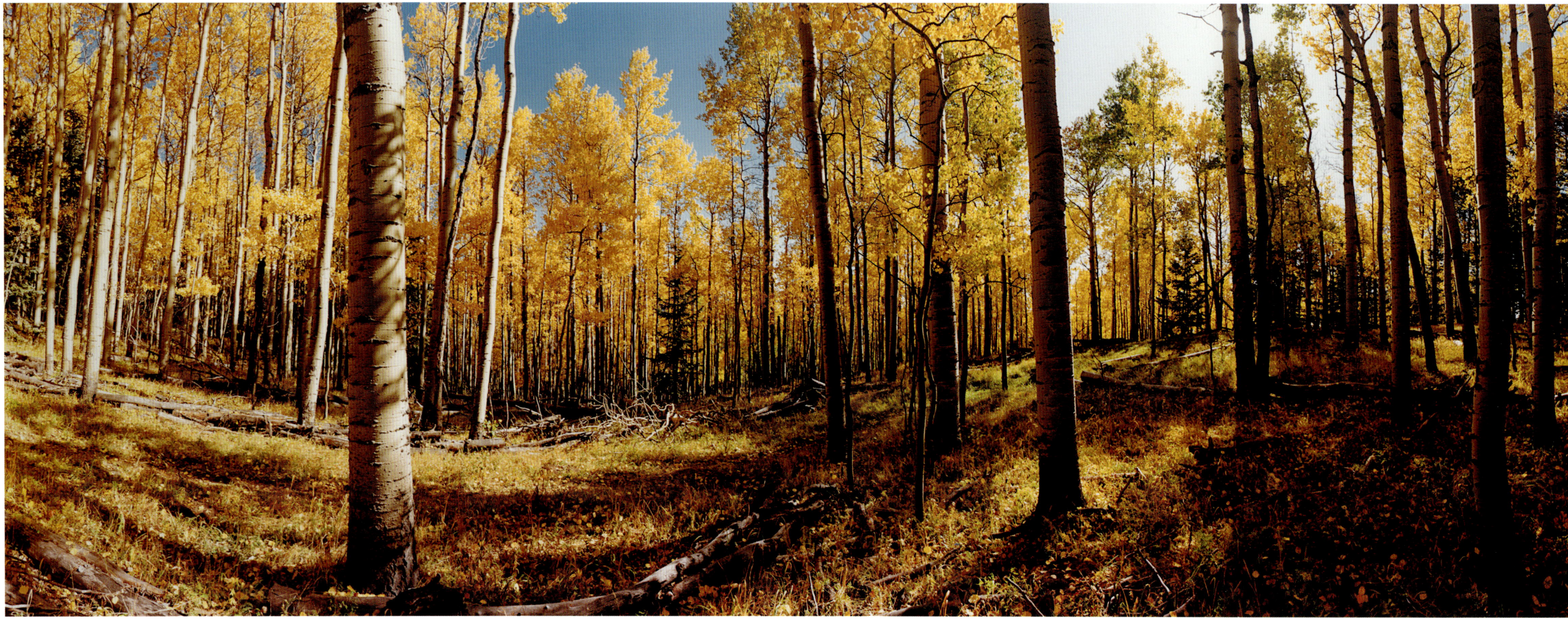

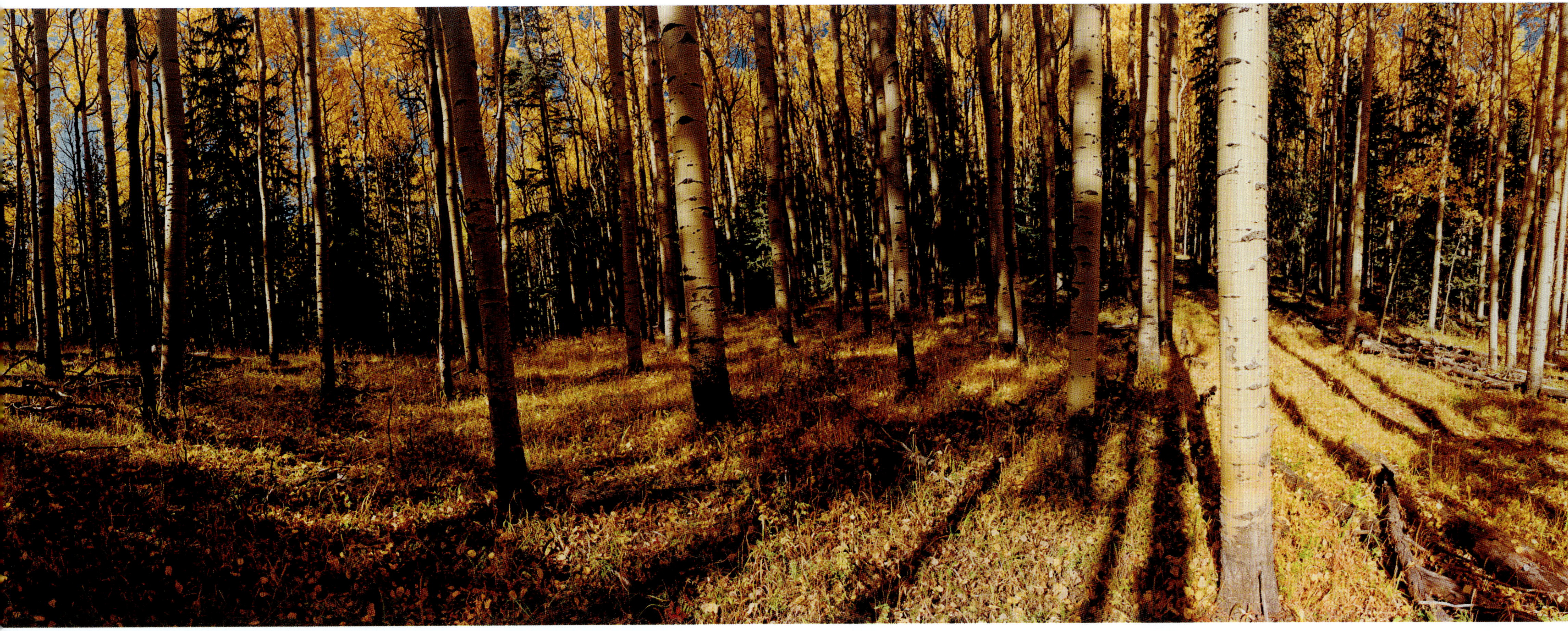

22 | ASPEN FOREST, SANTA FE NATIONAL FOREST, NEW MEXICO | 1993 | 374°

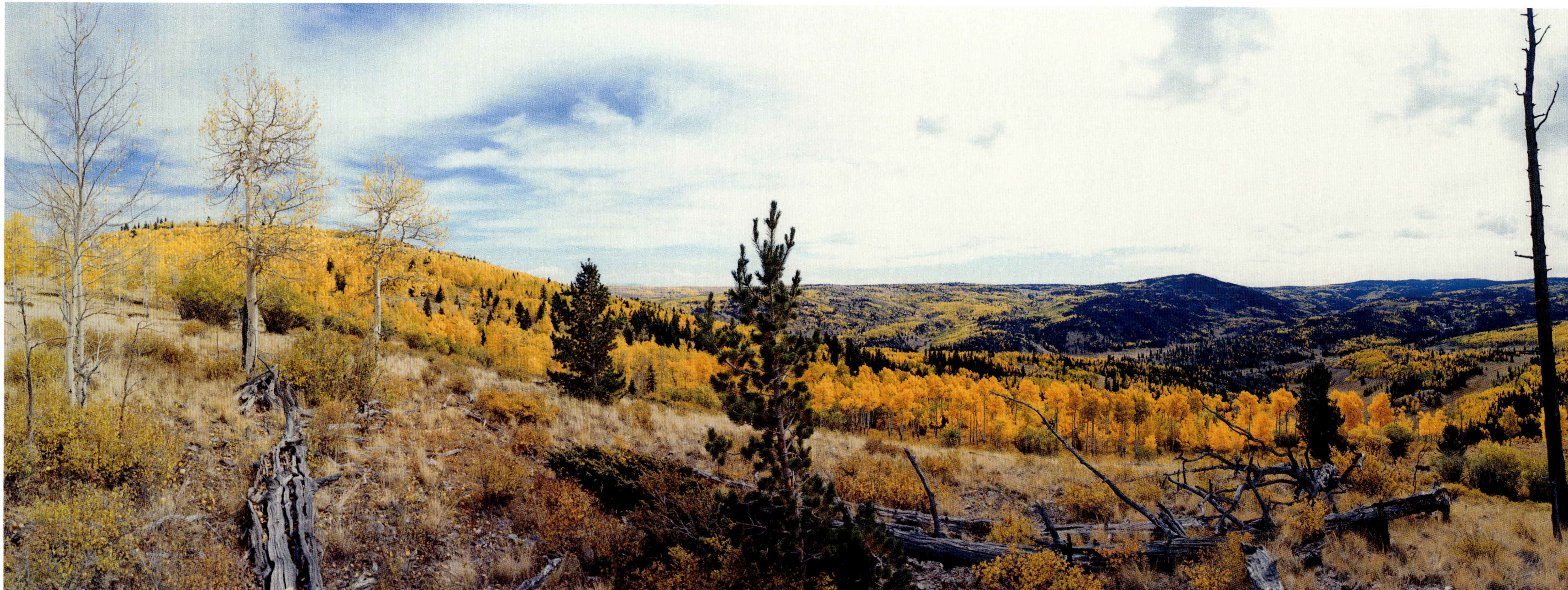

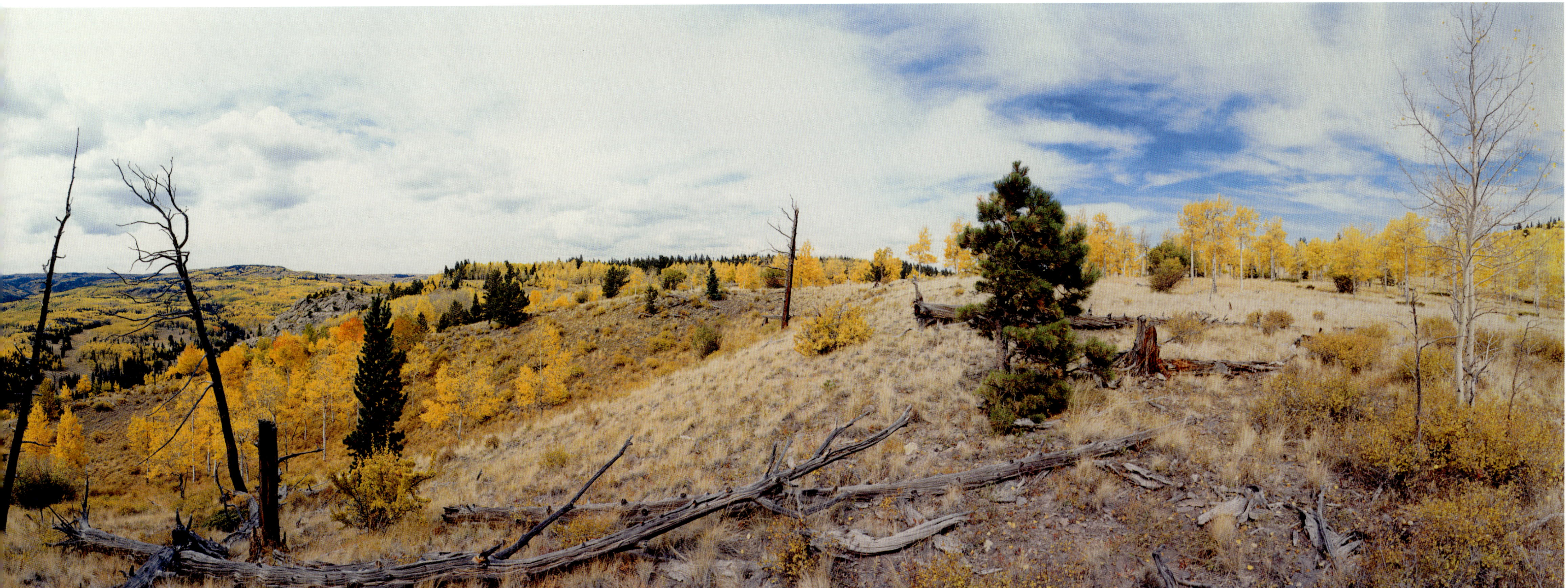

23 | CRUCES BASIN WILDERNESS, KIT CARSON NATIONAL FOREST, NEW MEXICO | 1988 | 384°

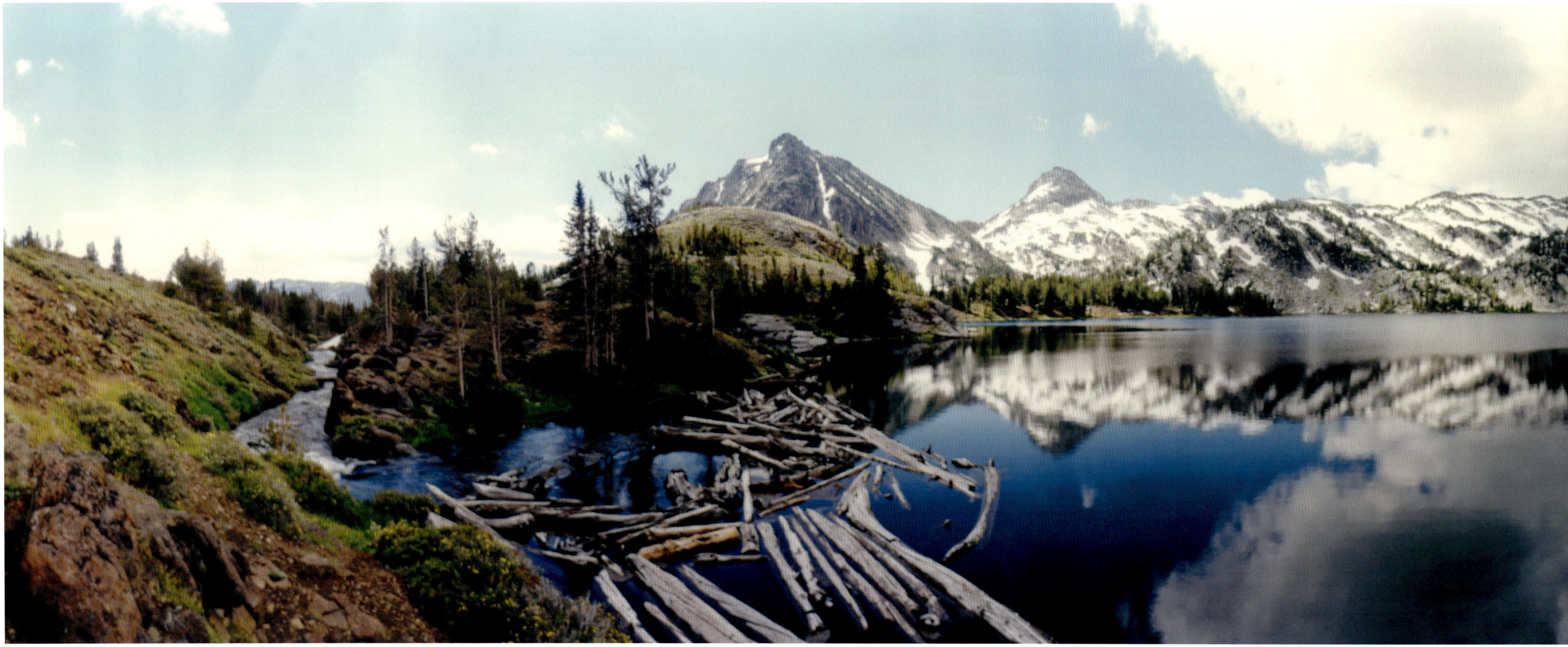

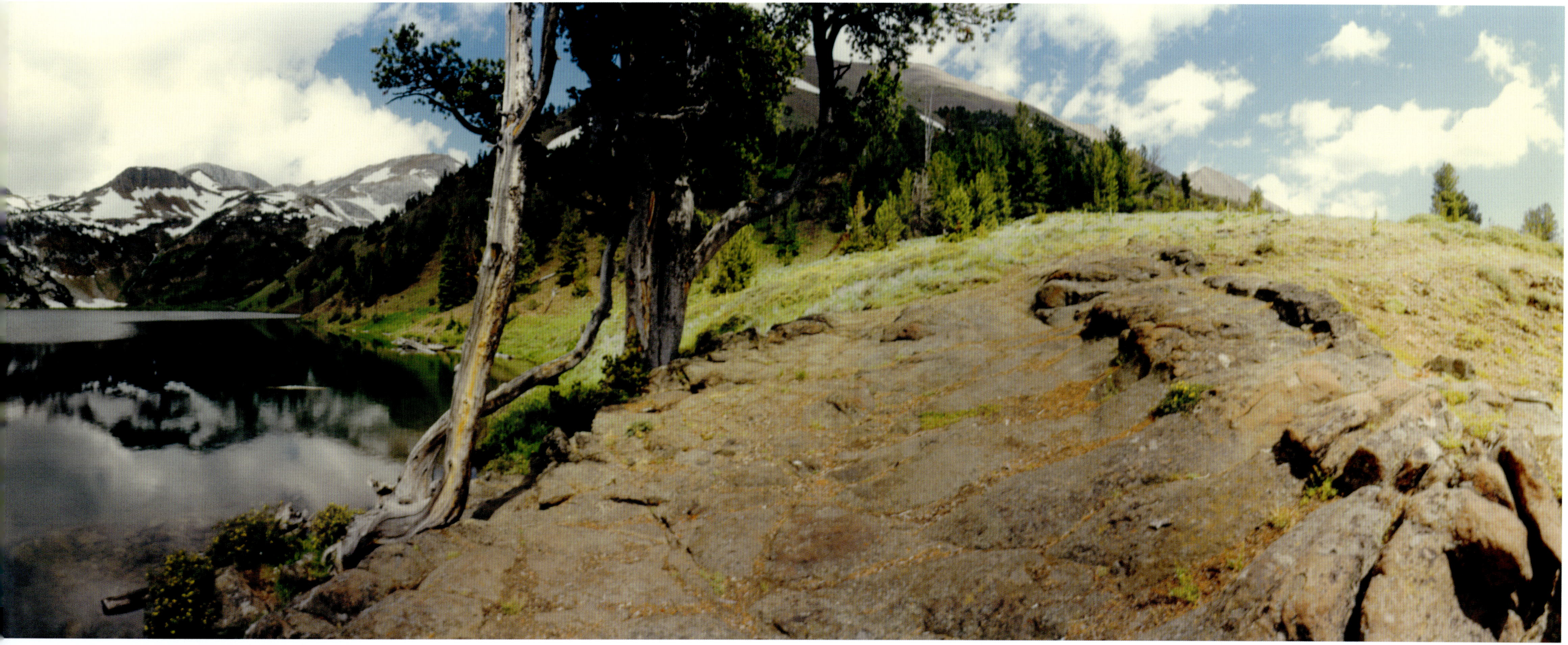

24 | ICE LAKE, WALLOWA WILDERNESS, OREGON | 1996 | 362°

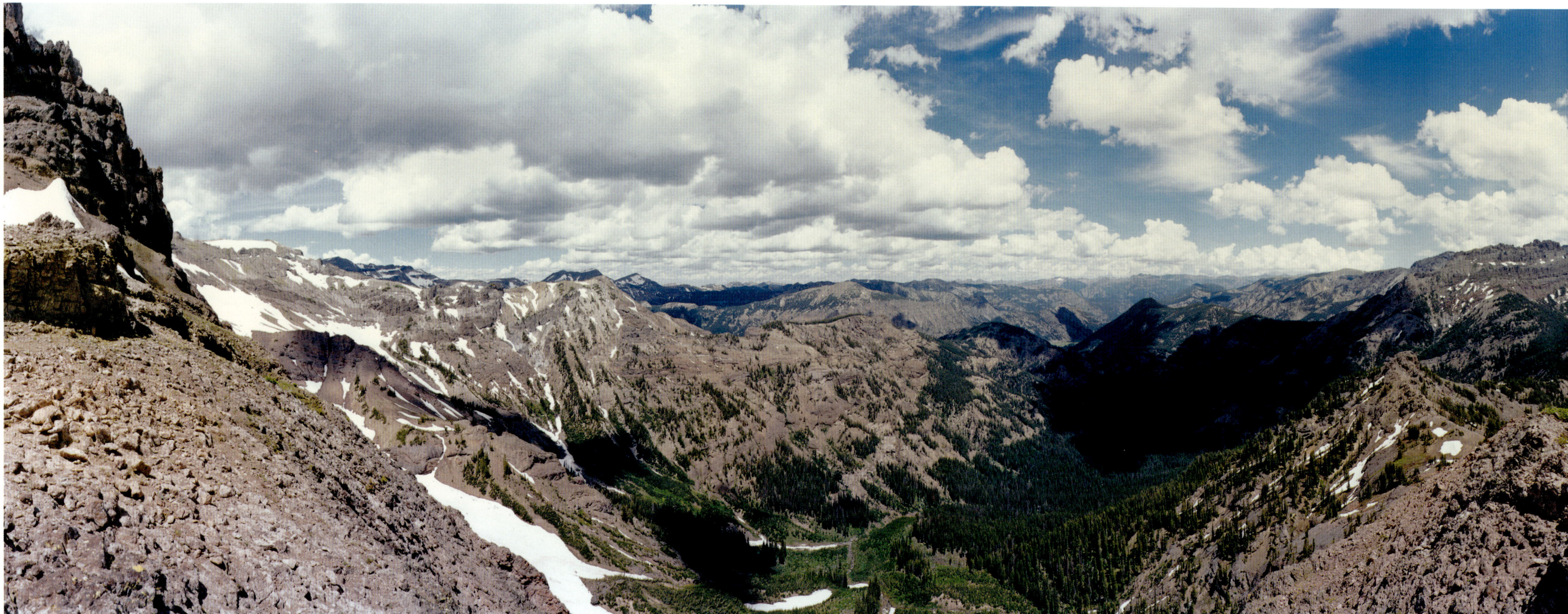

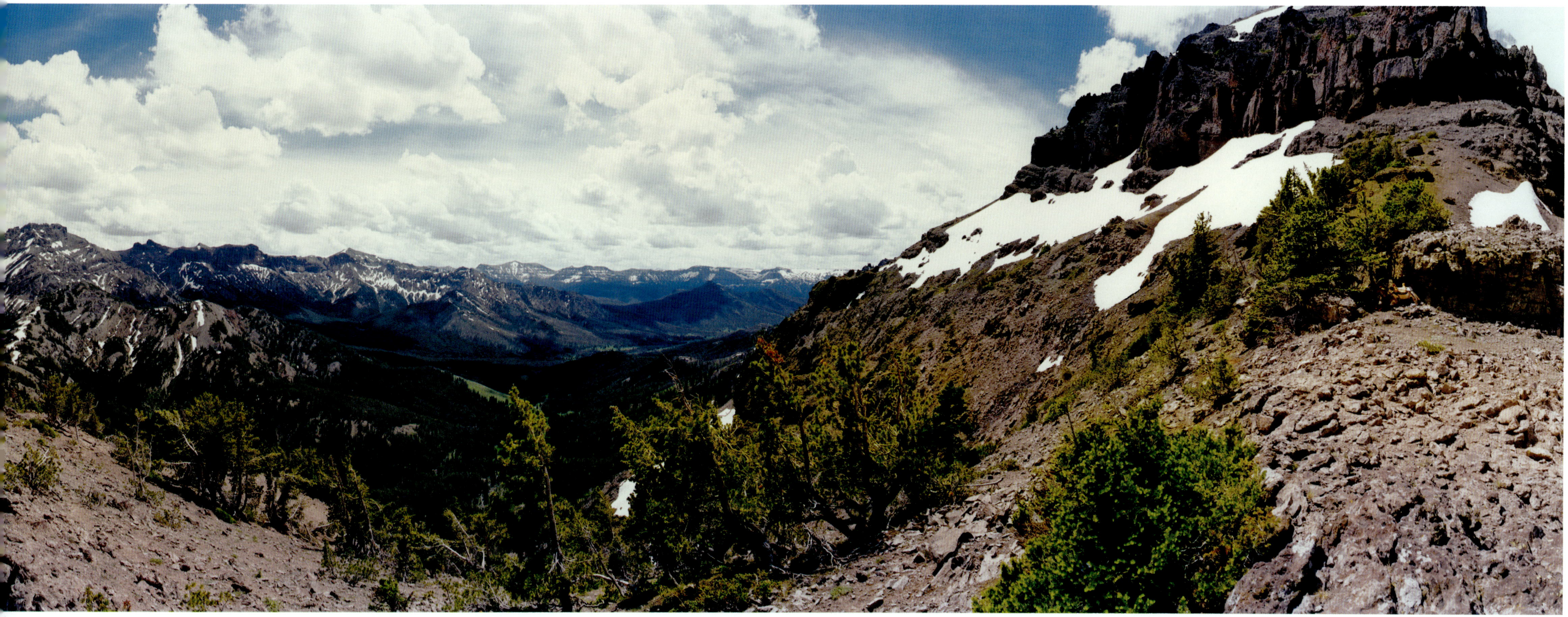

25 | EAGLE PEAK RIDGE, YELLOWSTONE NATIONAL PARK, WYOMING | 1997 | 377°

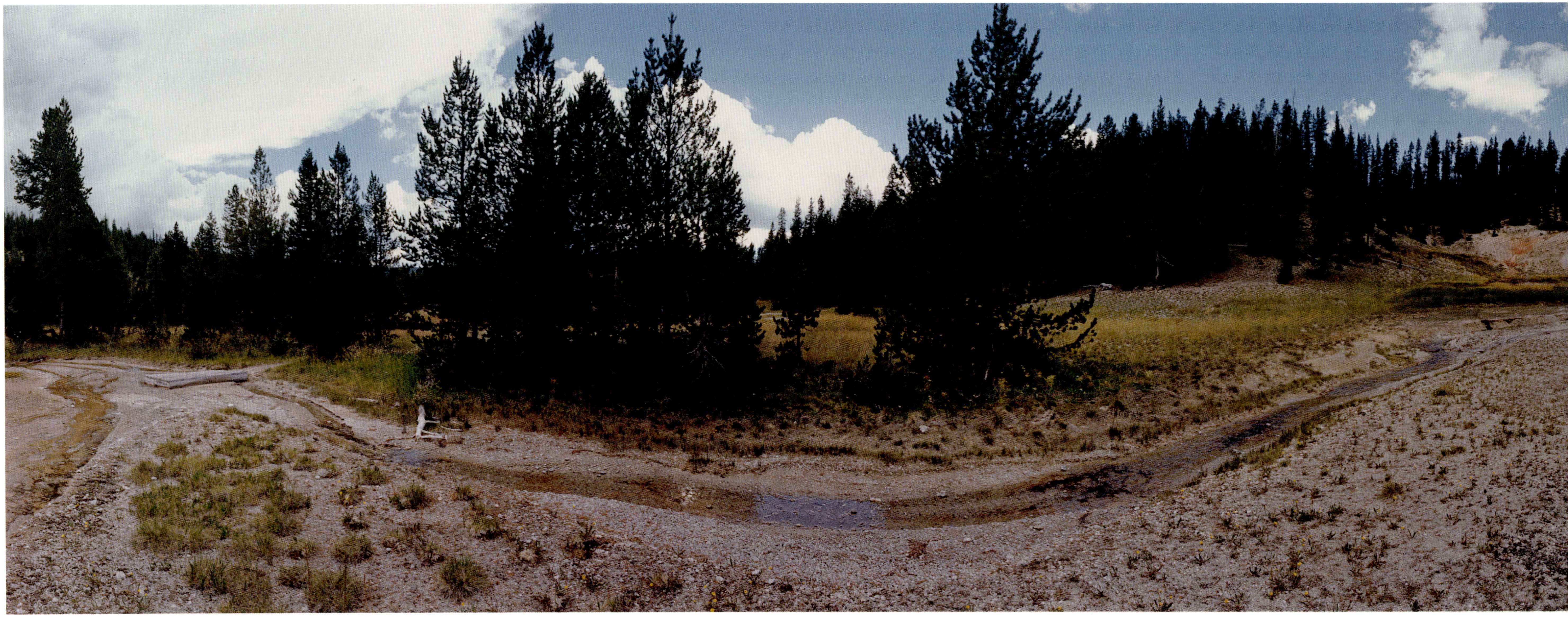

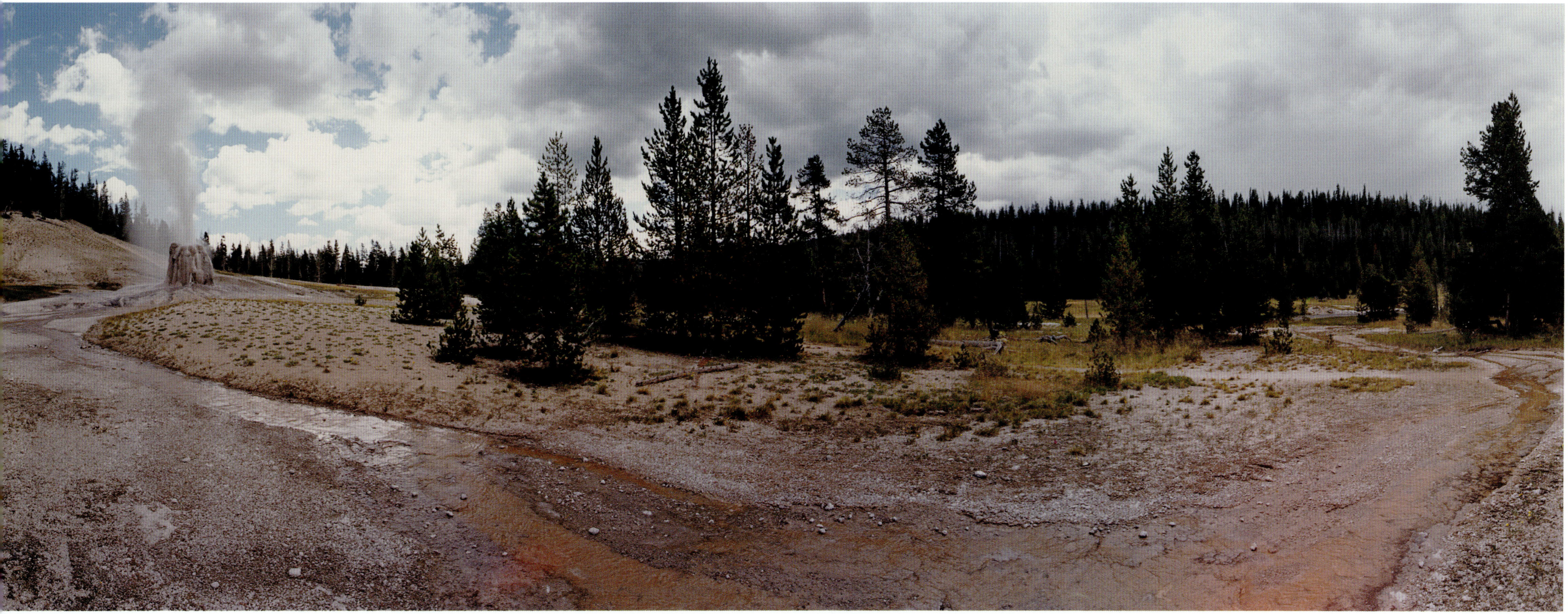

26 | LONESTAR GEYSER, YELLOWSTONE NATIONAL PARK, WYOMING | 1990 | 375°

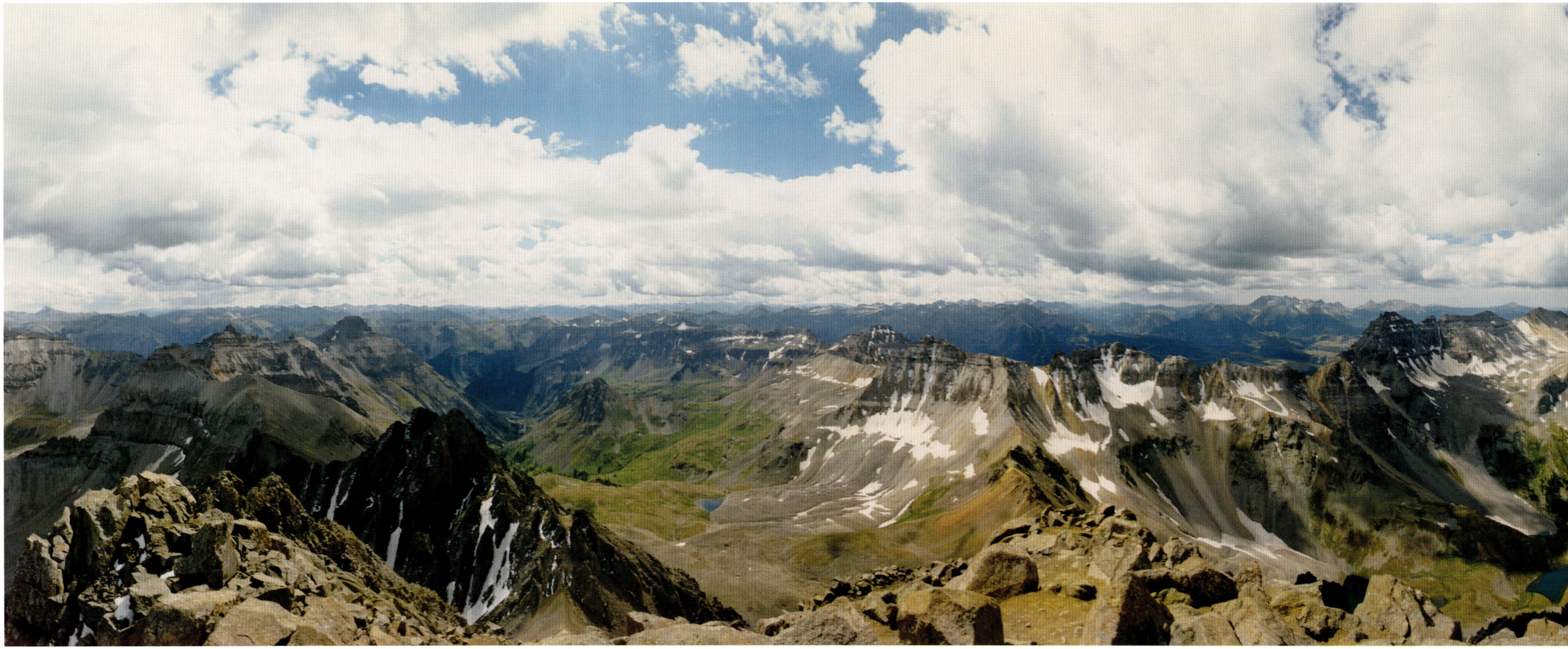

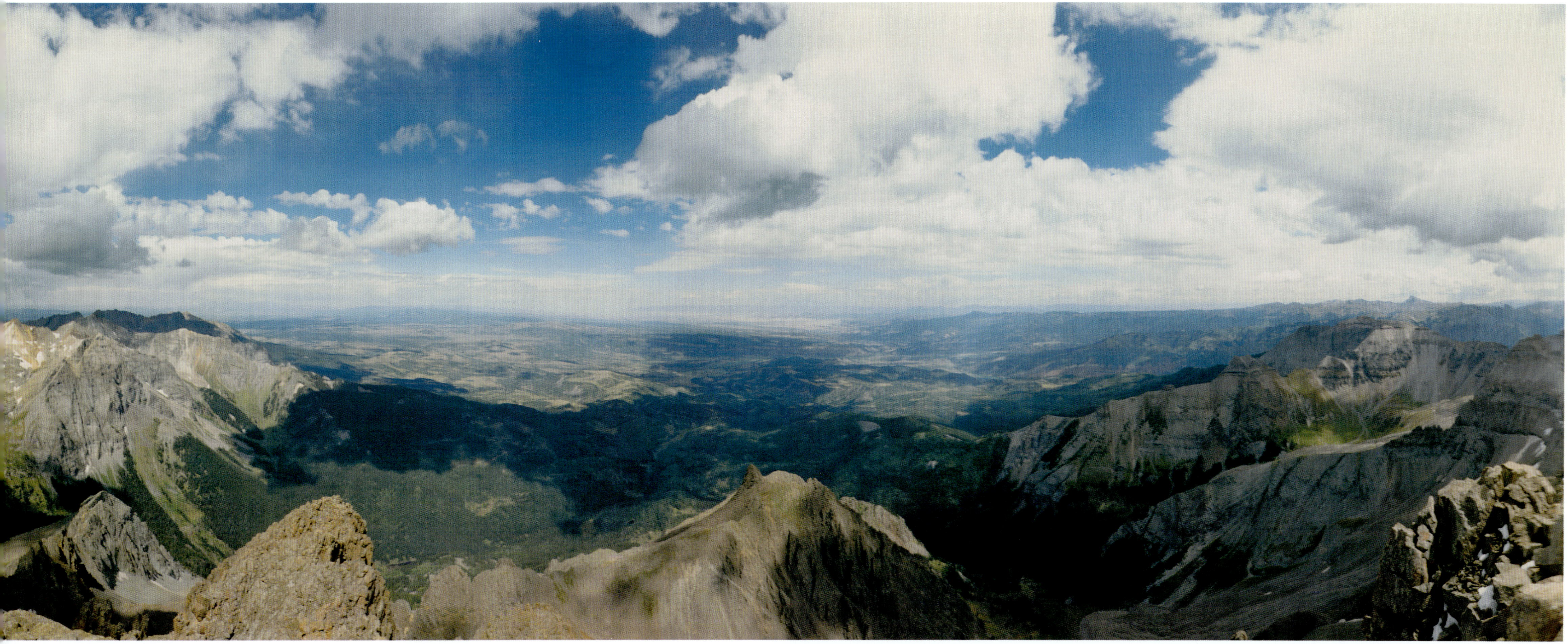

27 | MOUNT SNEFFELS, MOUNT SNEFFELS WILDERNESS, COLORADO | 1986 | 384°

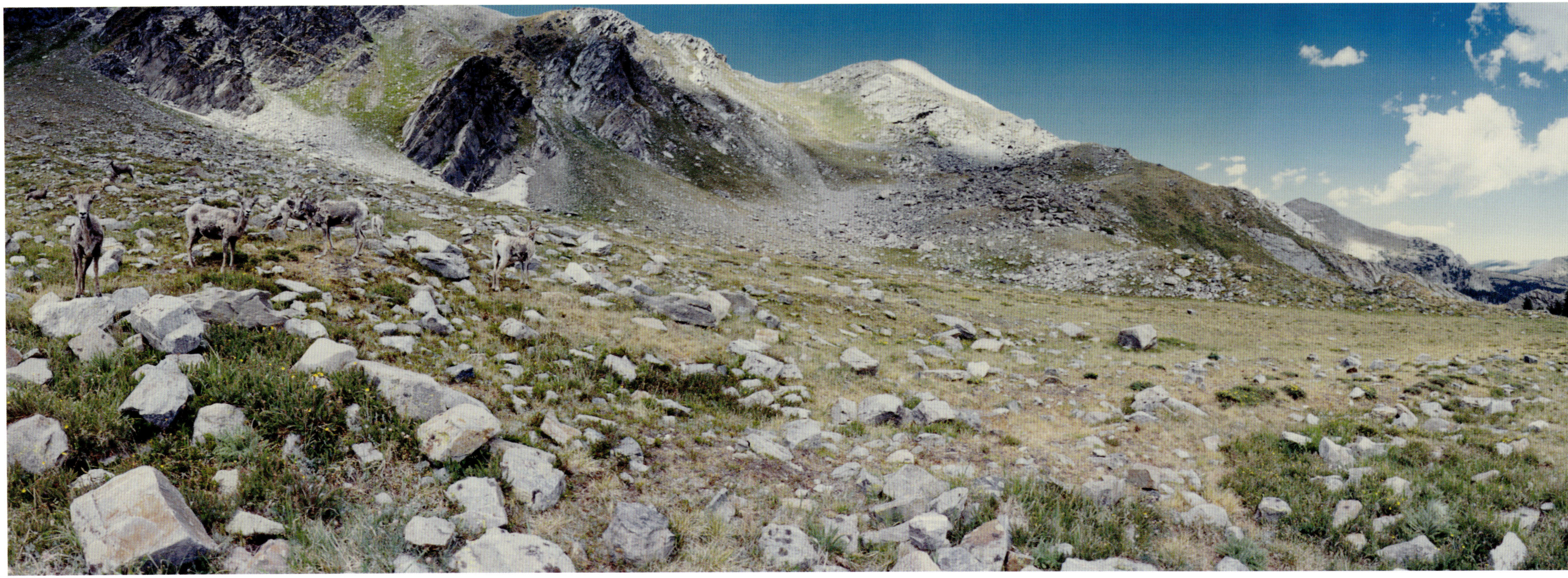

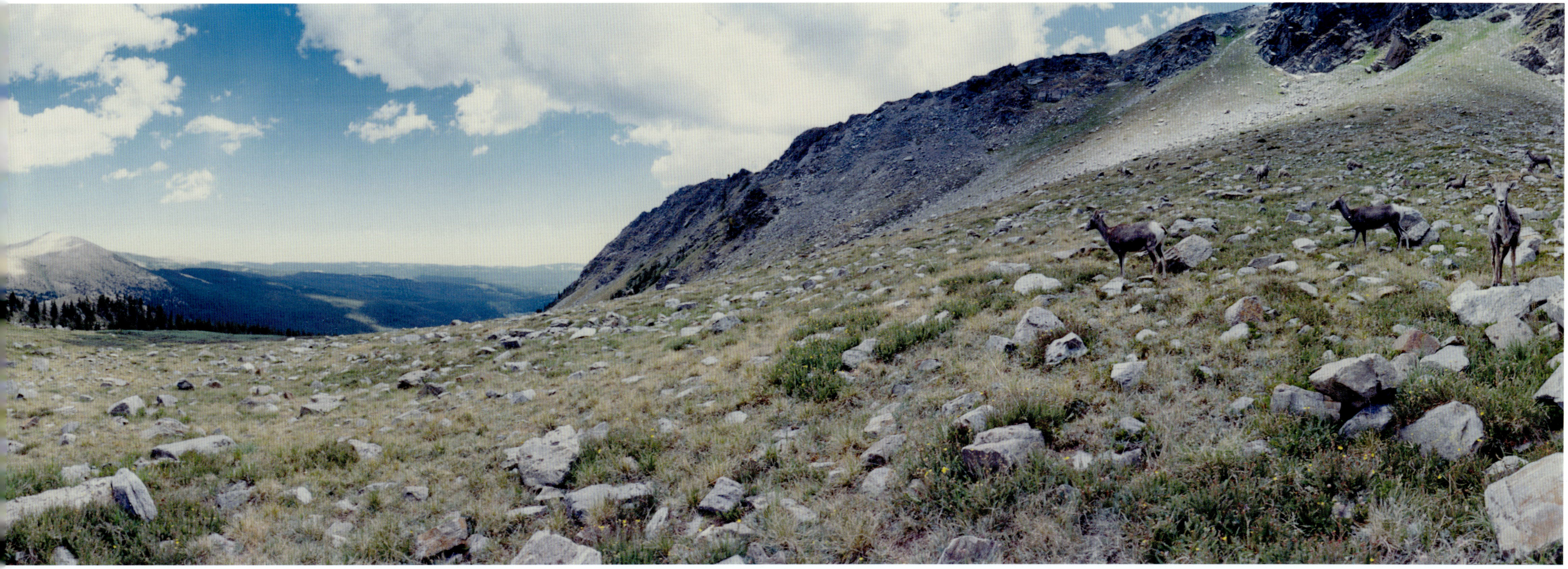

28 | PECOS BIG HORNS, PECOS WILDERNESS, NEW MEXICO | 1989 | 377°

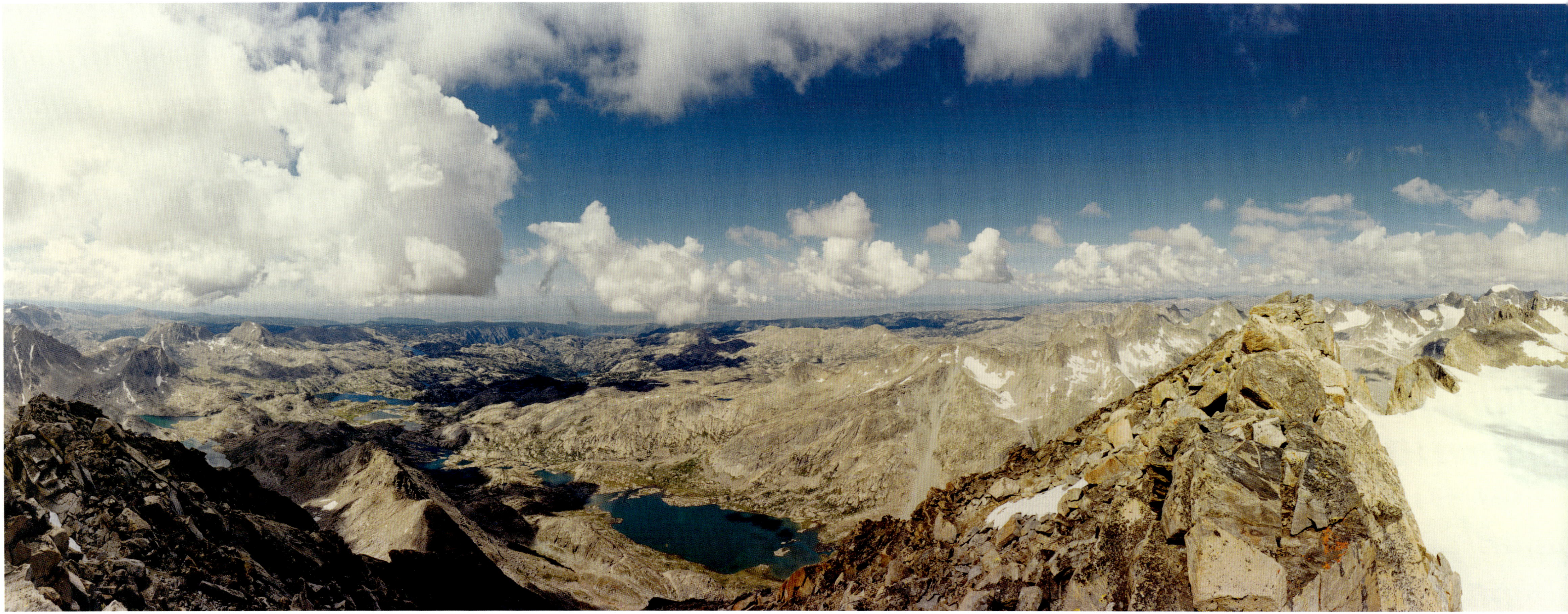

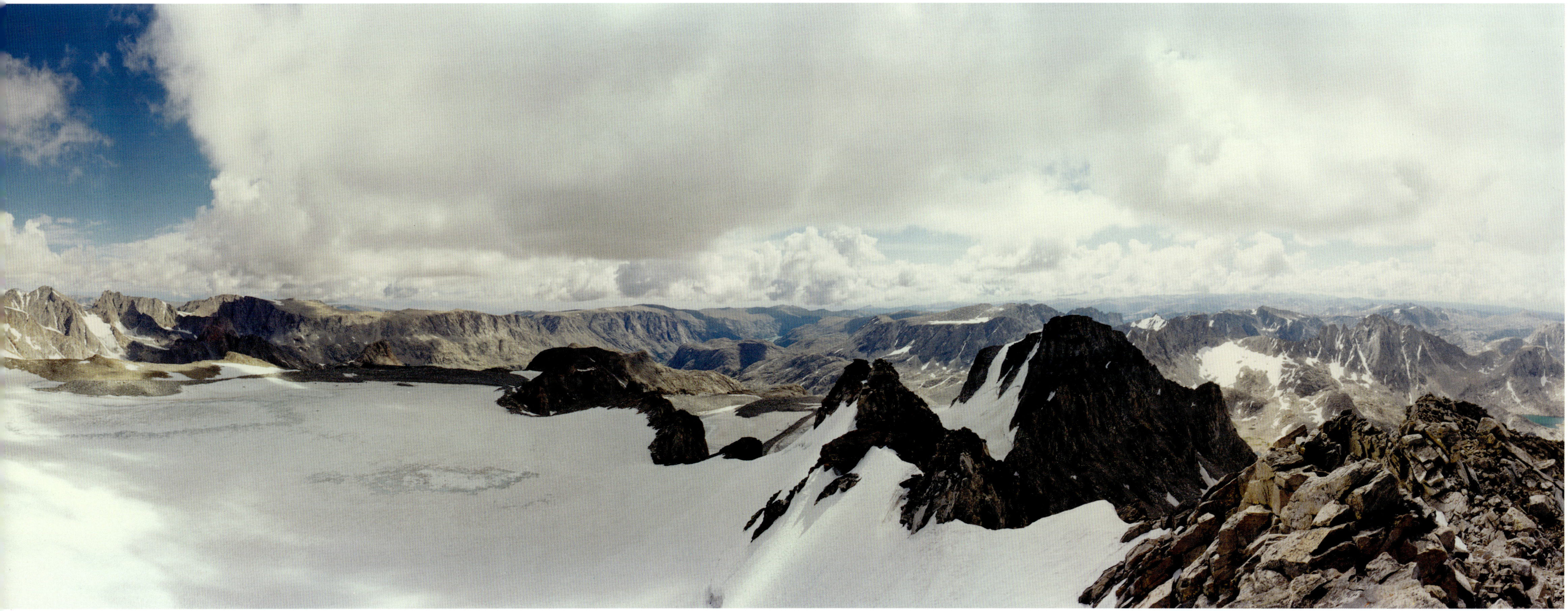

29 | FREMONT PEAK, BRIDGER WILDERNESS, WYOMING | 1994 | 377°

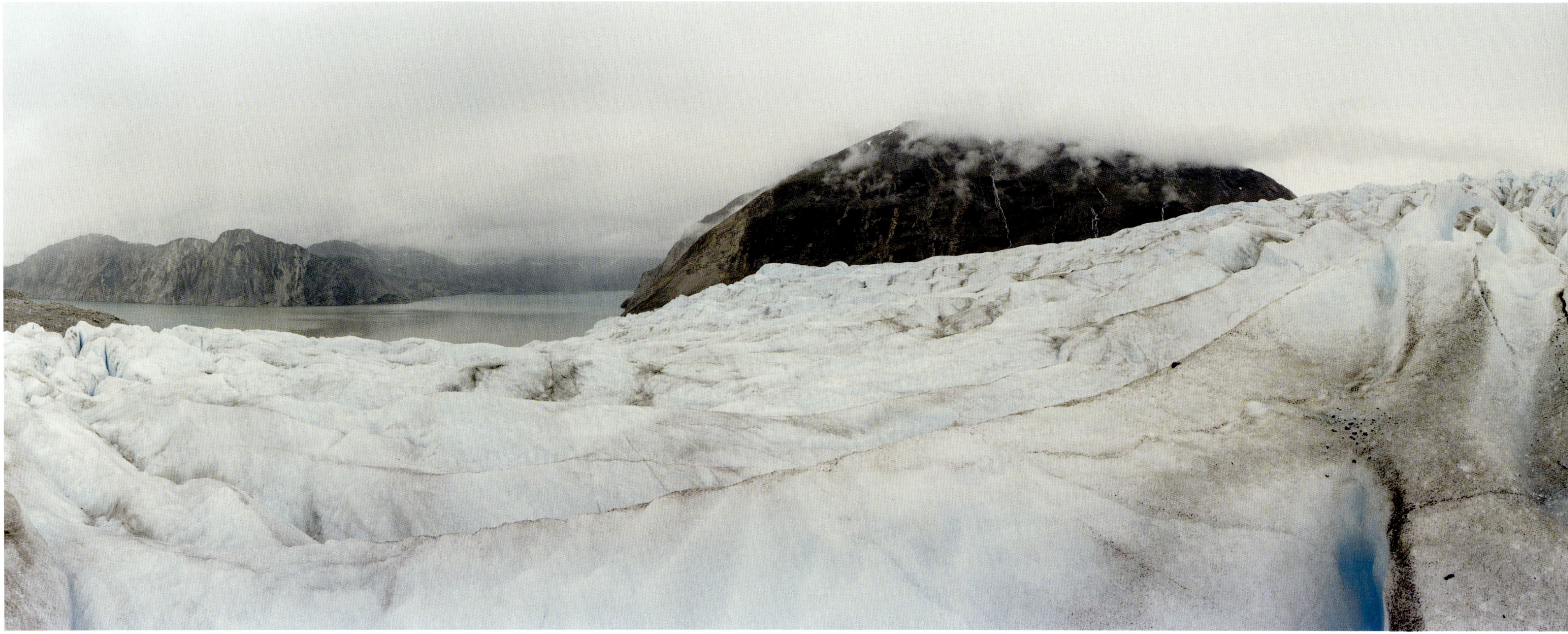

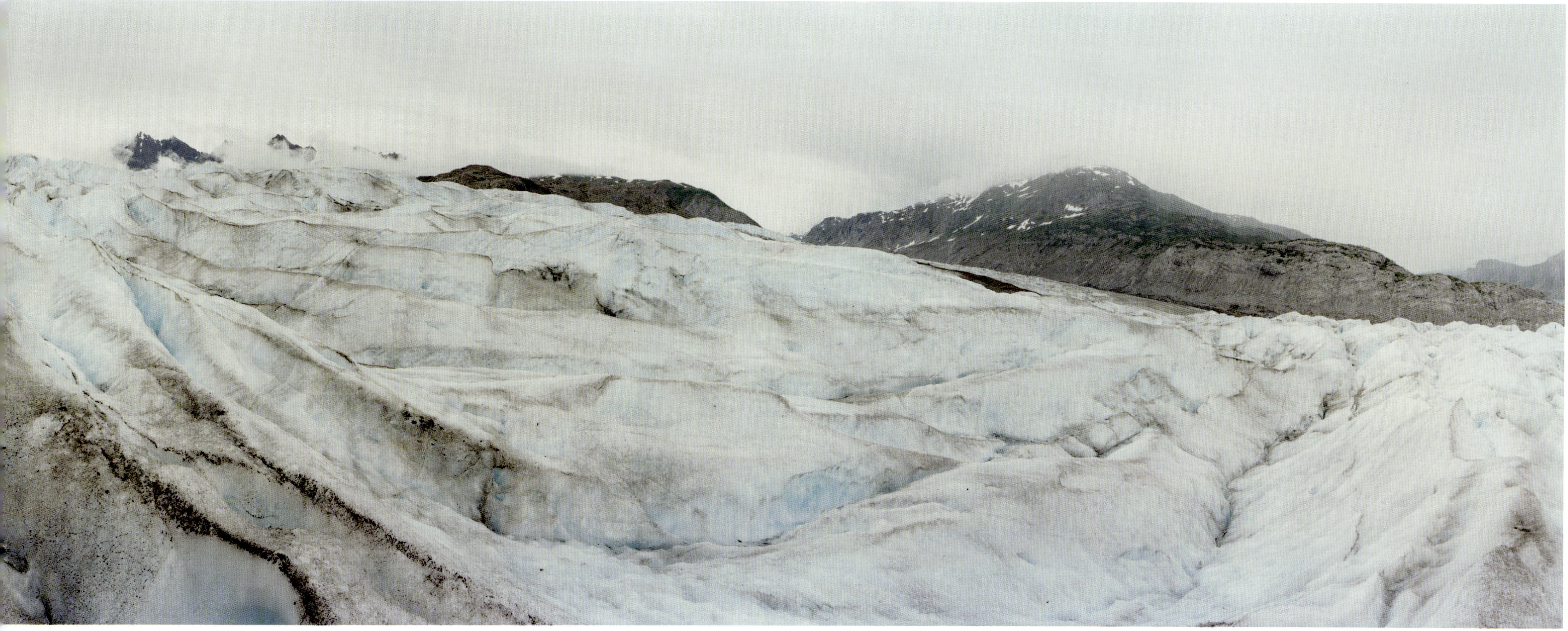

30 | RIGGS GLACIER, GLACIER BAY WILDERNESS, ALASKA | 1991 | 366°

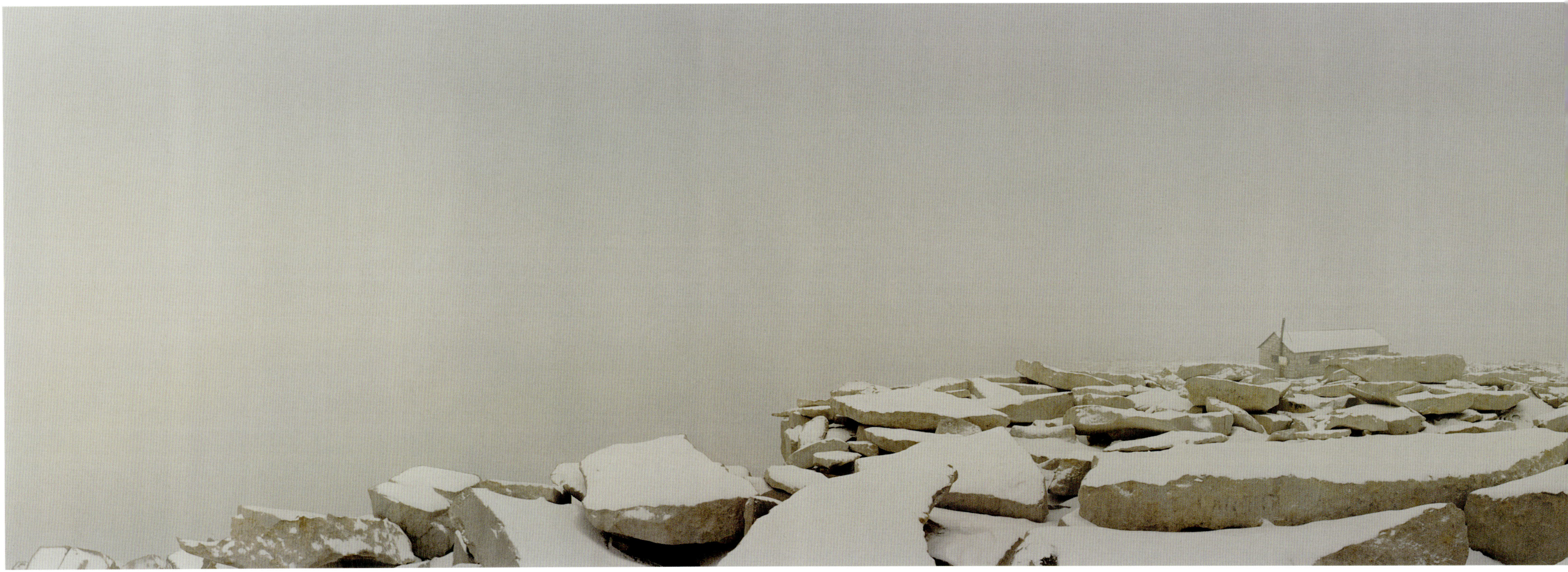

31 | MOUNT WHITNEY, INYO NATIONAL FOREST, CALIFORNIA | 1990 | 374°

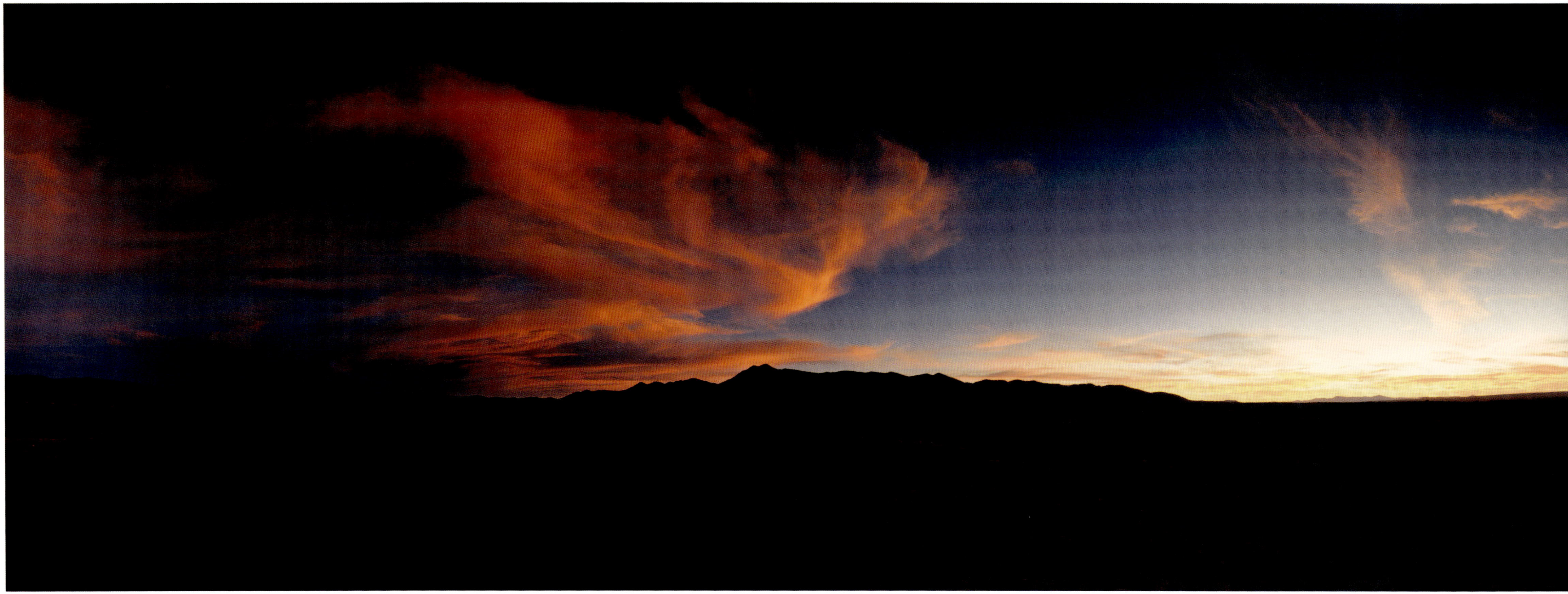

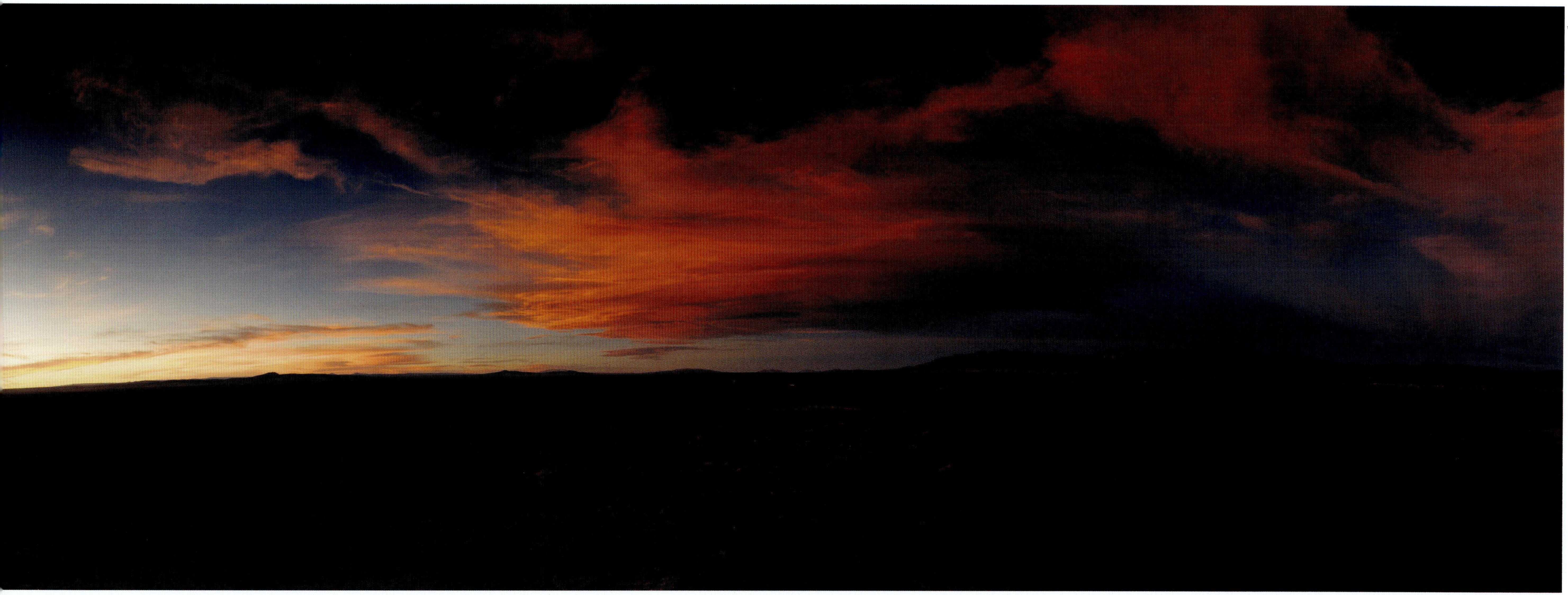

32 | MESA SUNSET, TAOS COUNTY, NEW MEXICO | 1988 | 355°

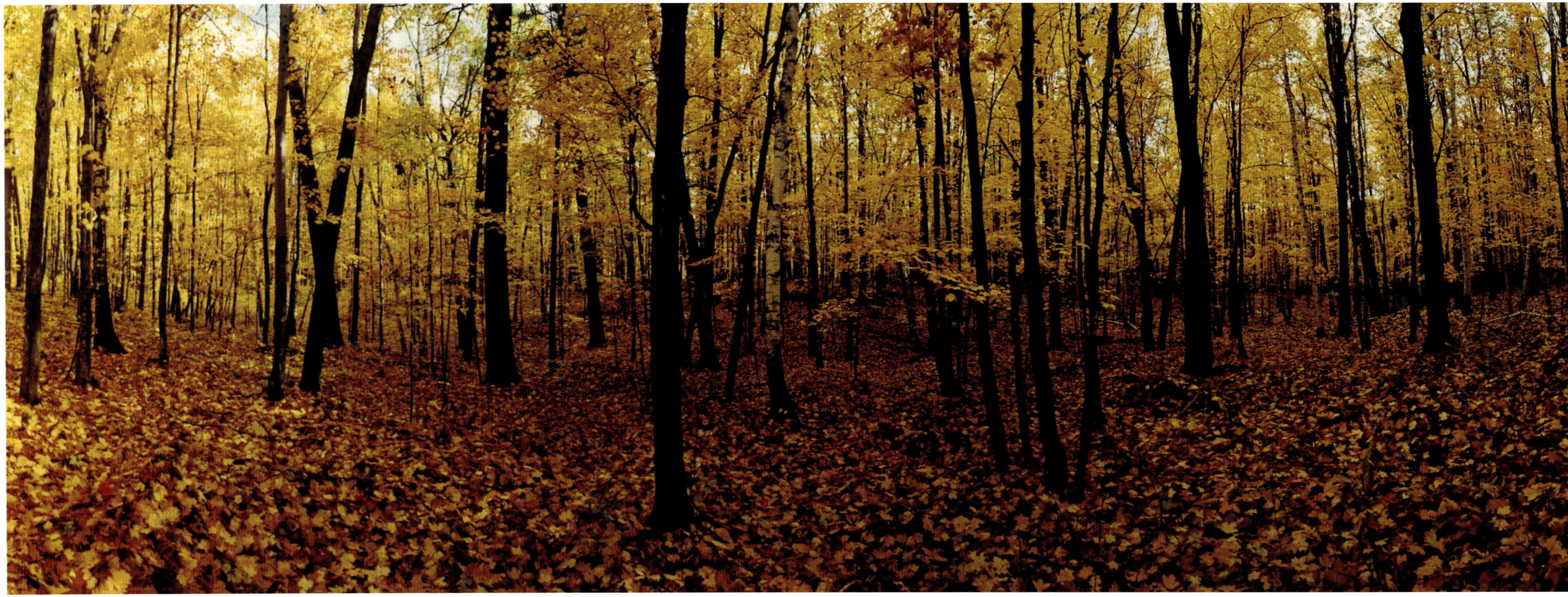

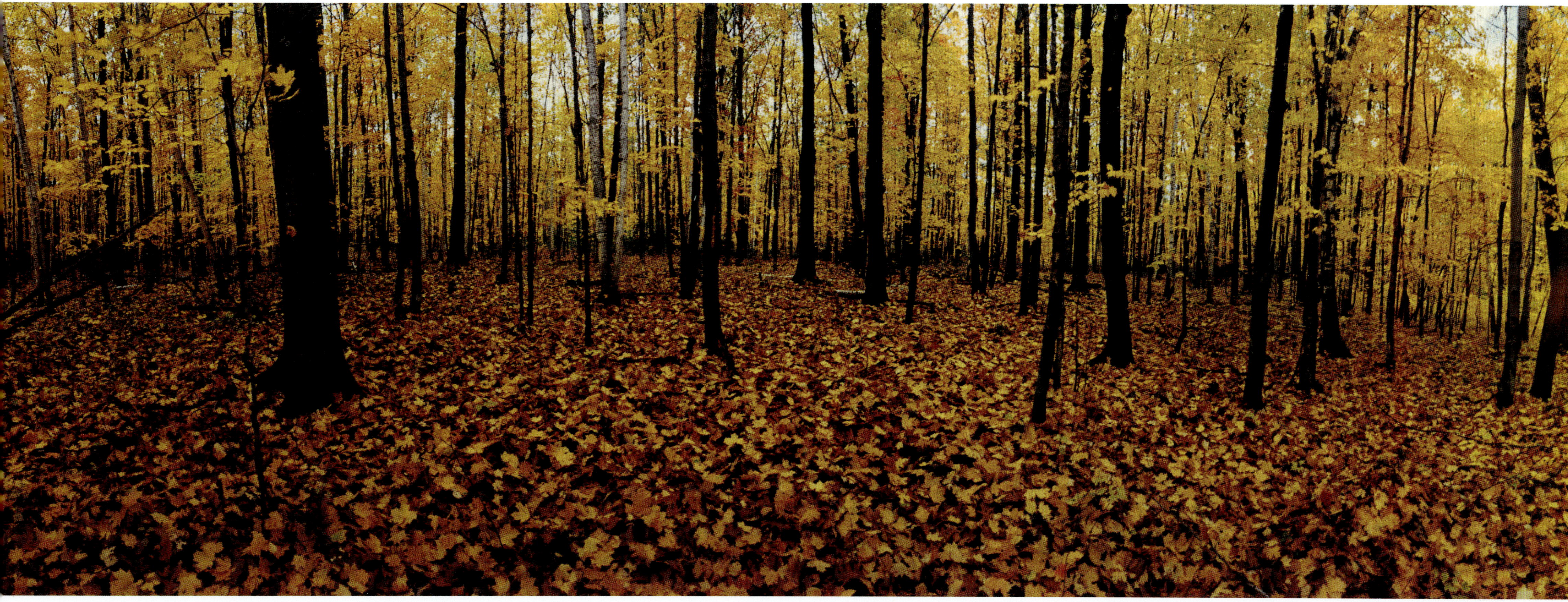

33 | NORTHWOODS, ONEIDA COUNTY, WISCONSIN | 1988 | 372°

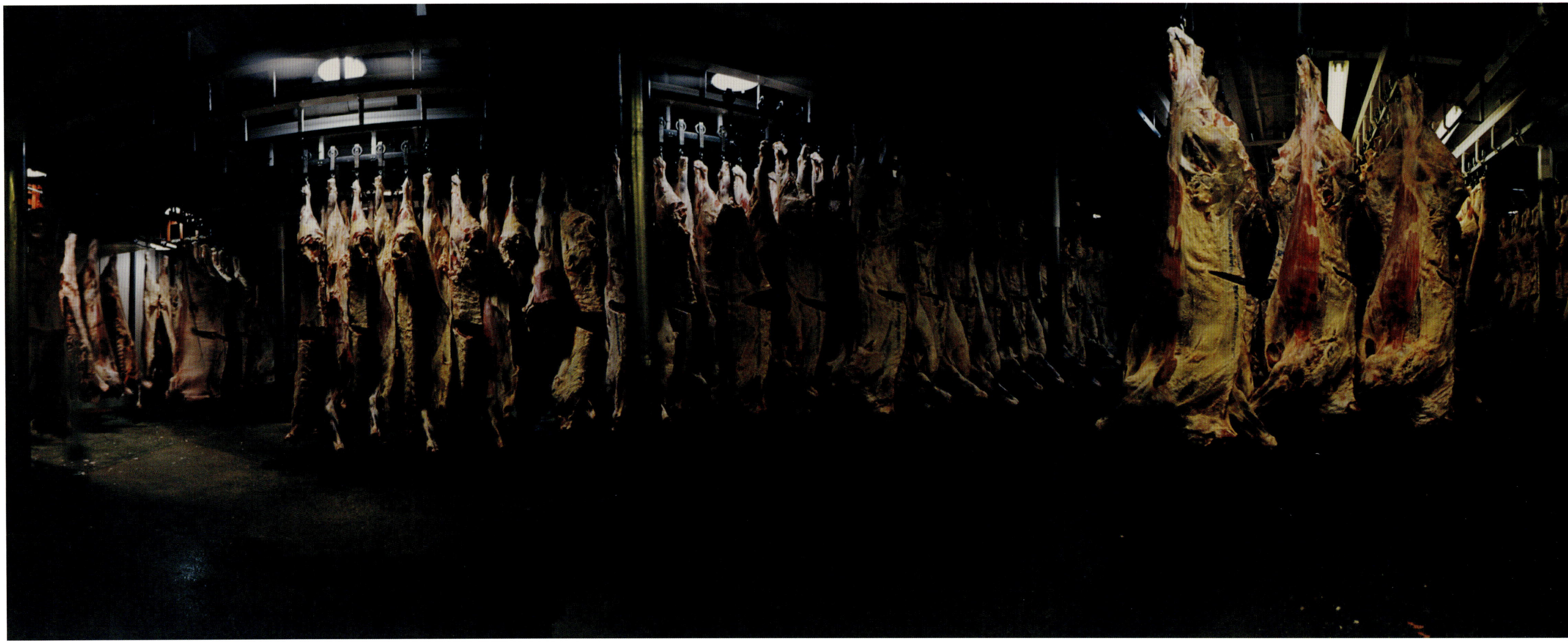

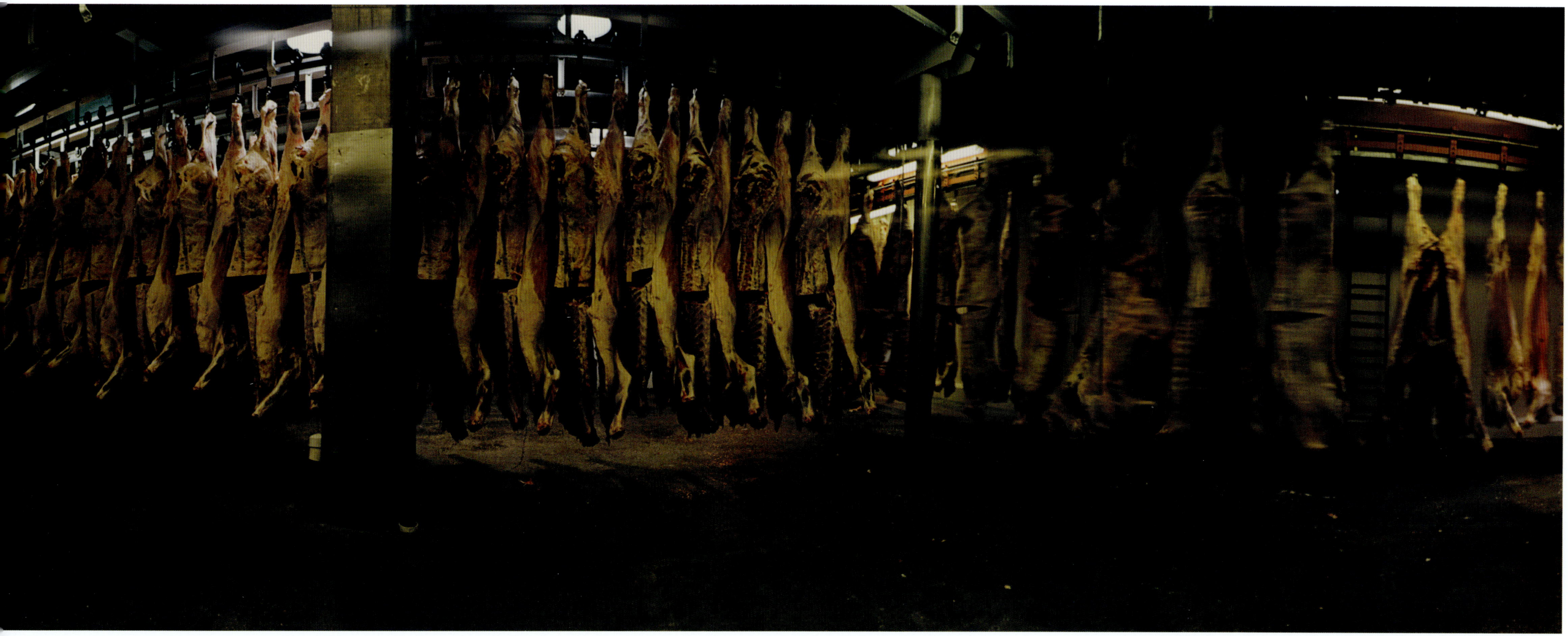

 | PACKERLAND BEEF, BROWN COUNTY, WISCONSIN | 1998 | 355°

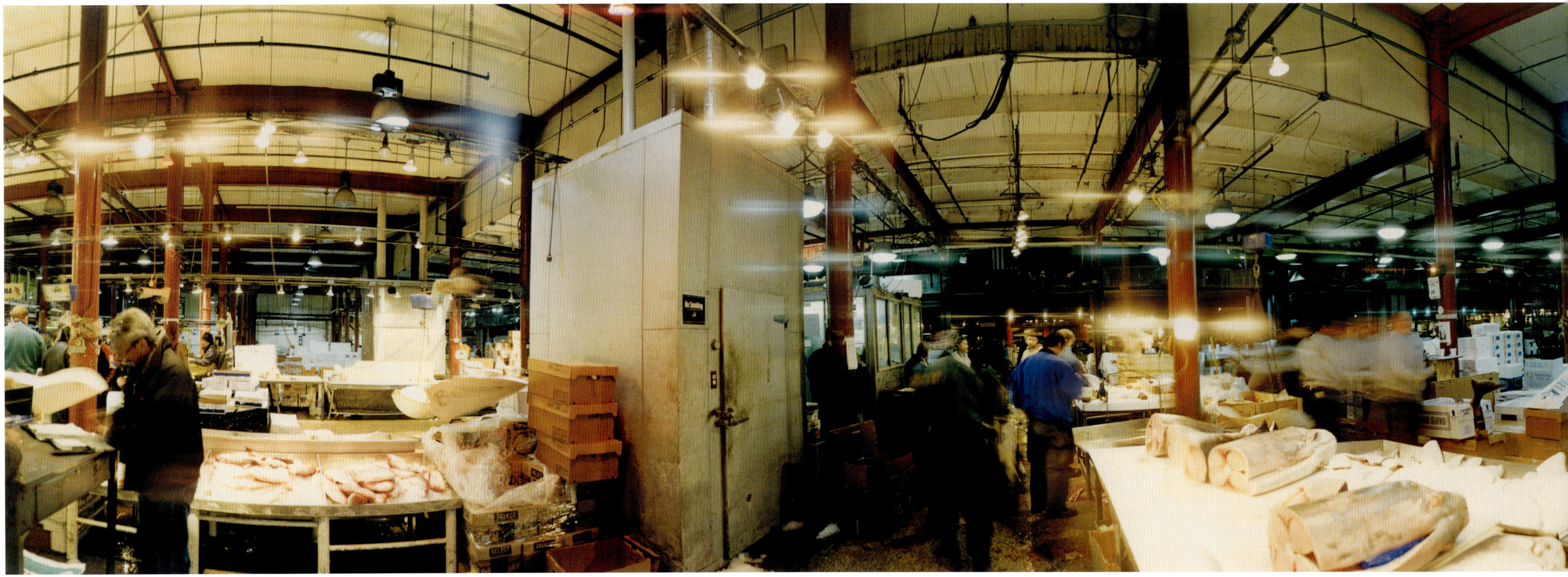

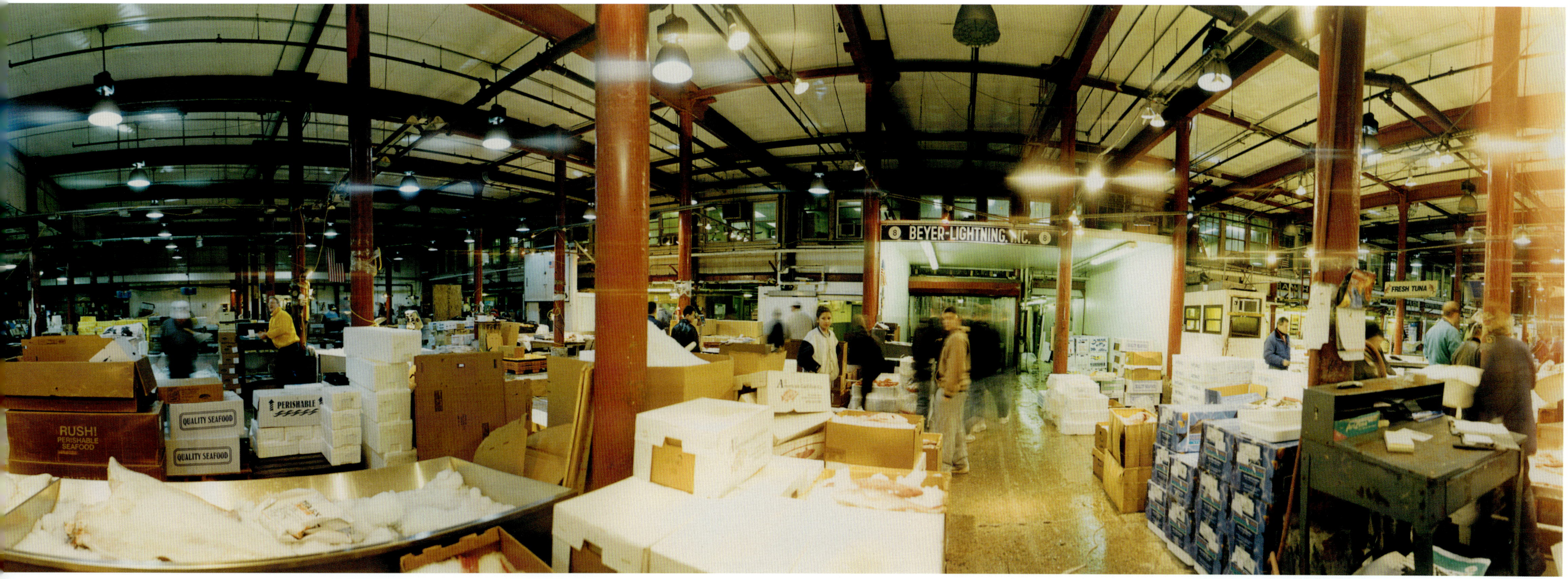

35 | FULTON STREET FISH MARKET, NEW YORK CITY, NEW YORK | 2004 | 377°

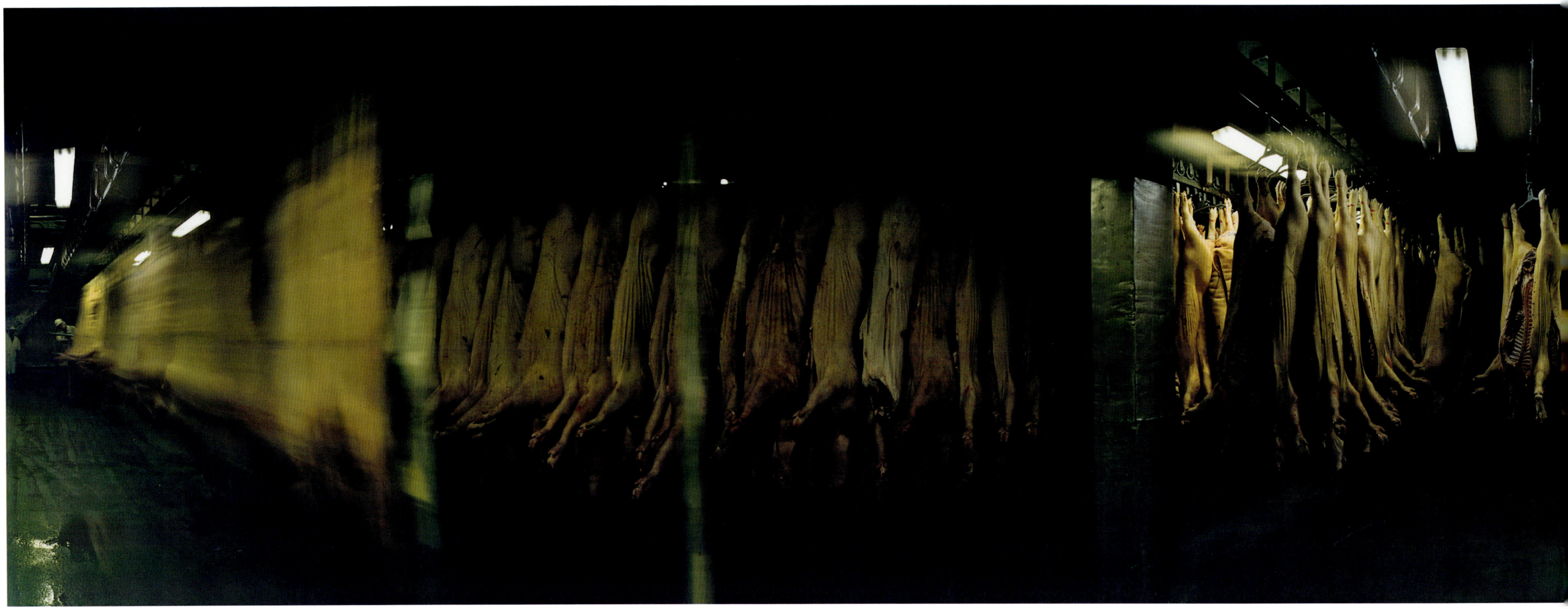

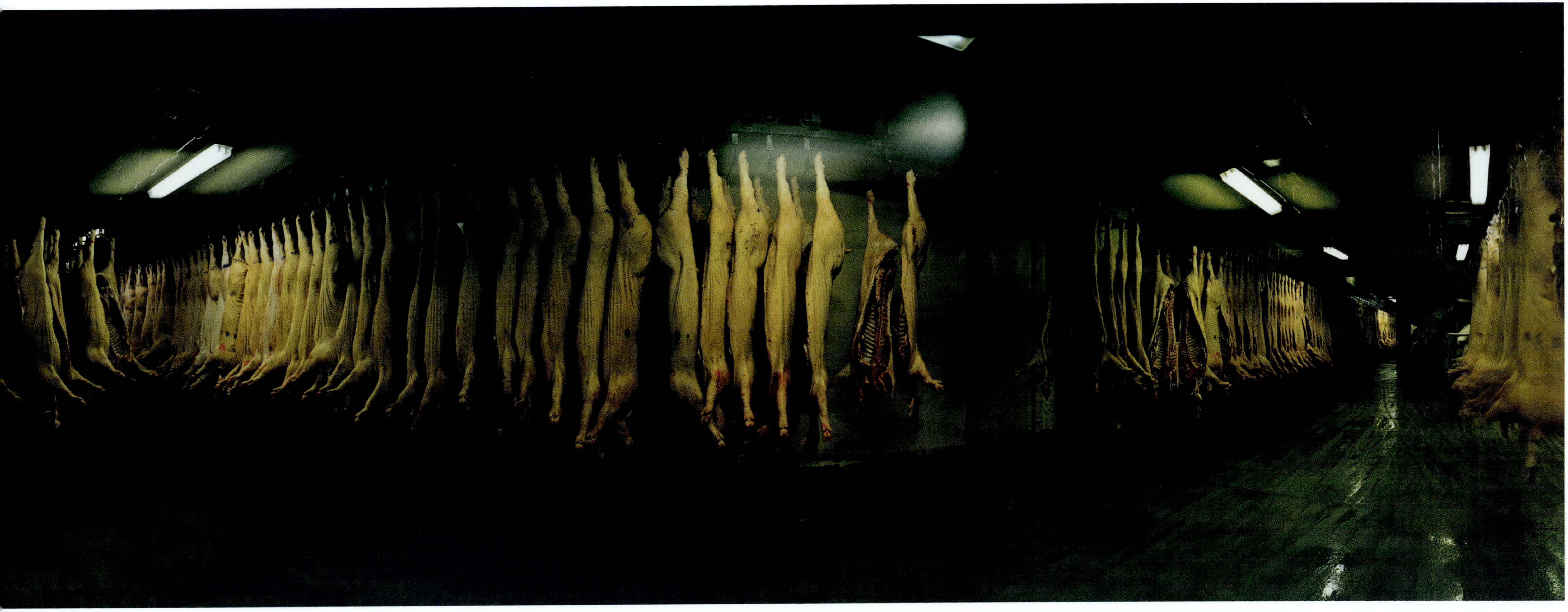

36 | PORK, MINNEHAHA COUNTY, SOUTH DAKOTA | 1998 | 377°

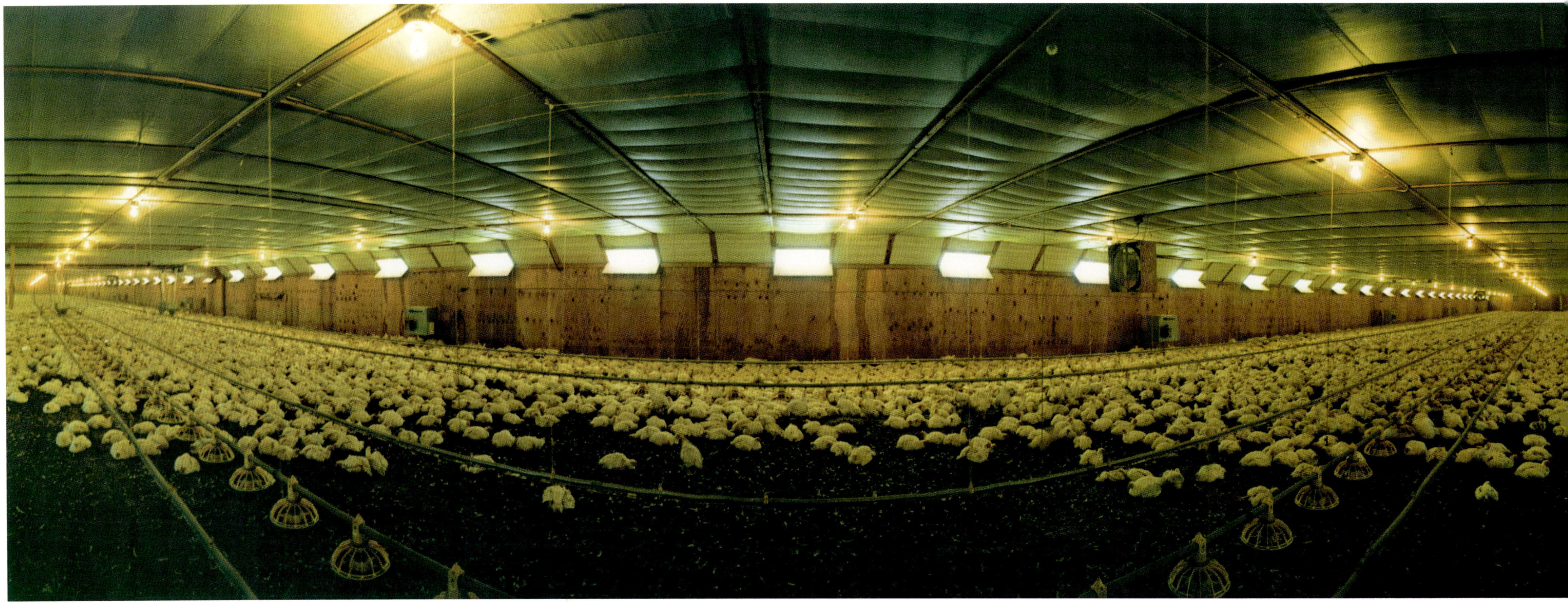

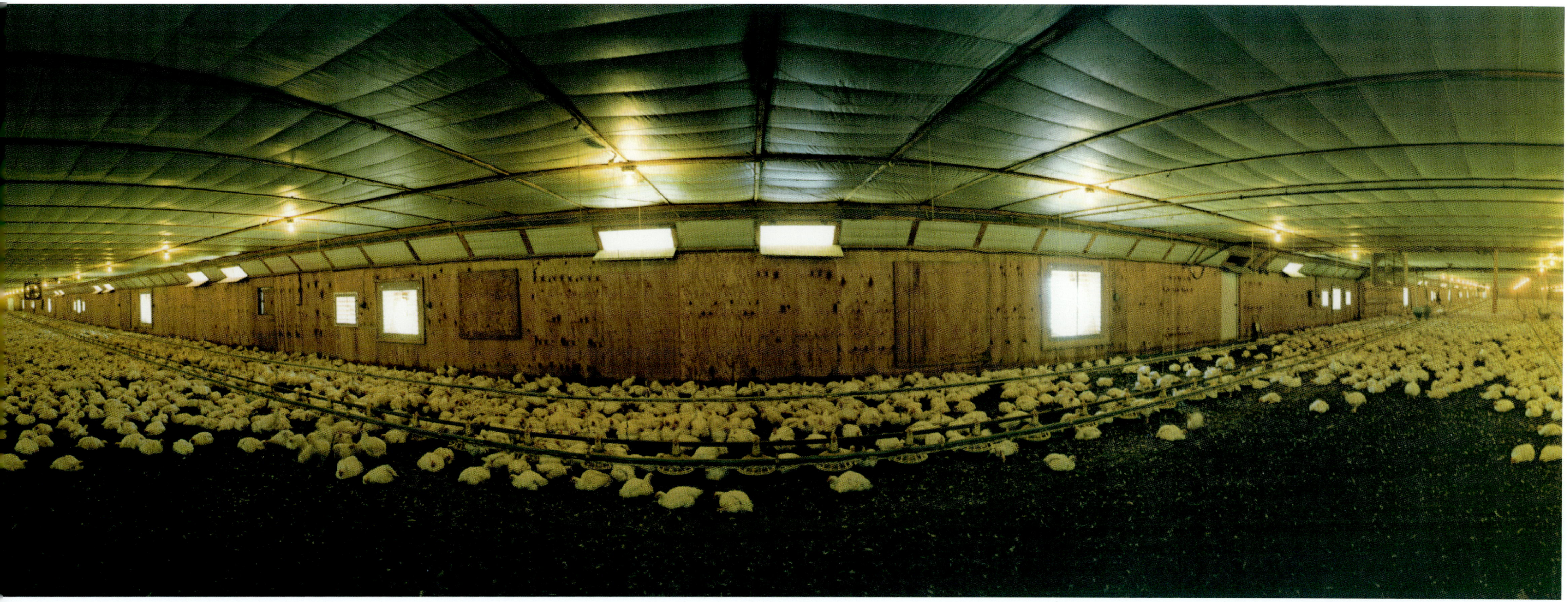

37 | FREE-RANGE CHICKENS, STEARNS COUNTY, MINNESOTA | 1998 | 369°

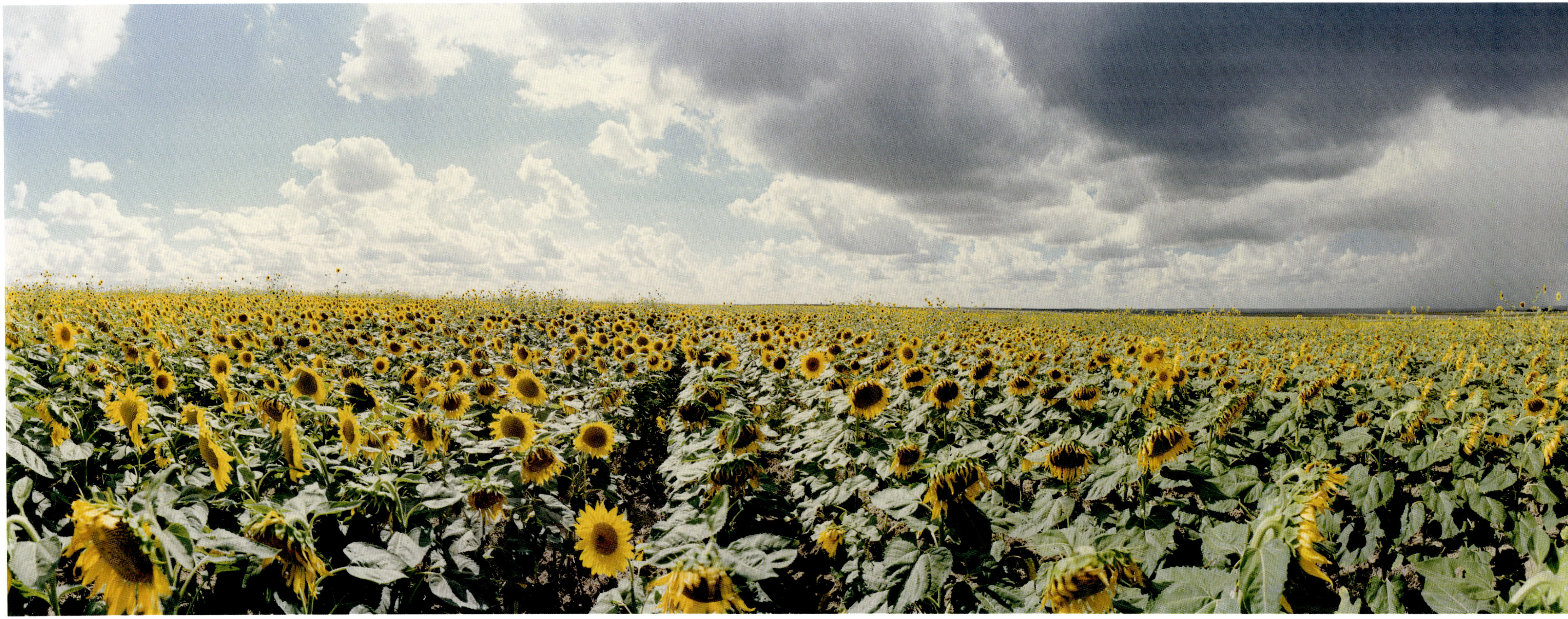

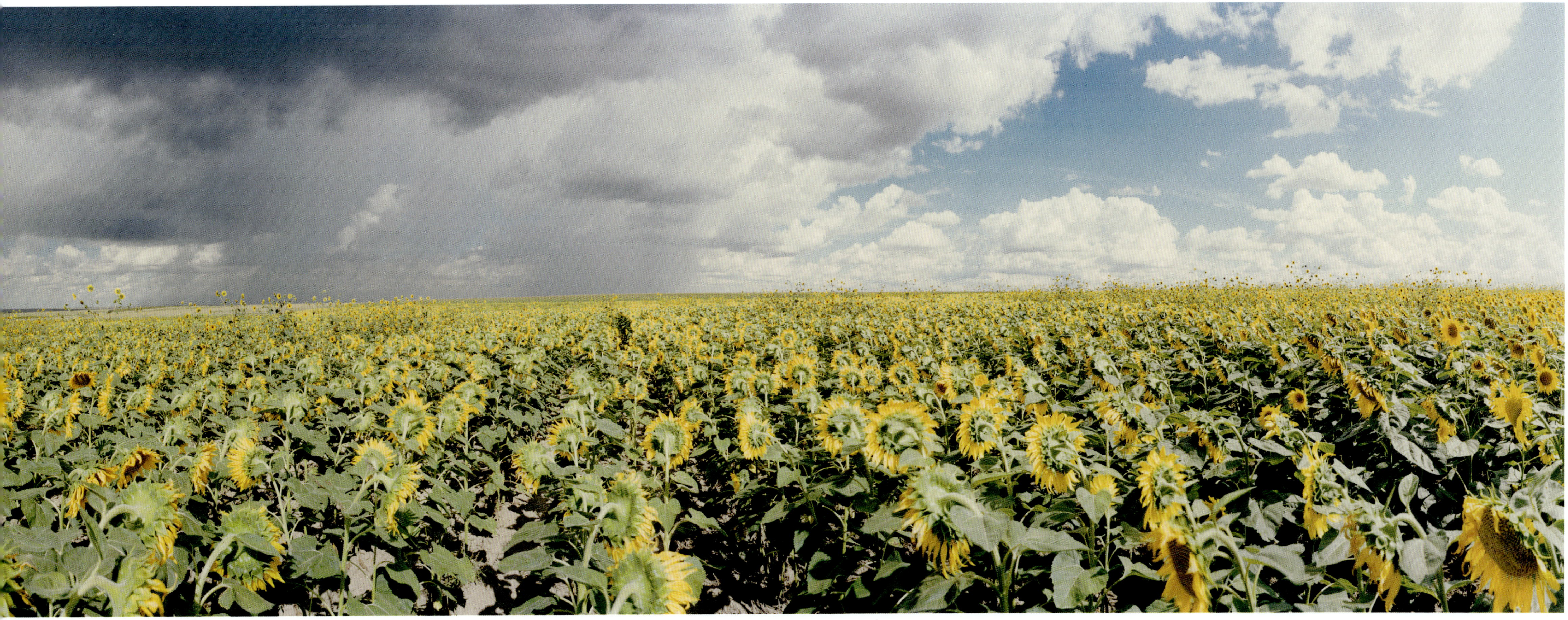

38 | SUNFLOWERS, WALLACE COUNTY, KANSAS | 1996 | 385°

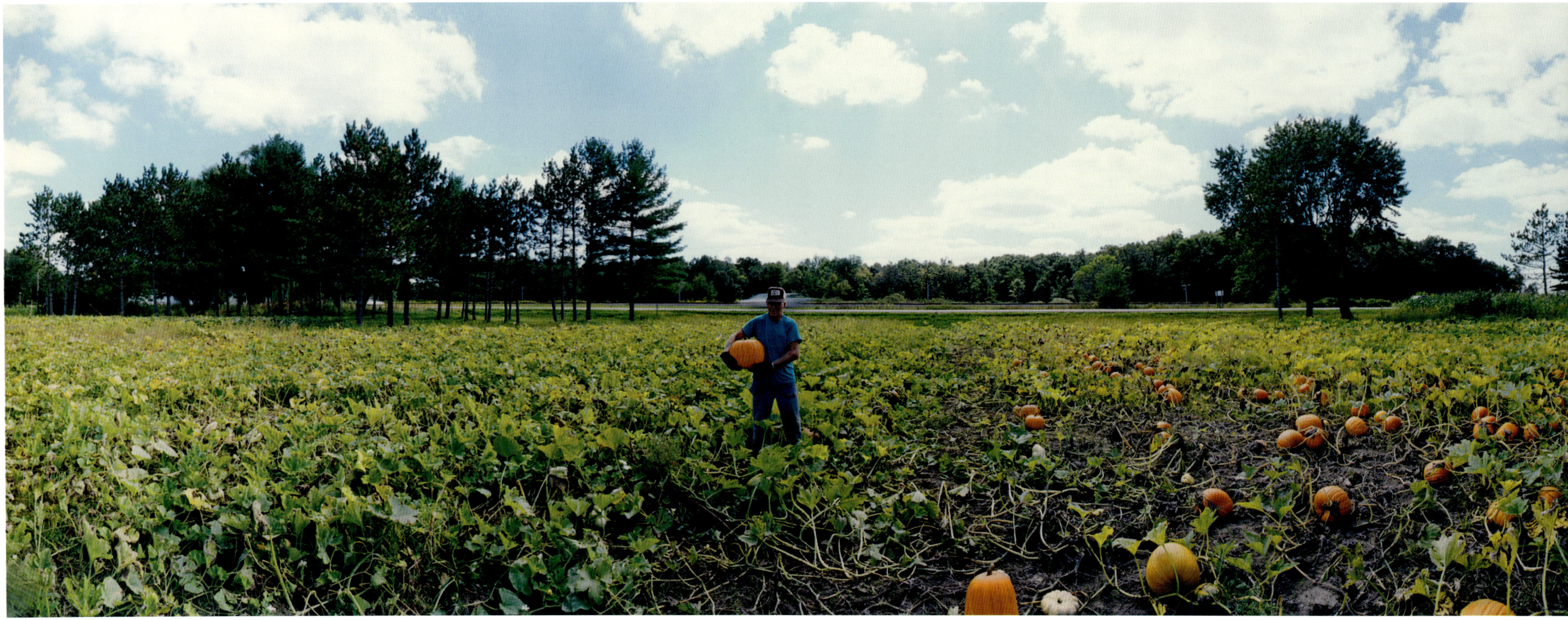

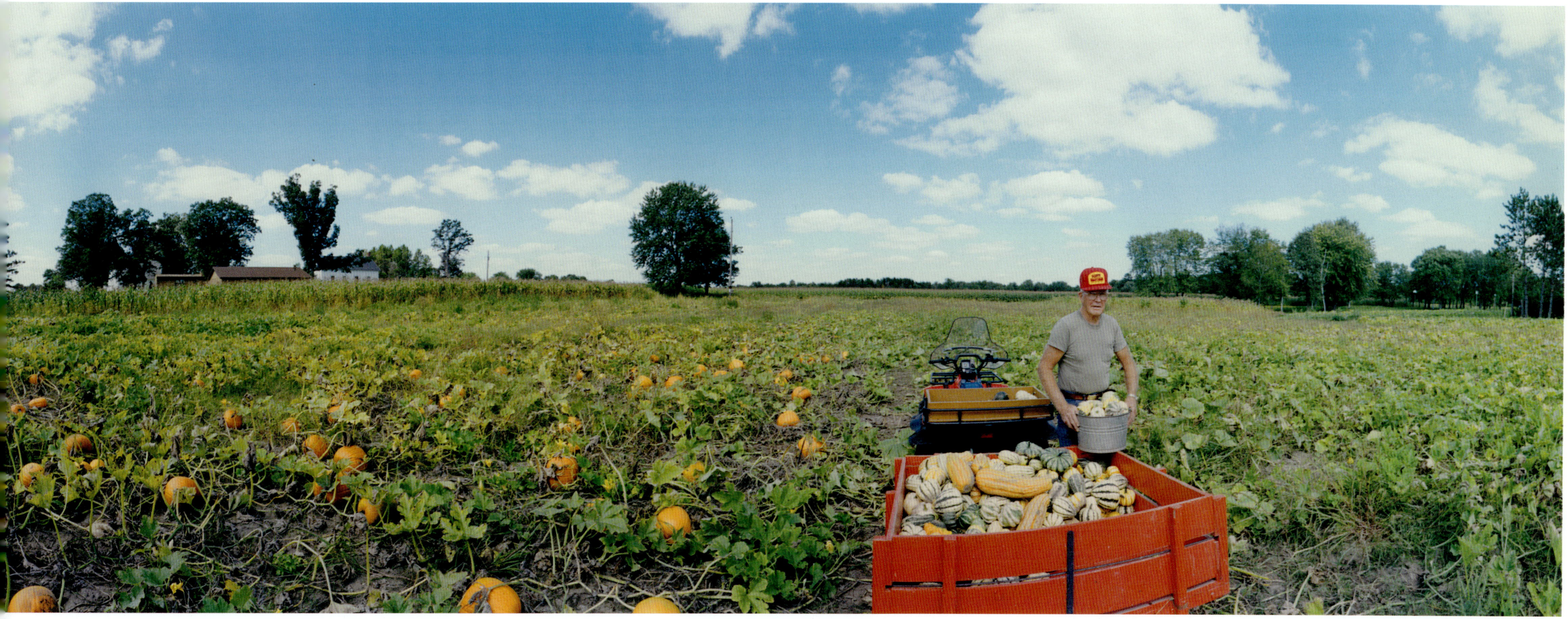

39 | PUMPKIN HARVEST, JUNEAU COUNTY, WISCONSIN | 1997 | 374°

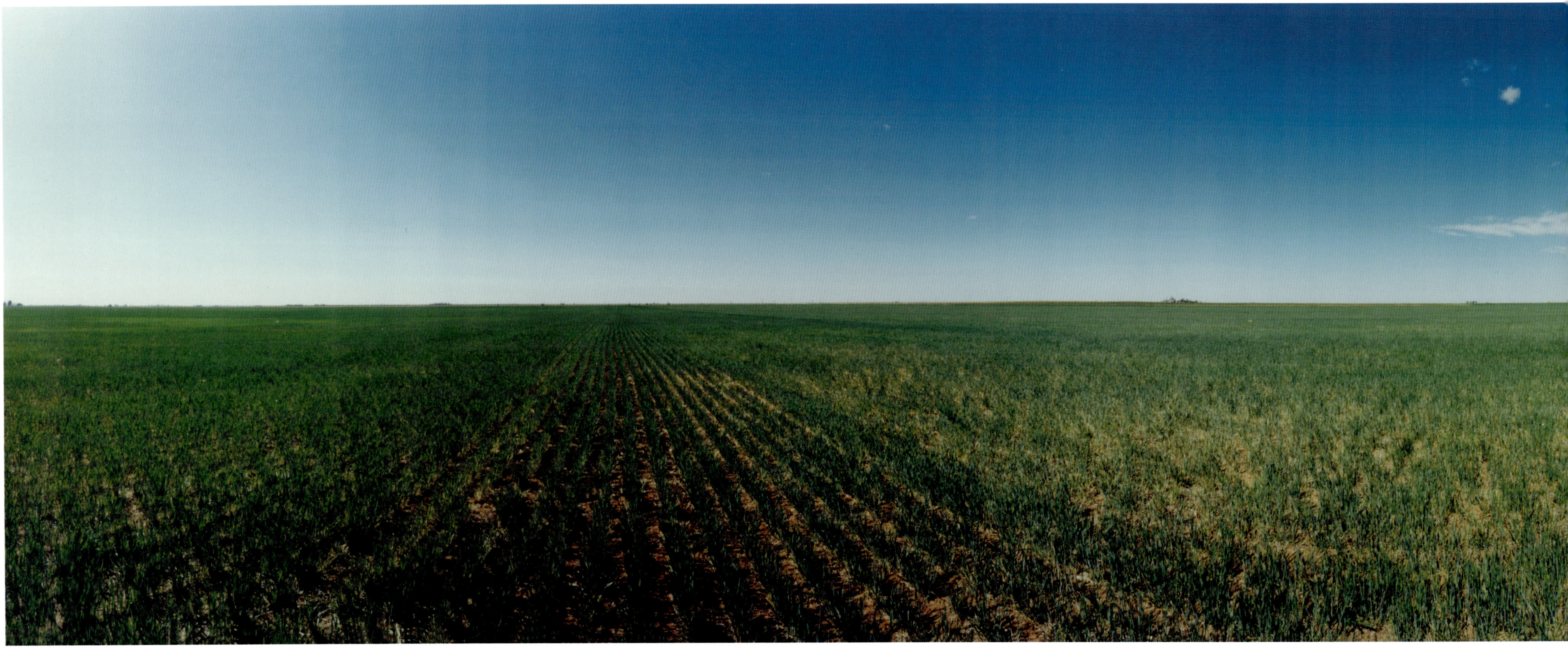

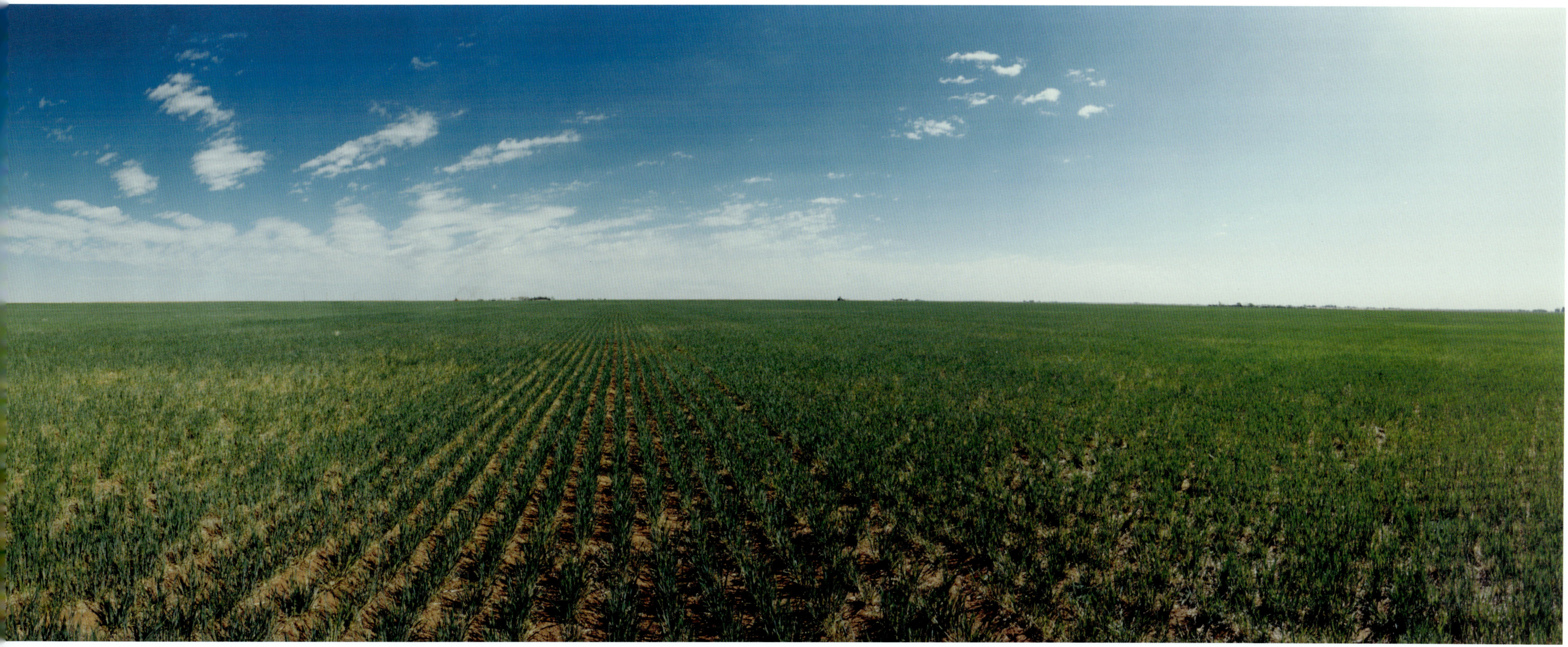

40 | NEW WHEAT, POTTER COUNTY, TEXAS | 1988 | 364°

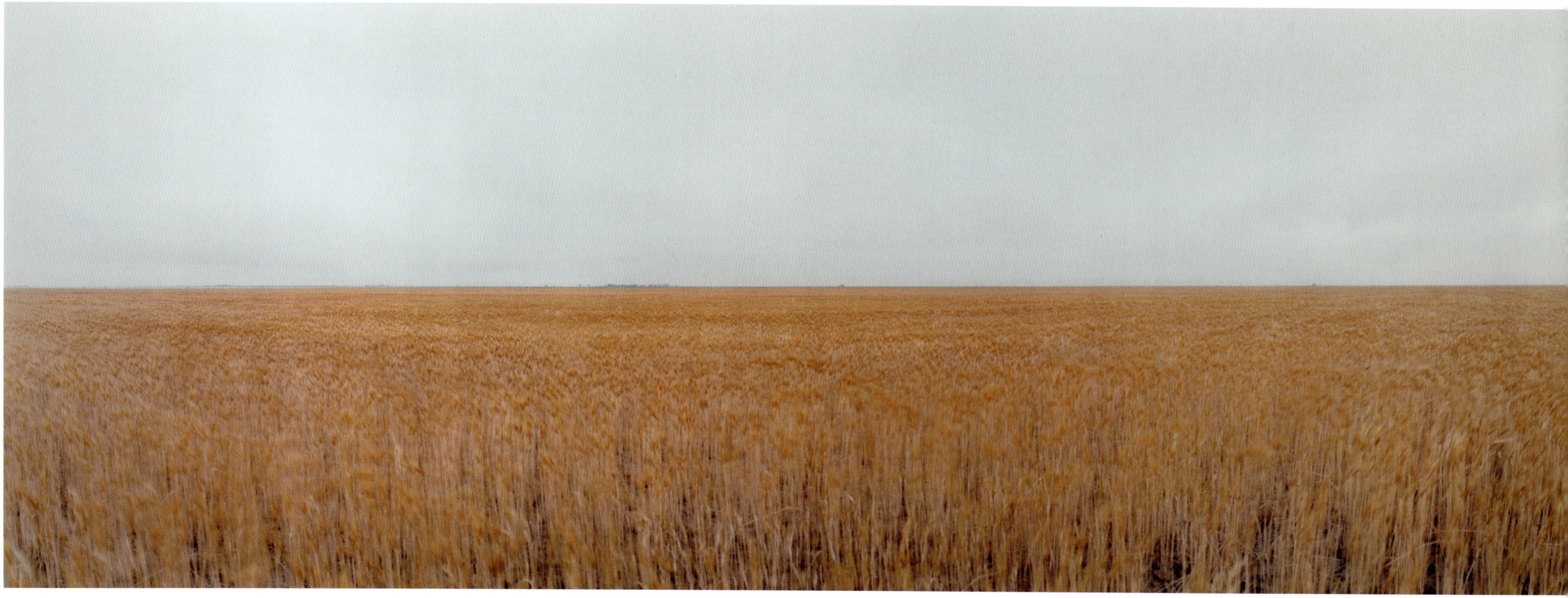

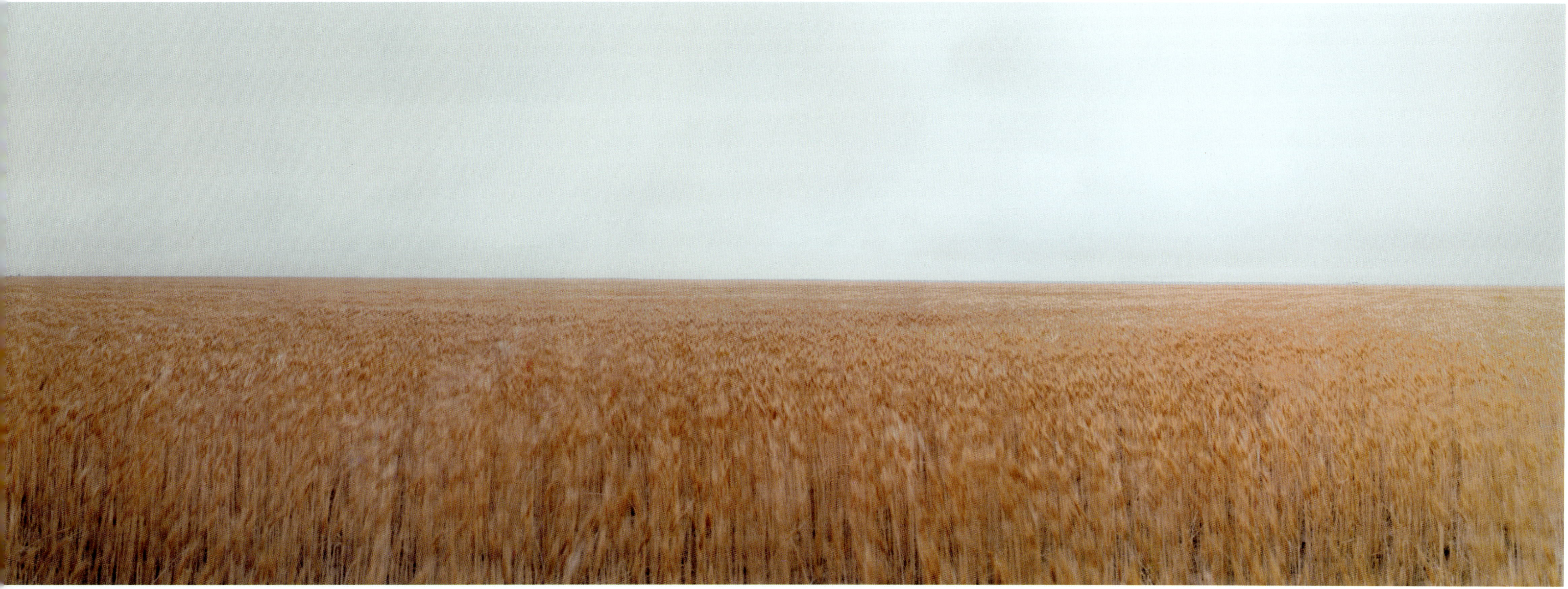

41 | WINTER WHEAT, QUAY COUNTY, NEW MEXICO | 2004 | 377°

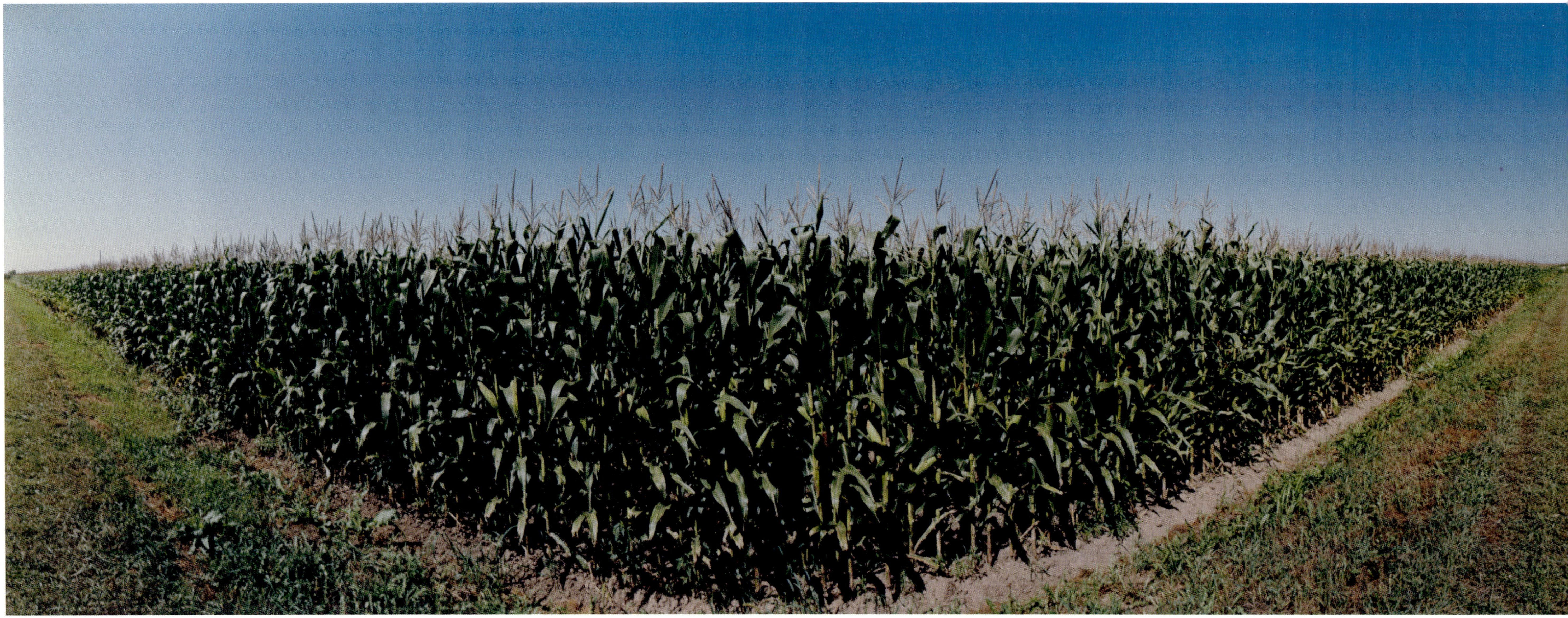

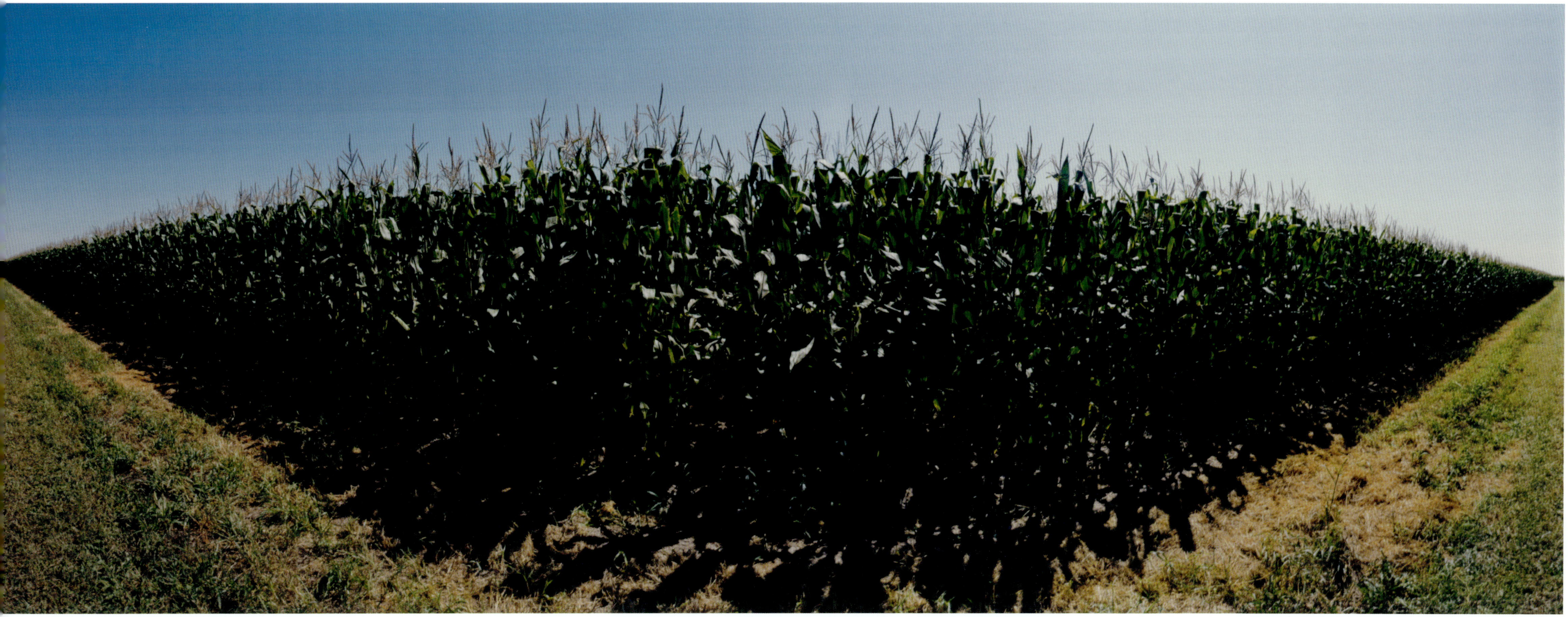

42 | CORN, SEWARD COUNTY, NEBRASKA | 1998 | 361°

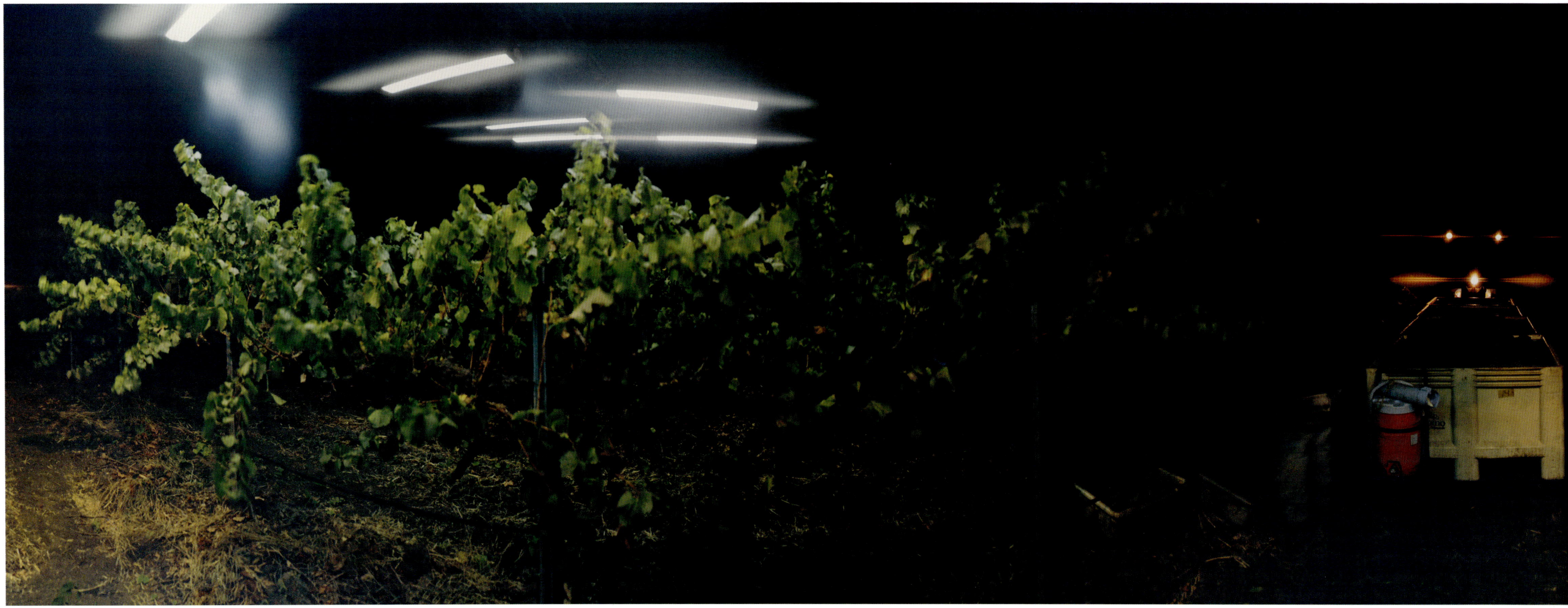

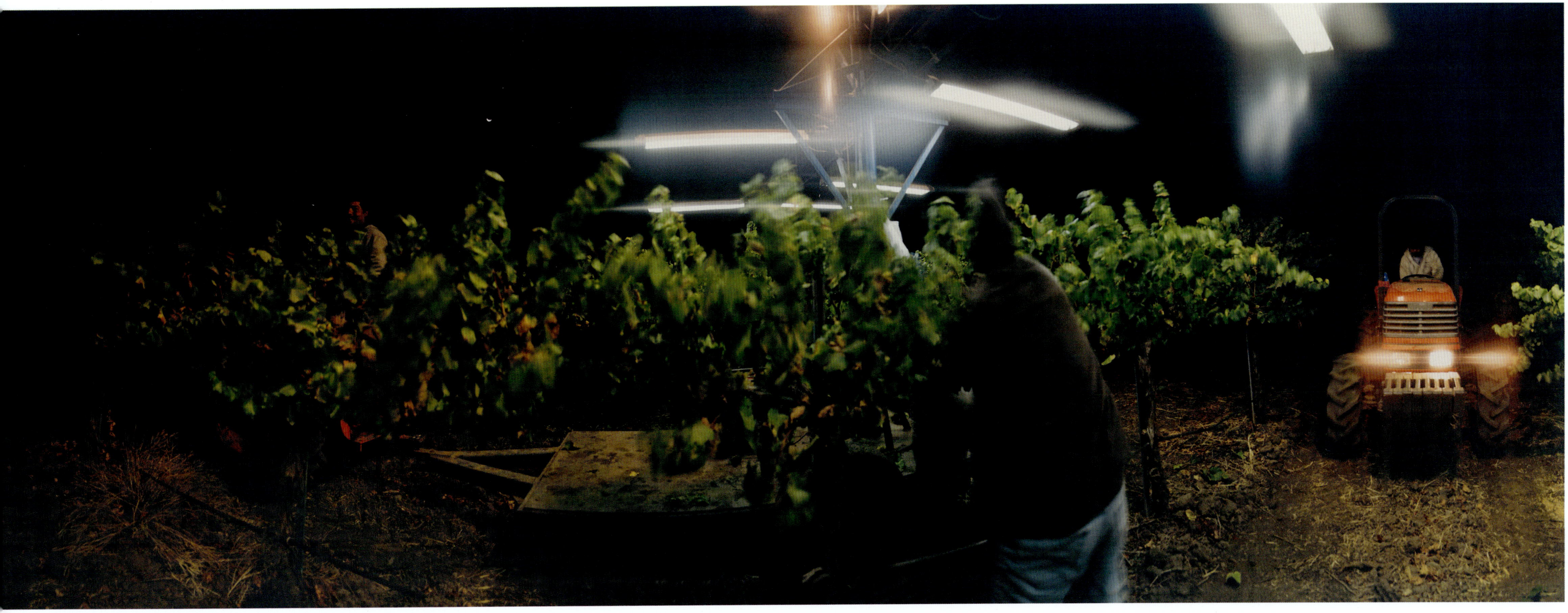

43 | CHARDONNAY HARVEST, SONOMA COUNTY, CALIFORNIA | 2002 | 370°

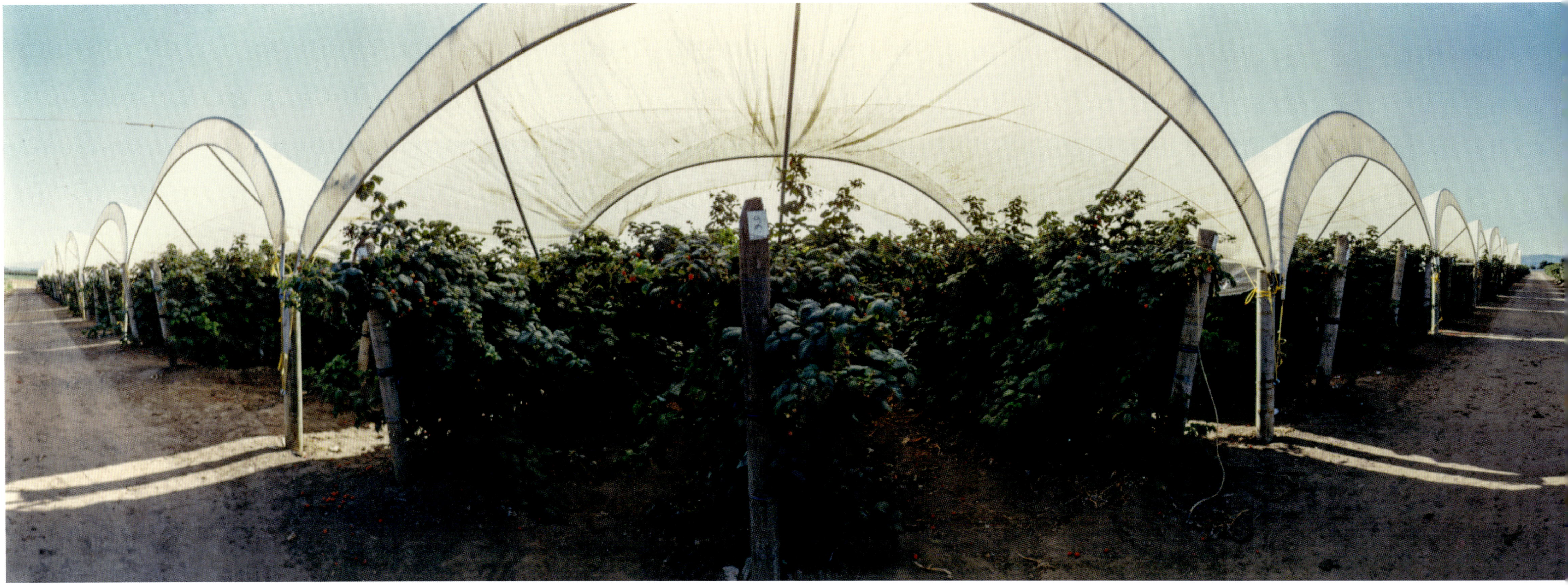

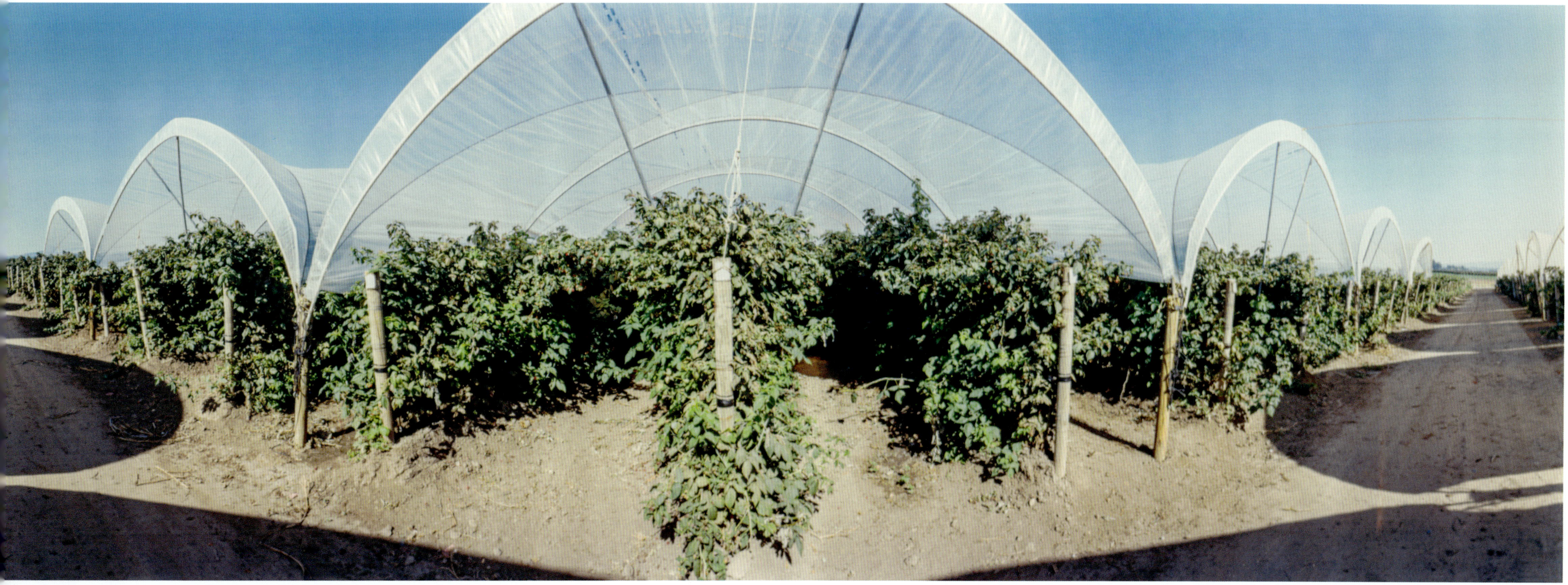

44 | RASPBERRIES, SANTA CRUZ COUNTY, CALIFORNIA | 2002 | 374°

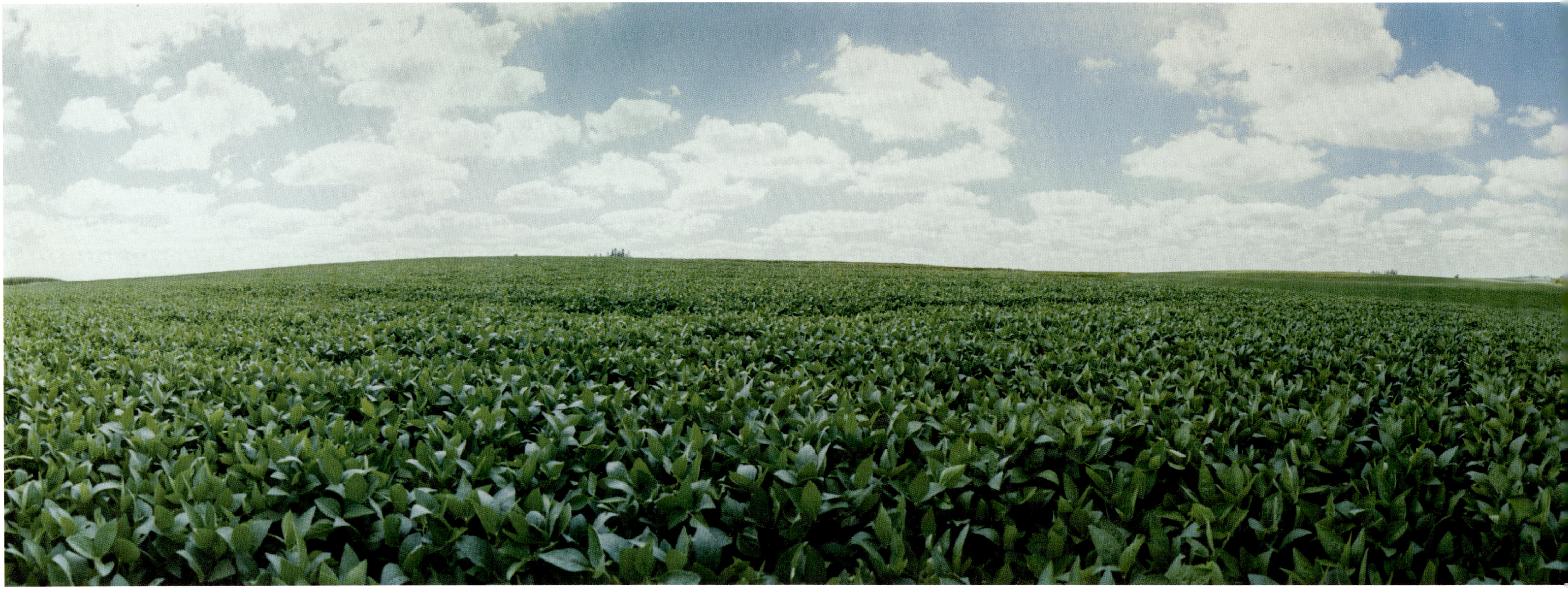

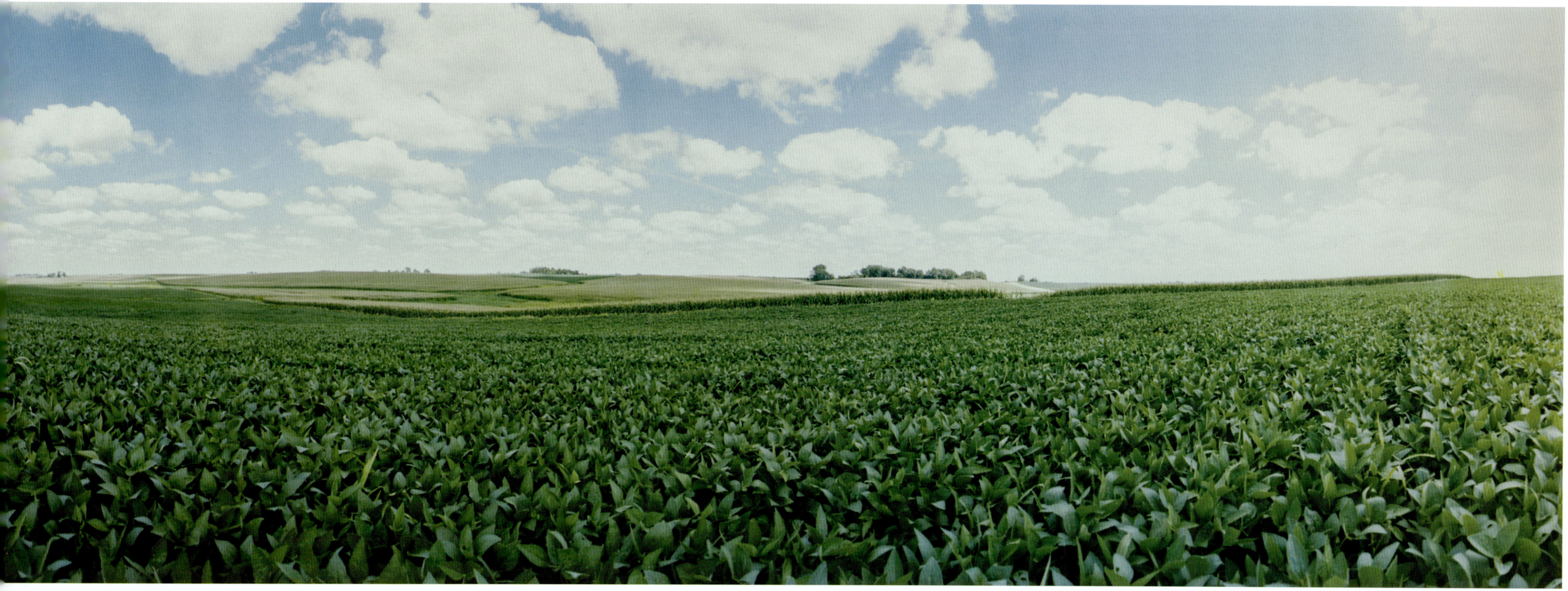

45 | SOYBEANS, GUTHRIE COUNTY, IOWA | 1998 | 378°

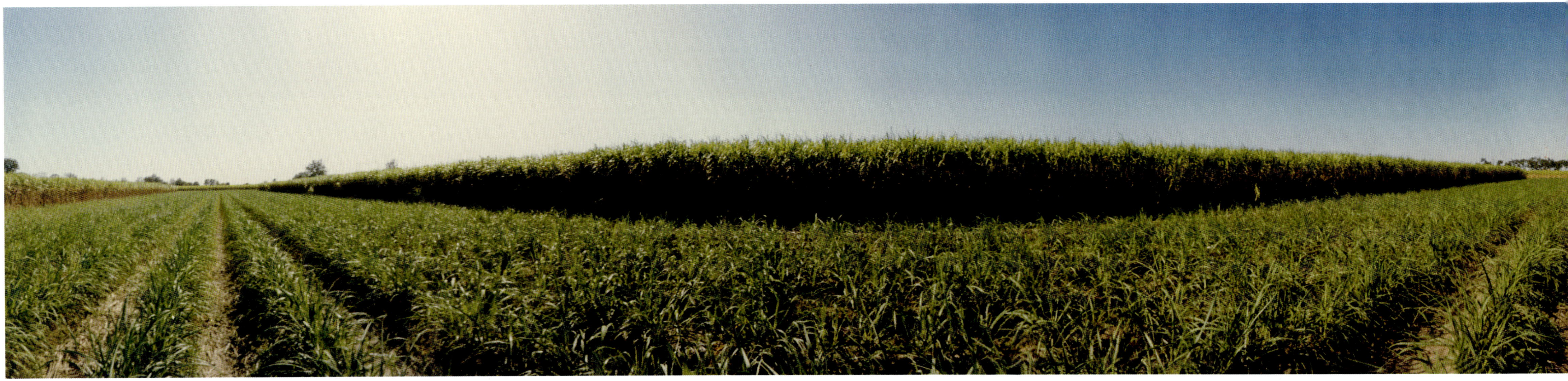

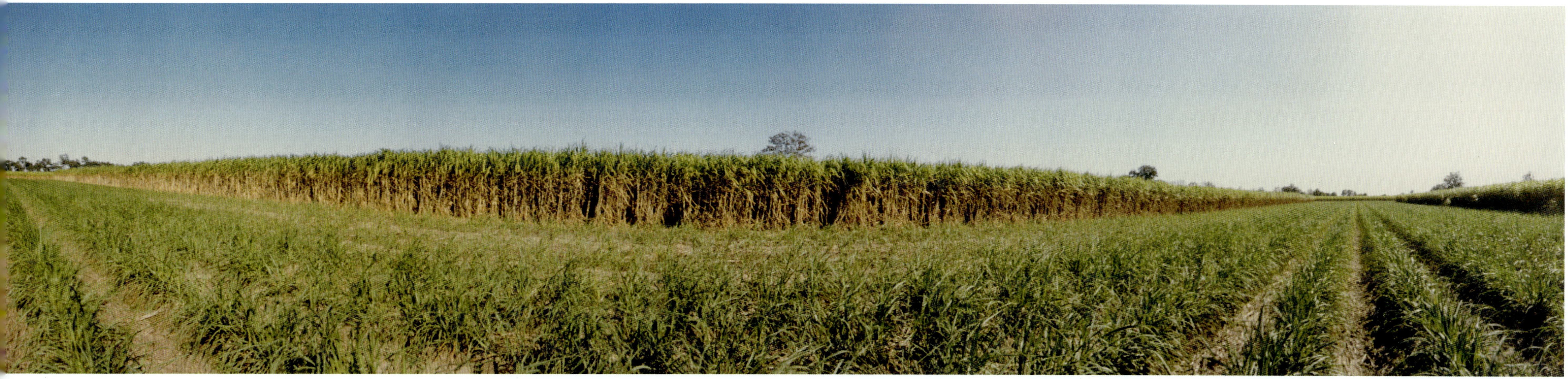

46 | SWEET LIGHT SUGARCANE, SAINT MARTIN PARISH, LOUISIANA | 1983 | 417°

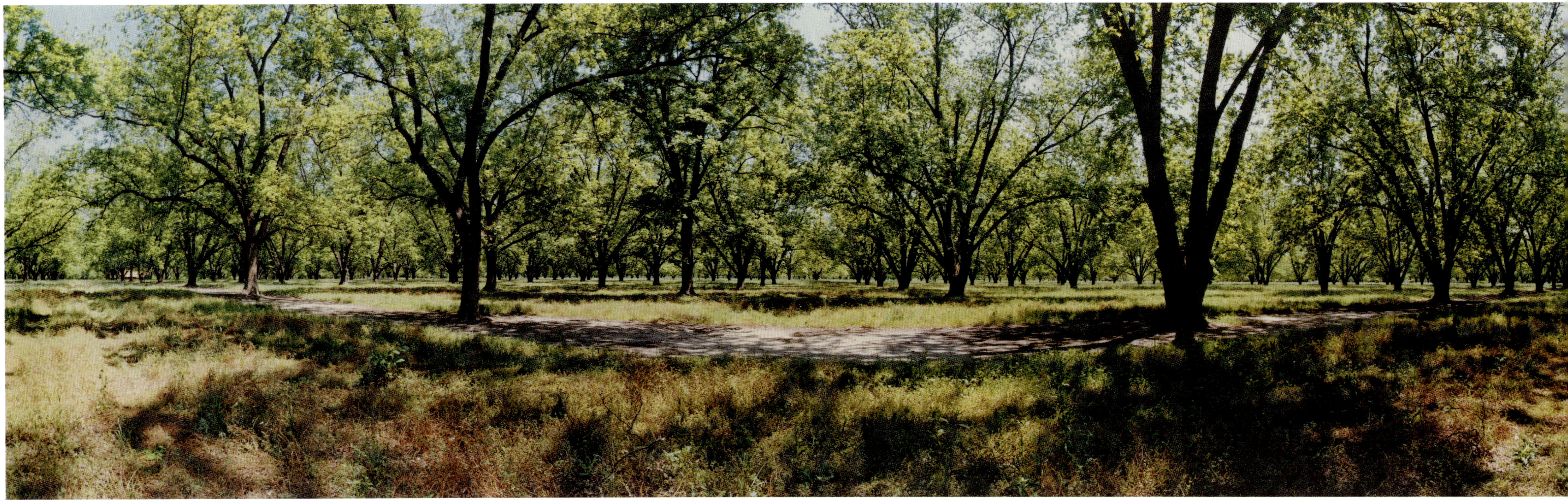

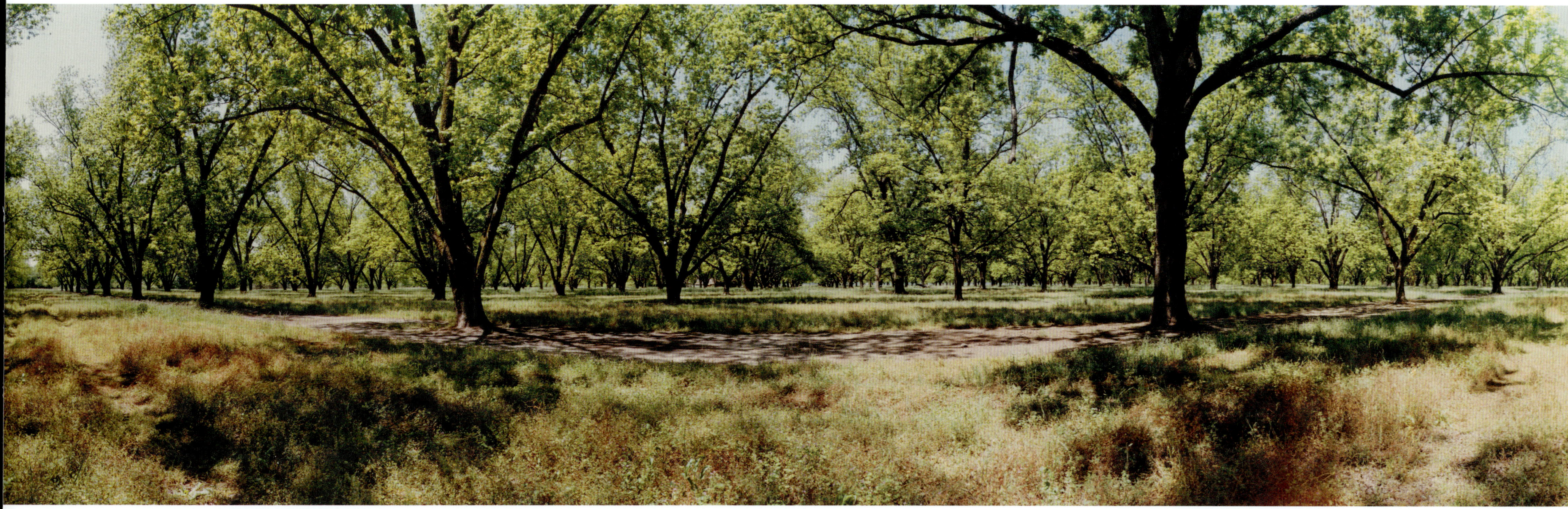

47 | PECAN GROVE, MERIWETHER COUNTY, GEORGIA | 2003 | 367°

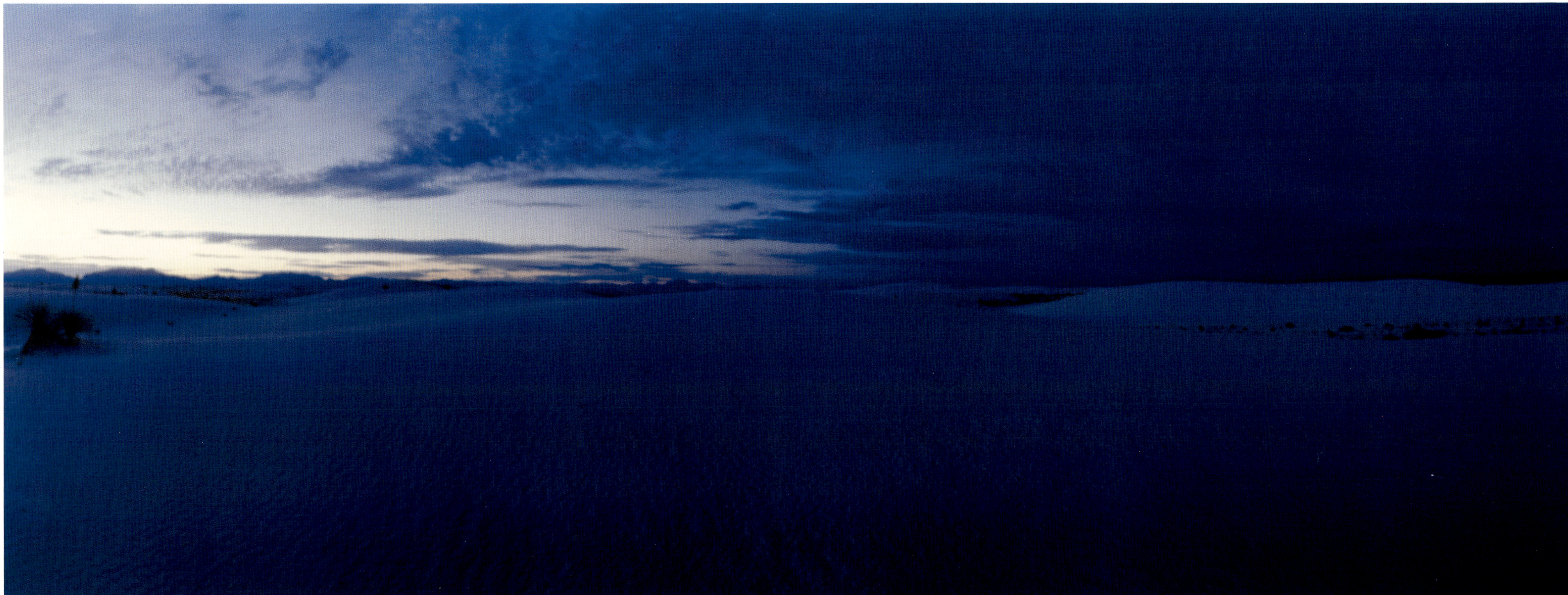

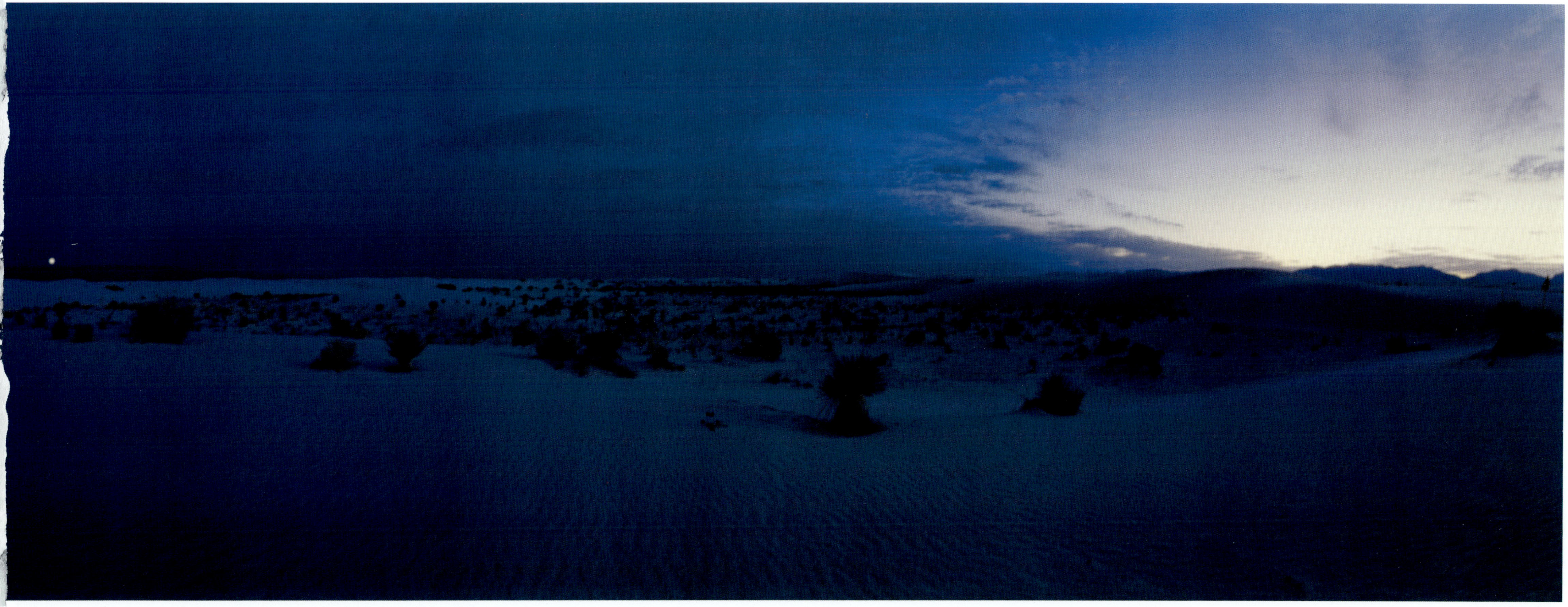

48 | MOONRISE AT WHITE SANDS, WHITE SANDS NATIONAL PARK, NEW MEXICO | 2002 | 370°

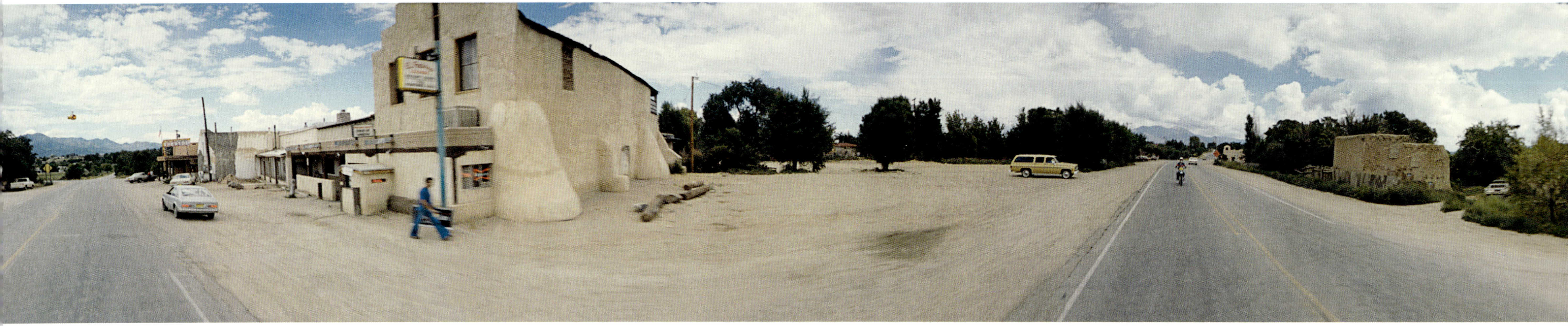

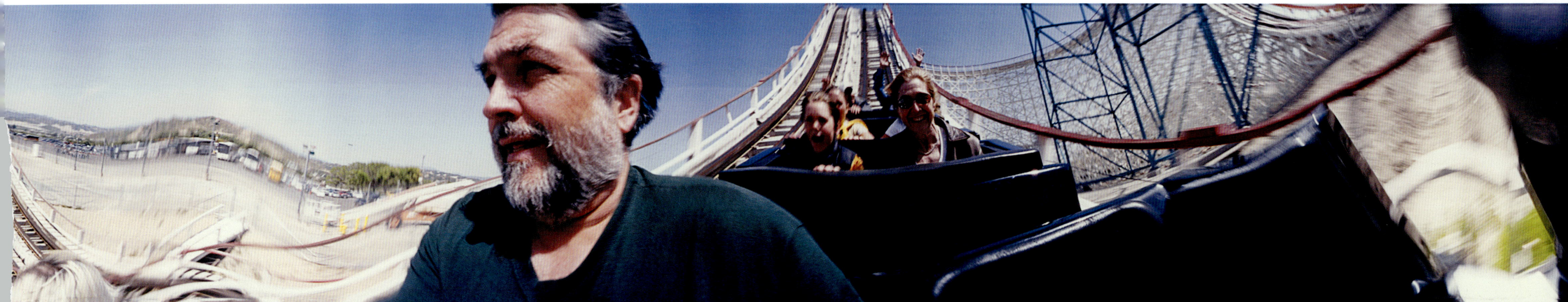

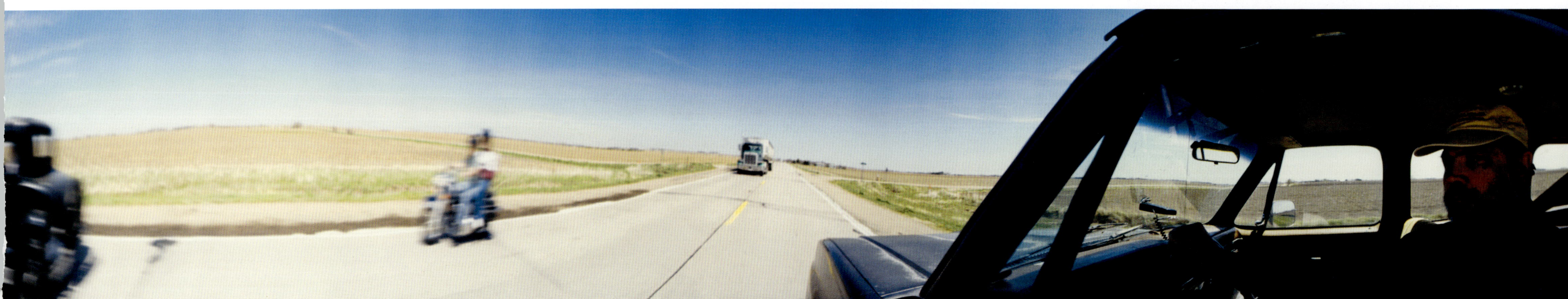

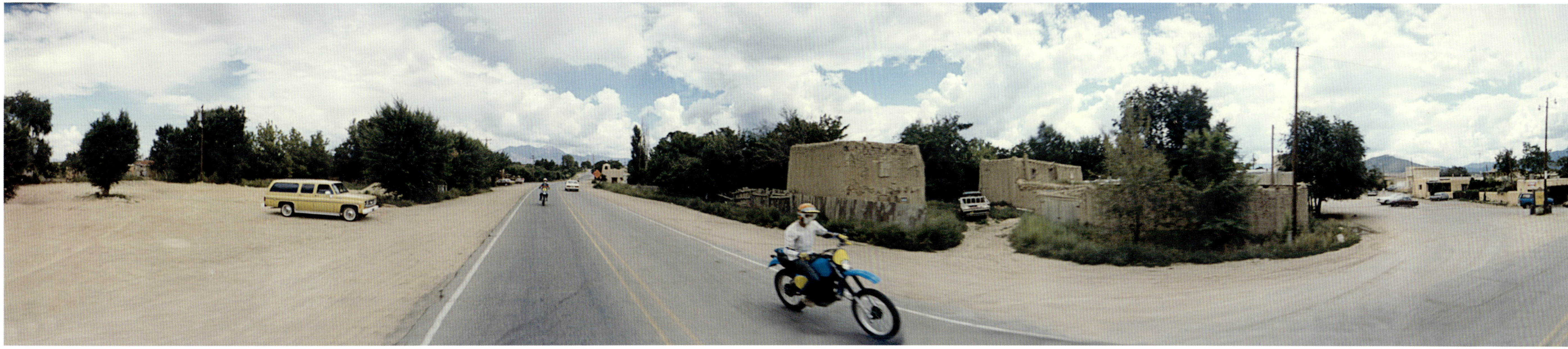

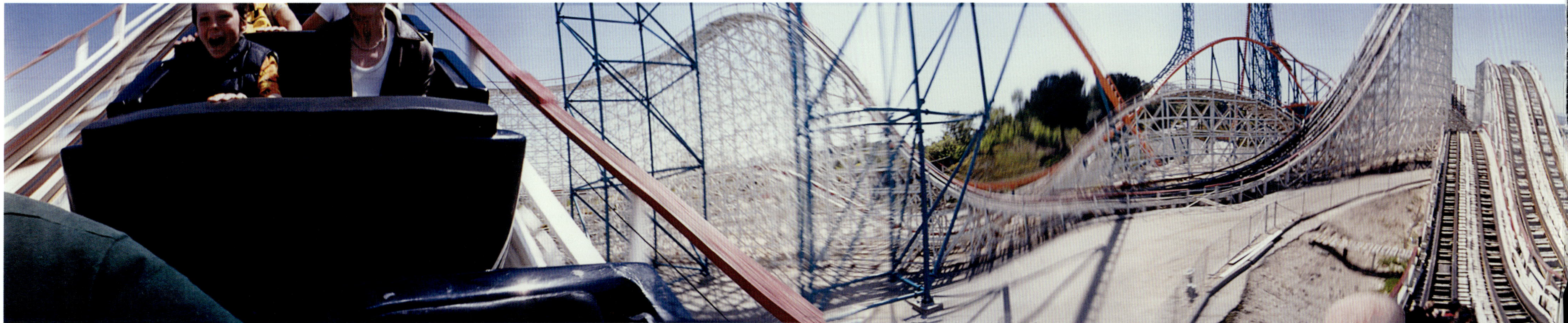

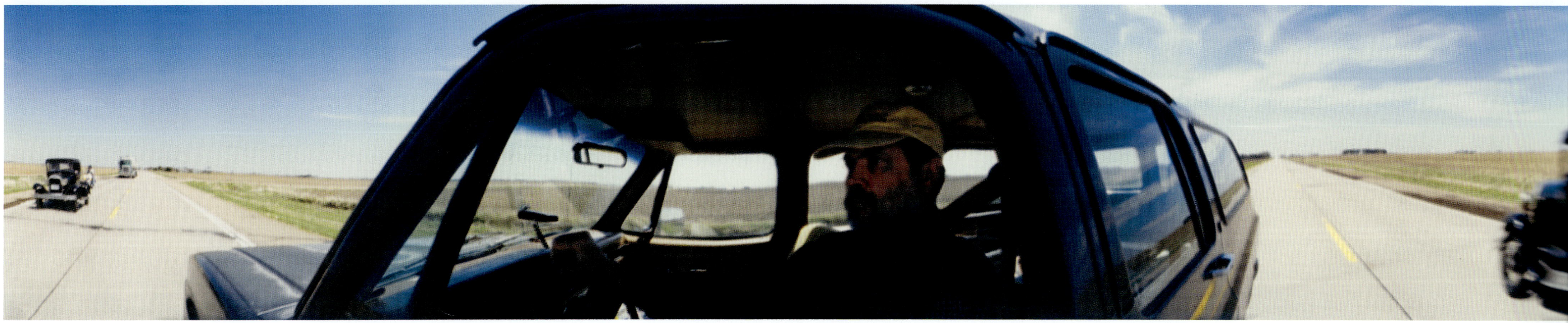

GUS FOSTER: CLOCKING IN WITH EINSTEIN

EDWARD T. HALL

Einstein held that time is what a clock says it is and a clock can be anything: the rotation of the earth, the phases of the moon, the seasons, sunspots, the sprouting time of crocuses, the rhythm of a jazz band, a Rolex or Timex watch, and the vibration of a cesium atom.
—ETH

This is a continuation of a series of articles on the role of the artist which I first published under the heading of "Visual Conventions and Conventional Vision."[1] Visual conventions change with the times, and art inevitably reflects (and records) these changes. The exceptional artist is ahead of the times while other more conservative types for various reasons lag behind and merely serve the interests of nostalgia. The function of those who are in the forefront is not so much to lead as it is to express visually things that are happening in society but which people have not put into words or found the means to articulate. In this way artists come to formulate the future so that the mass of humanity can begin to deal with the reality it will soon face in more tangible form.

Because Gus Foster has chosen a format associated with the late nineteenth and early twentieth centuries—the panorama photograph, used for recording large groups of people gathered for various occasions—there is a risk that his work will mentally be tossed into the nostalgia bin when it would better be described as futuristic.

My wife and I were first introduced to Foster's work in Taos some seven years ago while visiting the studio of his neighbor Larry Bell. We met Foster and were immediately drawn to his work. Having walked or ridden on horseback over a good portion of north central New Mexico, I found Foster's 360-degree panoramic views of the area conveyed a special, very personal message to me. Taken from the tops of mountains I had climbed, they provided me with a visual notebook of events, scenes, and emotions that I was pleased to recall.

As it turned out, Foster and I shared many interests. In addition to mechanical things, photography, and the outdoors, we were both fascinated by certain aspects of Albert Einstein's thought. It was Einstein's observation that the man on the streetcar and the man on the sidewalk looking at the passing streetcar do not see time in the same way. This notion, this insight originally written for physicists, had burrowed into Gus Foster's mind and wouldn't leave. Ultimately it motivated him to extend his obsession for the stationary panoramic view to the panorama recorded from a moving vehicle or platform.

It is the relationship between Foster's "Time Photographs" and his panoramas taken with the camera rotating around a single spot that forms the corpus of his current passion. In one instance he and his partner, Ruth, actually reproduced Einstein's argument as they photographed each other with panoramic cameras: one of them stood by the side of the road while the other drove by (see pages 154-155). The effect of viewing each image and concentrating on it revealed that they were qualitatively quite different. In precisely what ways they were different is not easy to describe because there is no vocabulary for this sort of thing. When I use the term "different" I do not just mean Foster's images are different from those of other photographers but they are also noticeably different from each other.

For years I have used photographs as a research tool when investigating unconscious behaviors such as the size of the bubble of personal space surrounding each human being as it occurs in a great variety of settings and contexts. For my purposes, even snapshots taken by others as souvenirs yield valuable data. It is the almost inexhaustible amount of information in photographs that makes them so valuable.

What Foster has done is to restructure photographic information in a unique way, providing us with new insights and feedback on how the world can be perceived. Now I must say something about what I mean by "restructuring" and why I use the term "unique." Let's begin with unique. I know of no one else who is doing what Foster does. He had to either make or design virtually all of the equipment that enables him to produce images up to twelve feet in length and thirty inches wide. In terms of restructuring how we use the information provided in photographs, it is first necessary to sort out how they differ from other uses of the medium that are concerned with freezing or slowing down time. Most students of photography are familiar with Eadweard Muybridge's nineteenth-century multiple images of racehorses and his series of naked men and women engaged in a variety of athletic activities such as running, jumping, boxing, and wrestling. To analyze the interplay of the muscles used, Muybridge employed a battery of separate cameras, set up serially. The shutters were tripped by strings as the subjects moved through space. Perhaps even more familiar to most of us is the use of "strobe" cameras to freeze motion: stroboscopic images of golfers swinging clubs (recorded in a single frame), or of bullets penetrating lightbulbs as glass shards explode into the surrounding space, and of the circular crowns formed by droplets of cream. The motion picture does a similar thing. But motion pictures (movies) are linear in the same way that a sentence is linear. This means that the viewer is held in the grip of the camera image as though it had a lock on the viewer's eyes. One cannot break the sequencing imposed by the linearity.

With Foster's "Time Photographs" (as well as with his more stationary panoramas) a modicum of control of perception and analysis is restored. That is, the panorama permits the viewer the same leeway that he/she has outdoors while taking in the actual scene. But for the time photograph the camera moves *through* space while *it* rotates in space so that one can see the same scene from different angles. Combining the two systems adds an entirely new dimension to photography, so that one can see both views simultaneously, as in the thought experiments conducted by Einstein.

Gus Foster has turned the camera into a new kind of clock, one which is rooted historically in the late nineteenth and early twentieth centuries. But, because of what Foster has done by tuning his clock to the dynamic universe, his camera is now more appropriate as an instrument for exploring the world of the future as it is forming than as a reminder of the past. Foster has given us a new way of recording the contemplating experience, trimming our visual sails to change.[2]

Notes

1. Edward T. Hall, "Visual Conventions and Conventional Vision," *El Palacio*, spring 1987.

2. This essay originally appeared in *Artspace Southwestern Contemporary Arts Quarterly*, fall 1988. It has been lightly edited for this book.

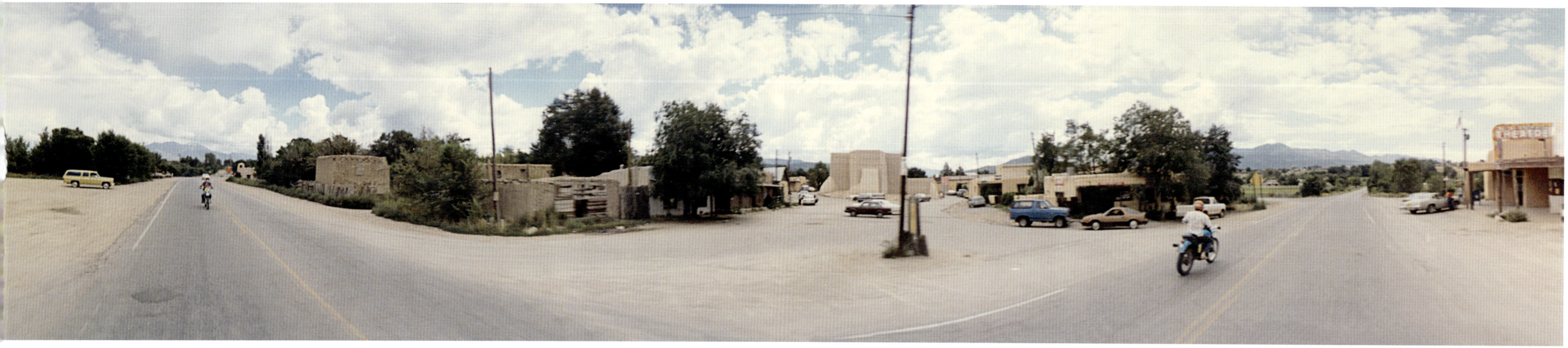

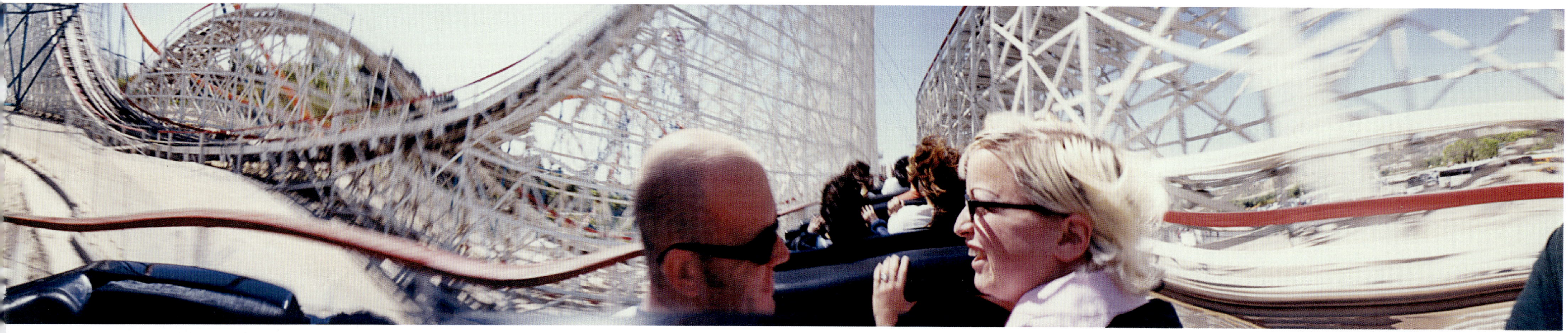

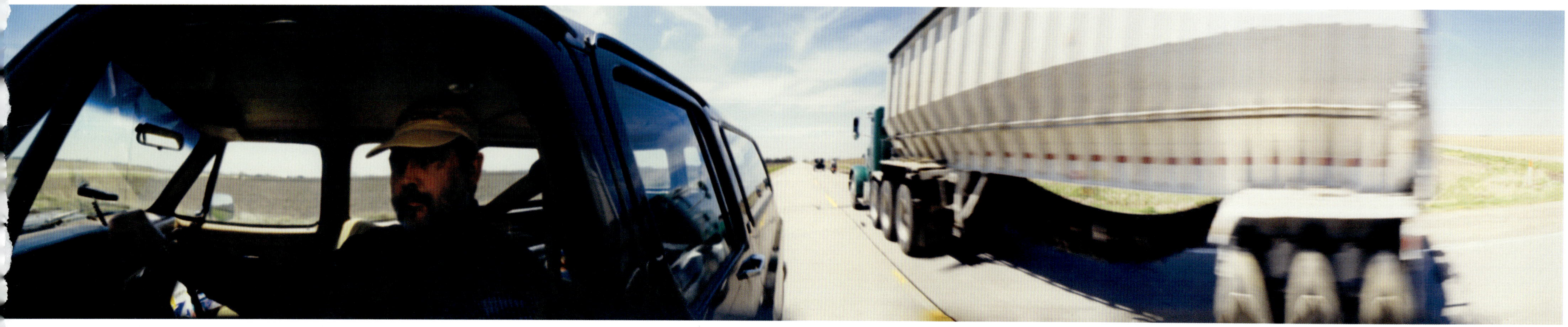

RANCHOS, TAOS COUNTY, NEW MEXICO | 1983 | 1015° • 50 | THE COLOSSUS, LOS ANGELES COUNTY, CALIFORNIA | 2001 | 1067° • 51 | ANTIQUES ROADSHOW NEBRASKA, KEARNEY COUNTY | 2000 | 1048°

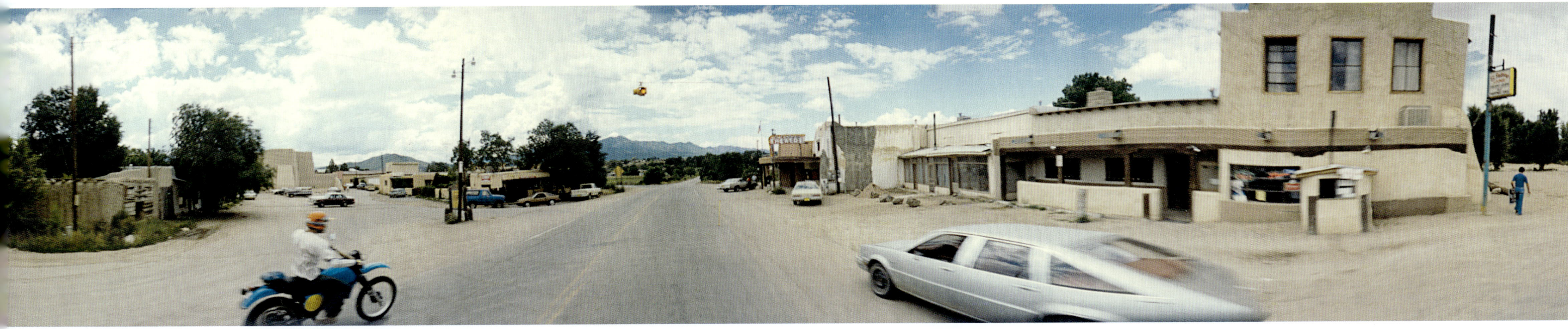

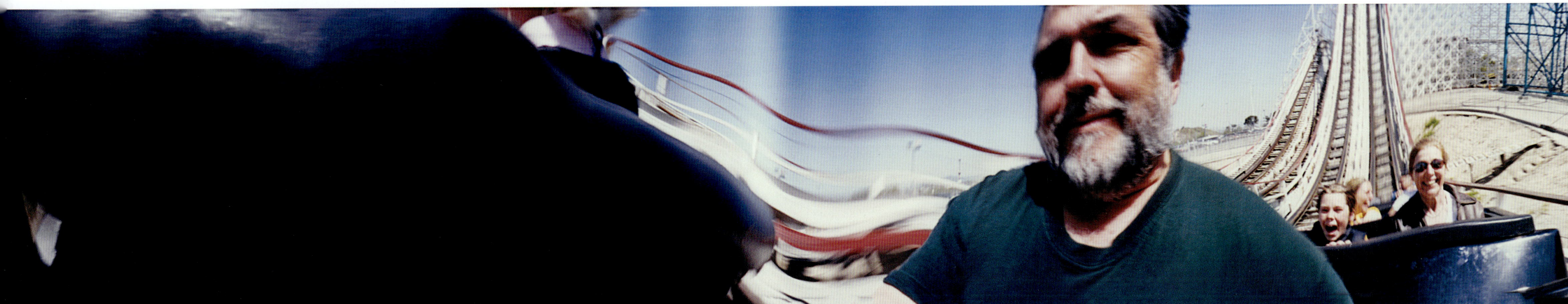

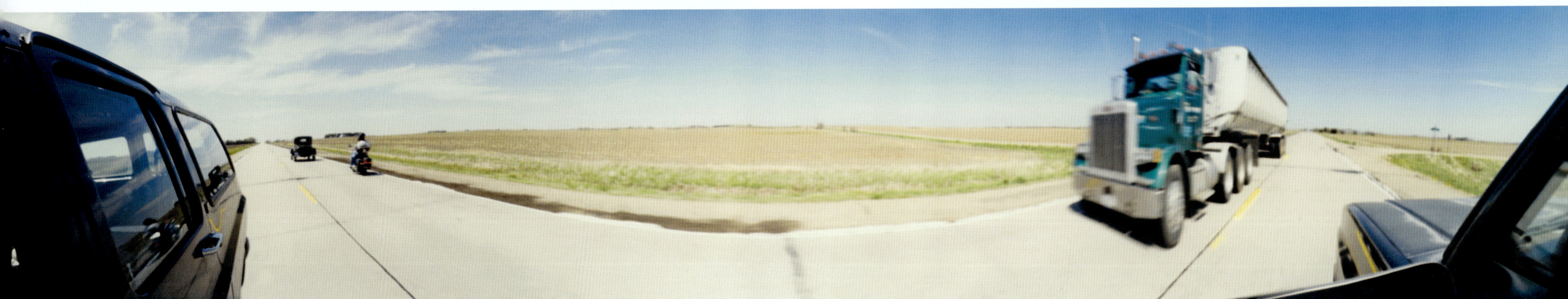

FROM TOP: 49 | PASSING TIME I

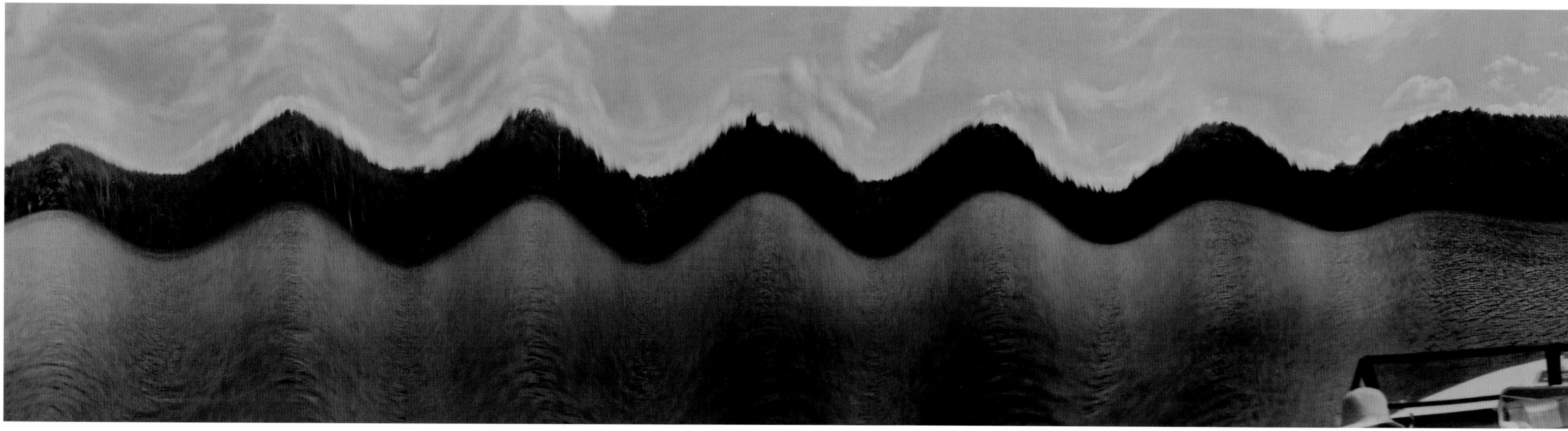

TIME PHOTOGRAPHS

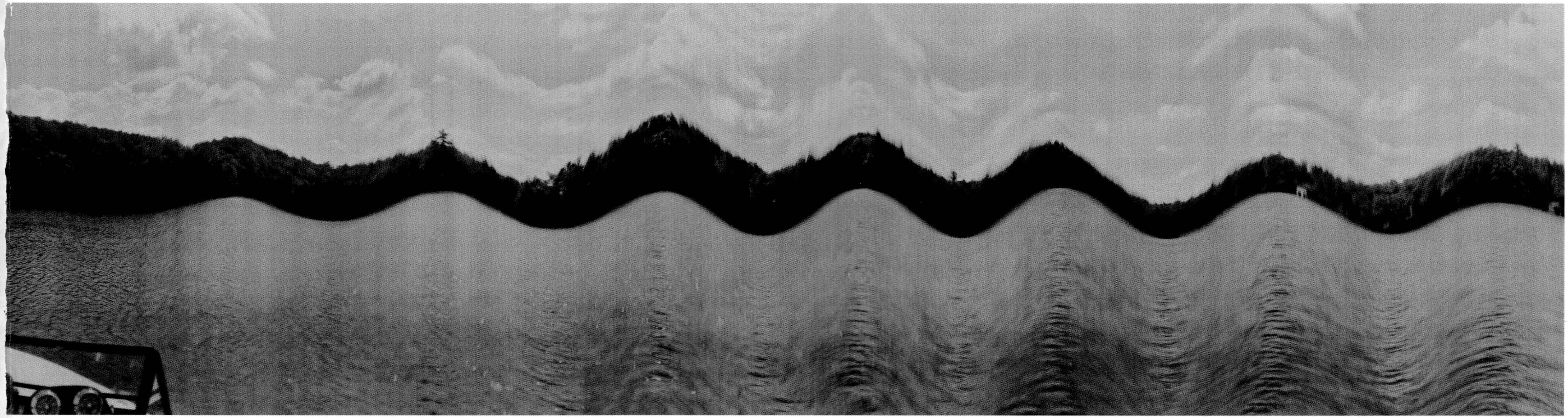

52 | ROCKING THE BOAT, ONEIDA COUNTY, WISCONSIN | 1979 | 318°

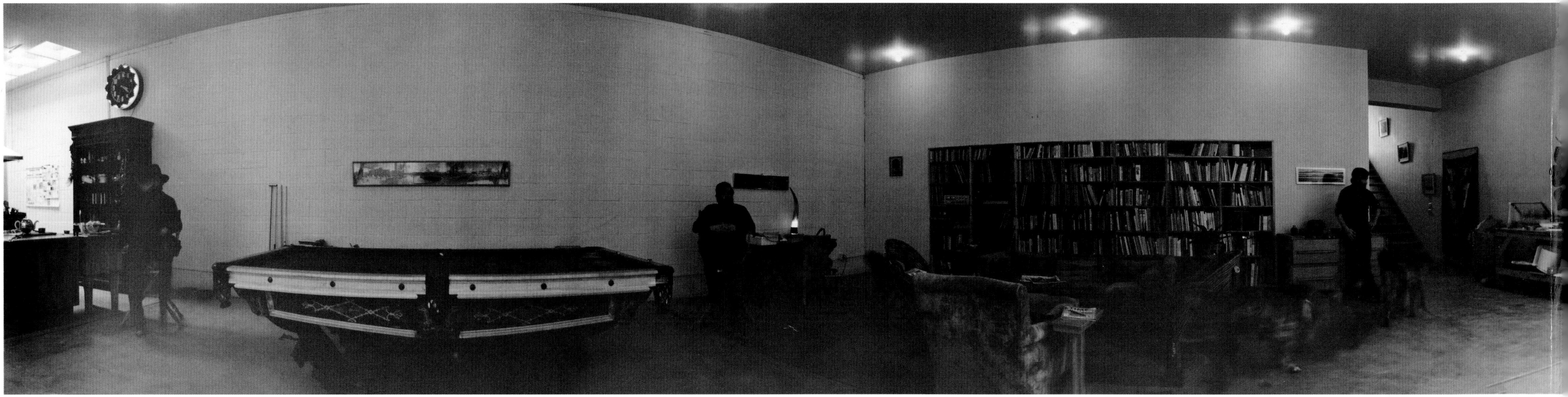

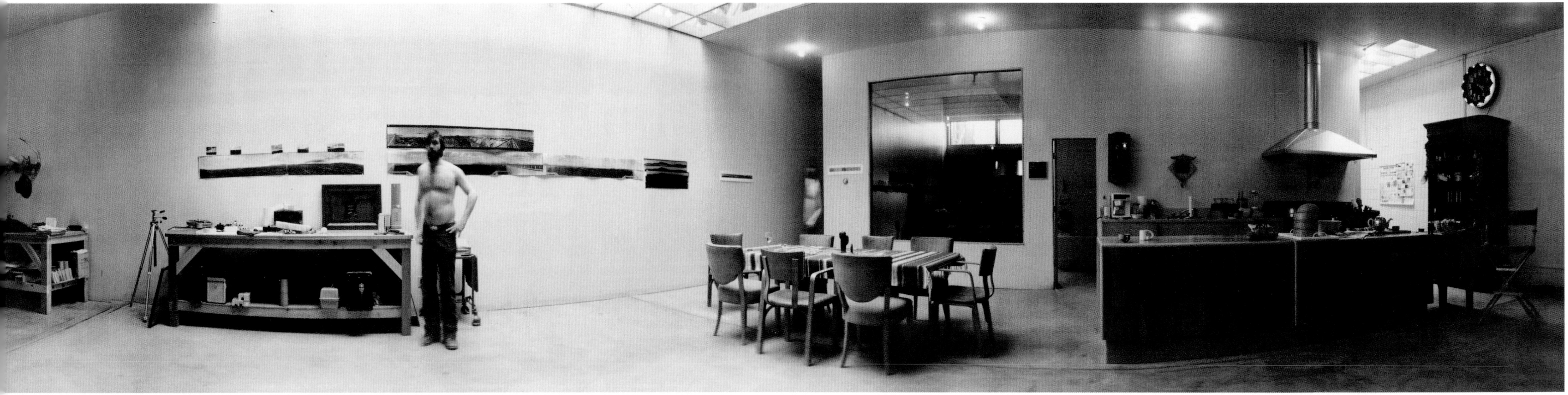

53 | STUDIO SELF-PORTRAIT, TAOS COUNTY, NEW MEXICO | 1980 | 386°

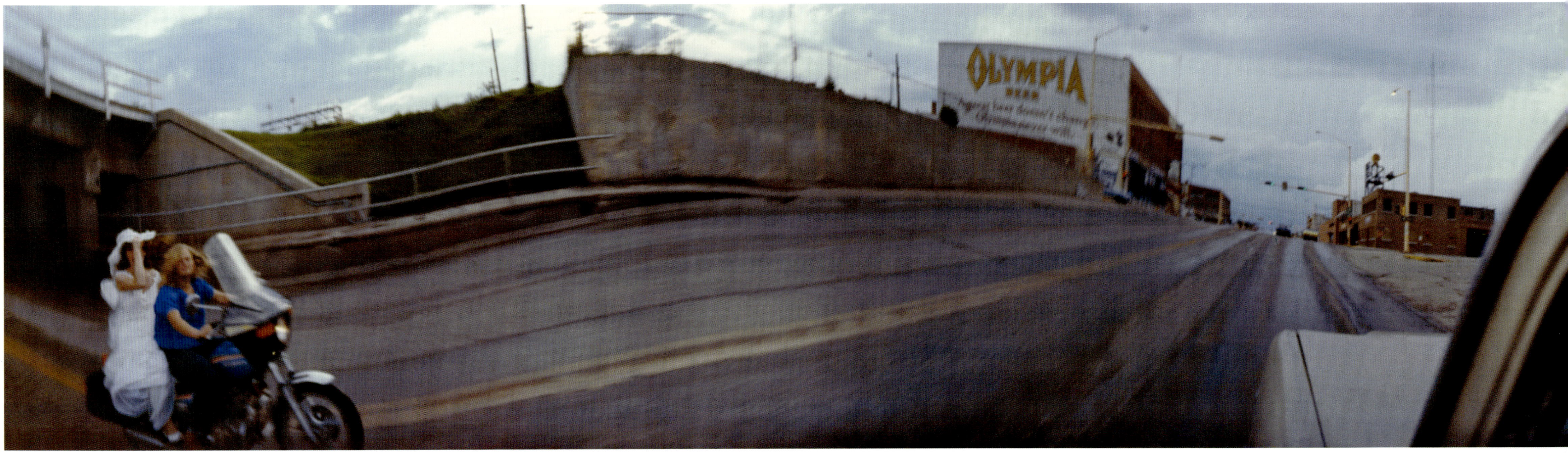
OLYMPIA
BEER

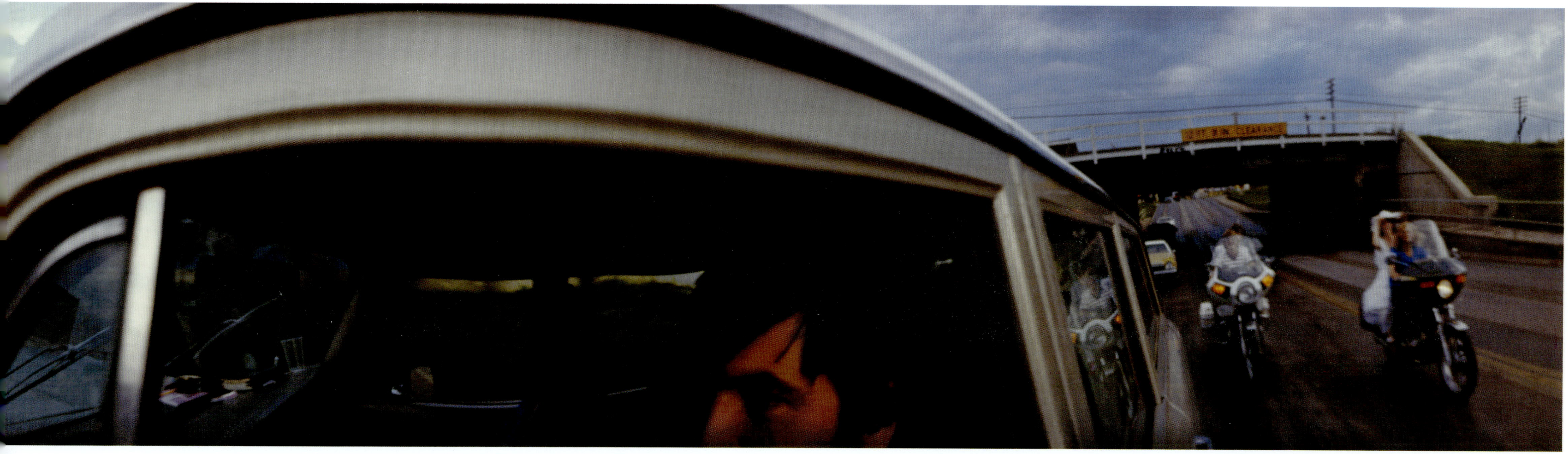

54 | NEBRASKA WEDDING, ADAMS COUNTY | 1982 | 424°

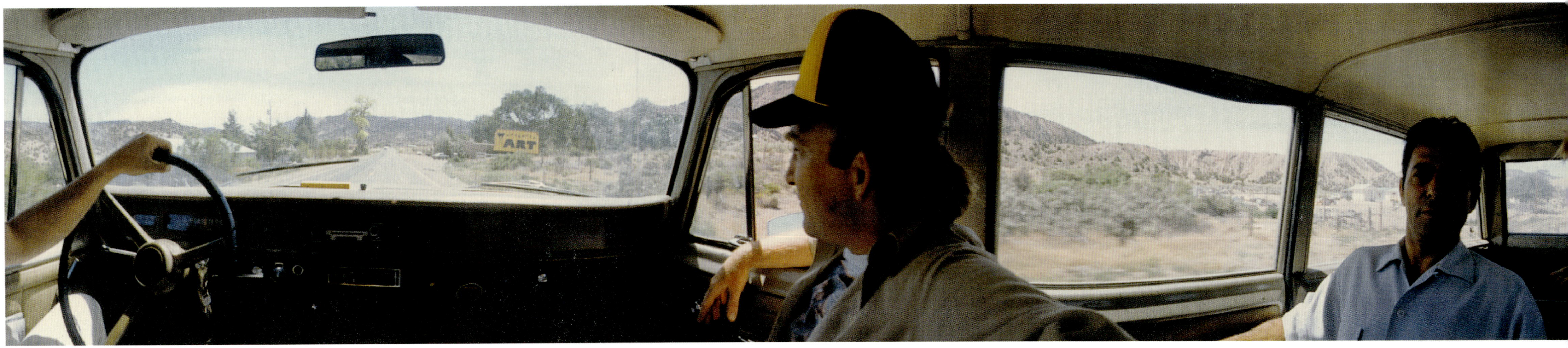
ART

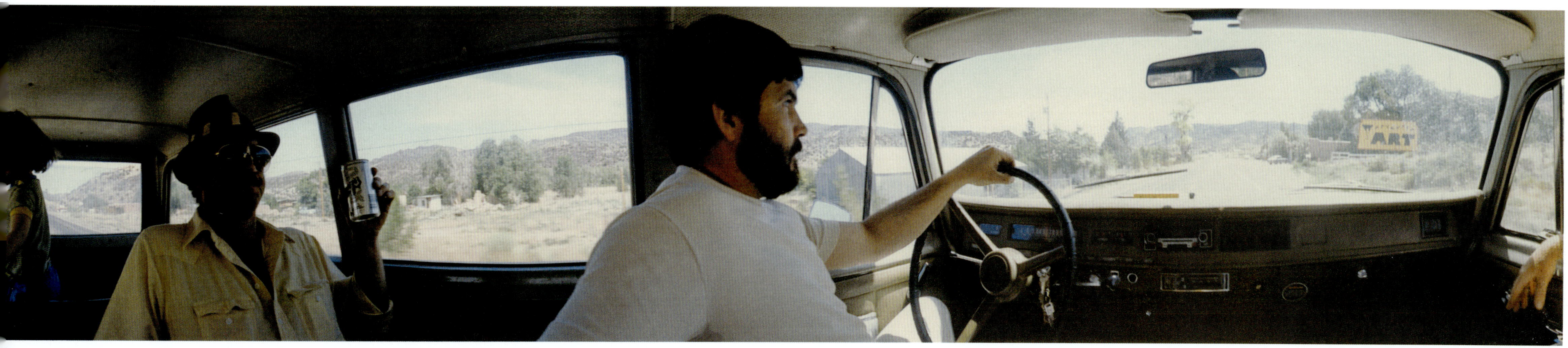

55 | ADVANCED ART ADVANCING, TAOS COUNTY, NEW MEXICO | 1983 | 469°

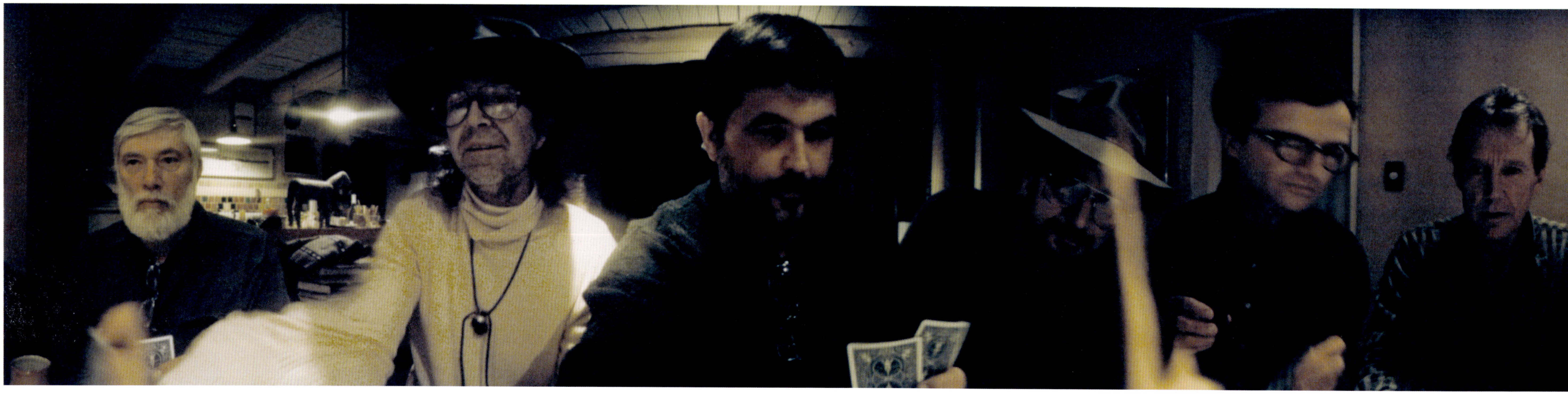

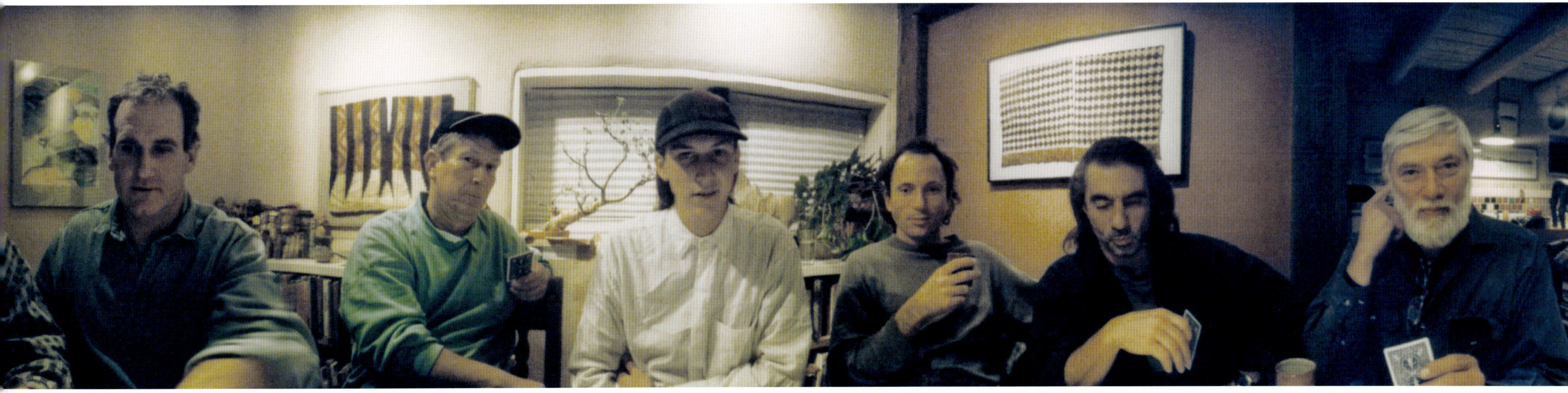

56 | POKER PORTRAITS, TAOS COUNTY, NEW MEXICO | 1992 | 398°

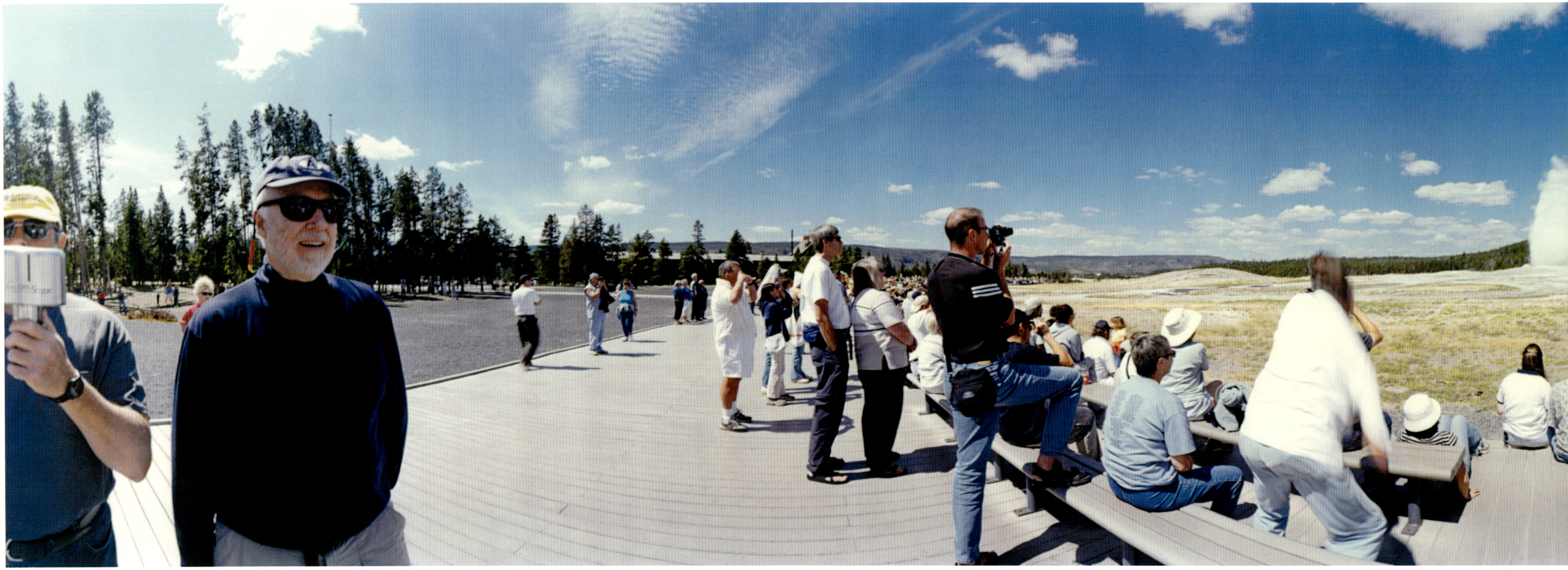

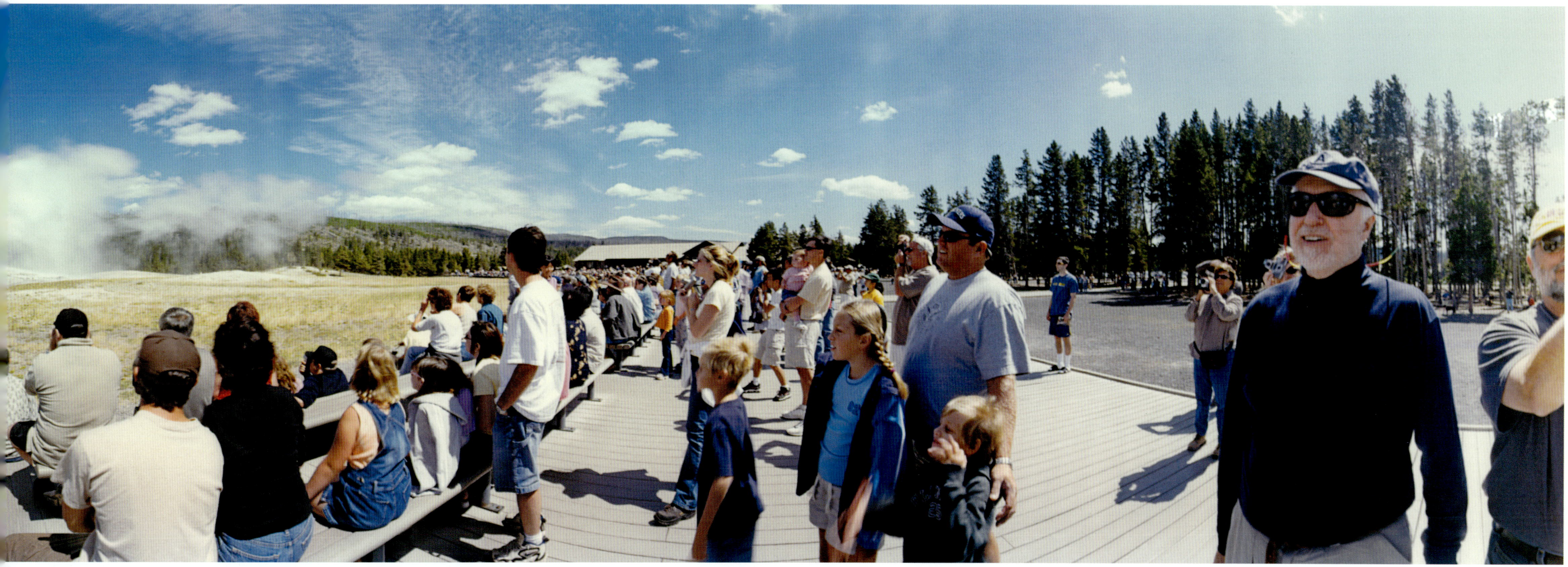

57 | OLD FAITHFUL, THE 1:26 P.M. SHOW, YELLOWSTONE NATIONAL PARK, WYOMING | 2002 | 376°

58 | 'ROUND TIMES SQUARE (OX□), NEW YORK CITY, NEW YORK | 1990 | 376°

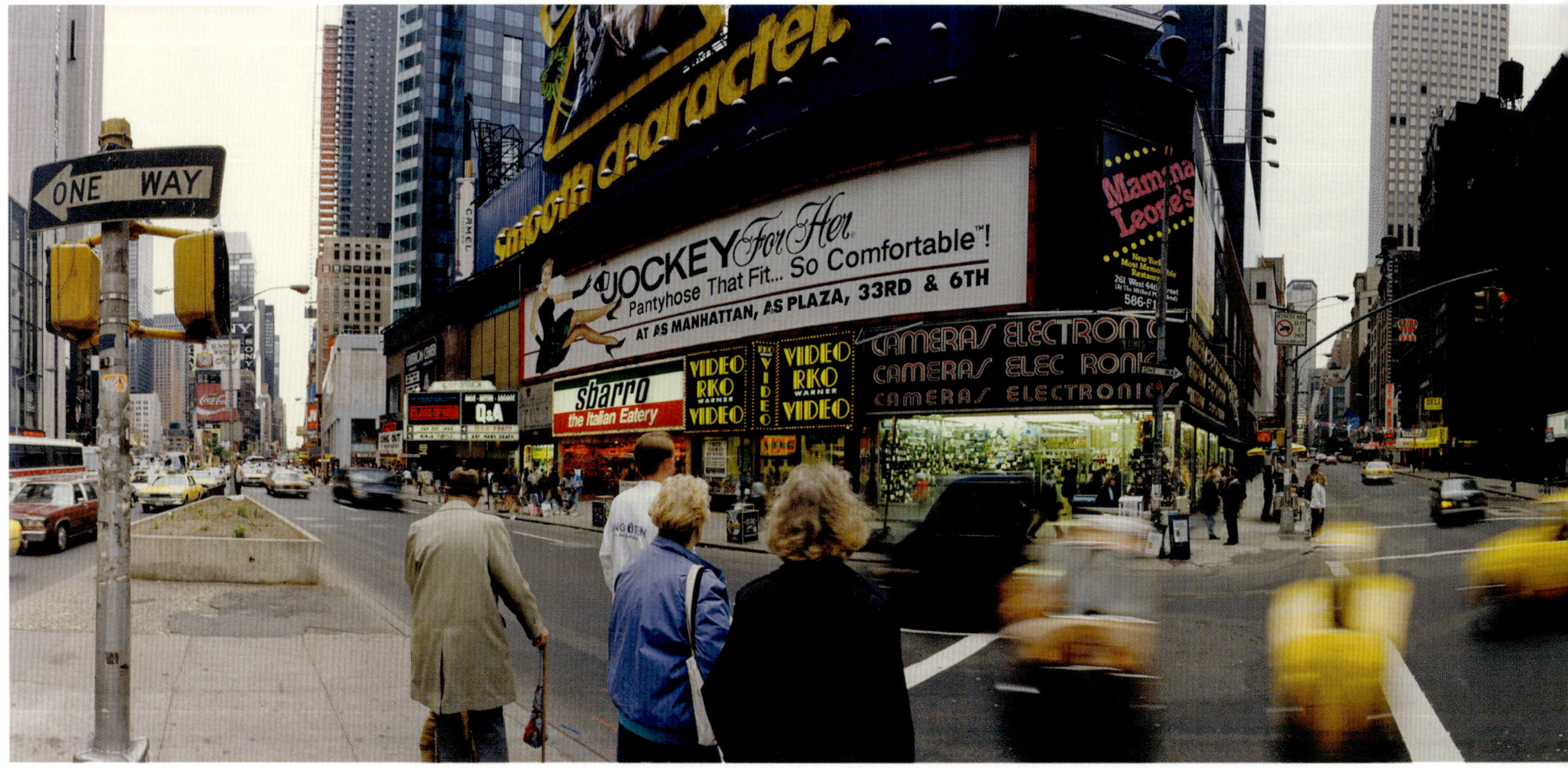

59 | 'ROUND TIMES SQUARE (OX□), NEW YORK CITY, NEW YORK | 2004 | 376°

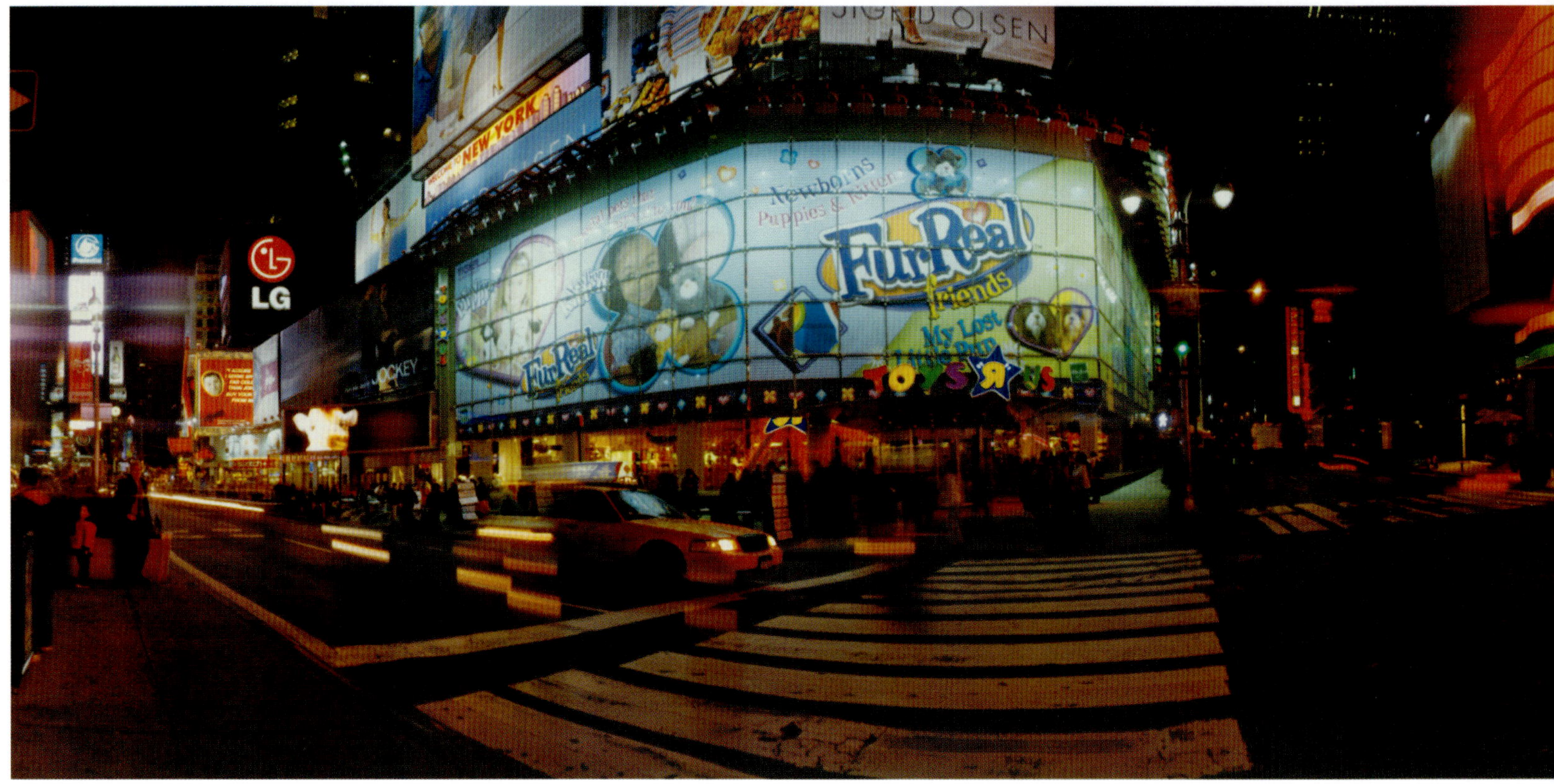

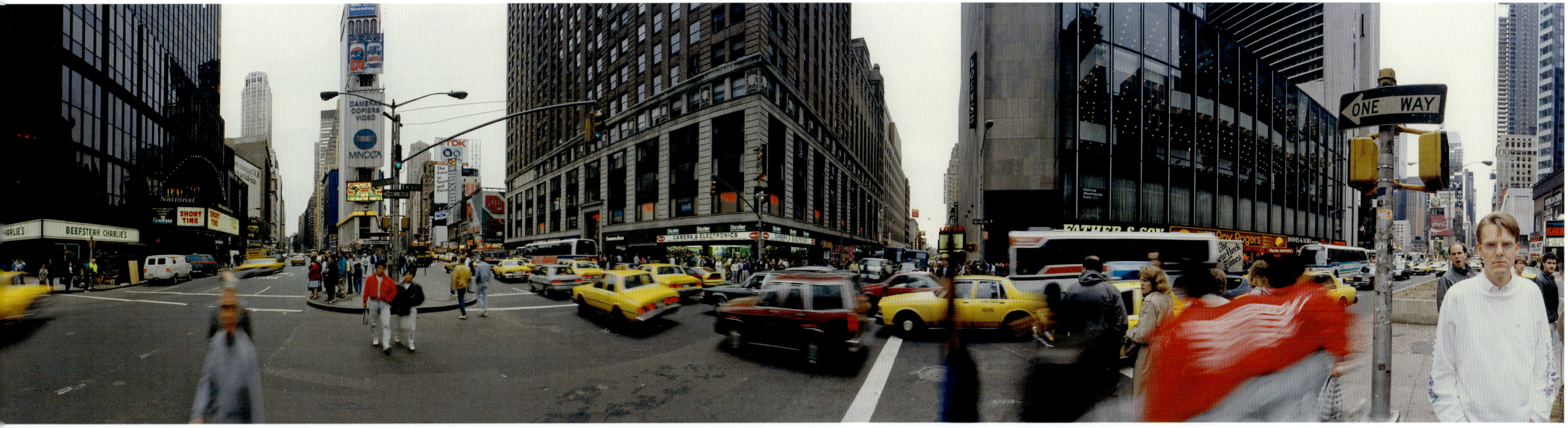

BEEFSTEAK CHARLIE'S
SHORT TIME
National
CAMERAS COPIERS VIDEO
MINOLTA
TDK
CAMERA & ELECTRONICS
FATHER & SON
ONE WAY

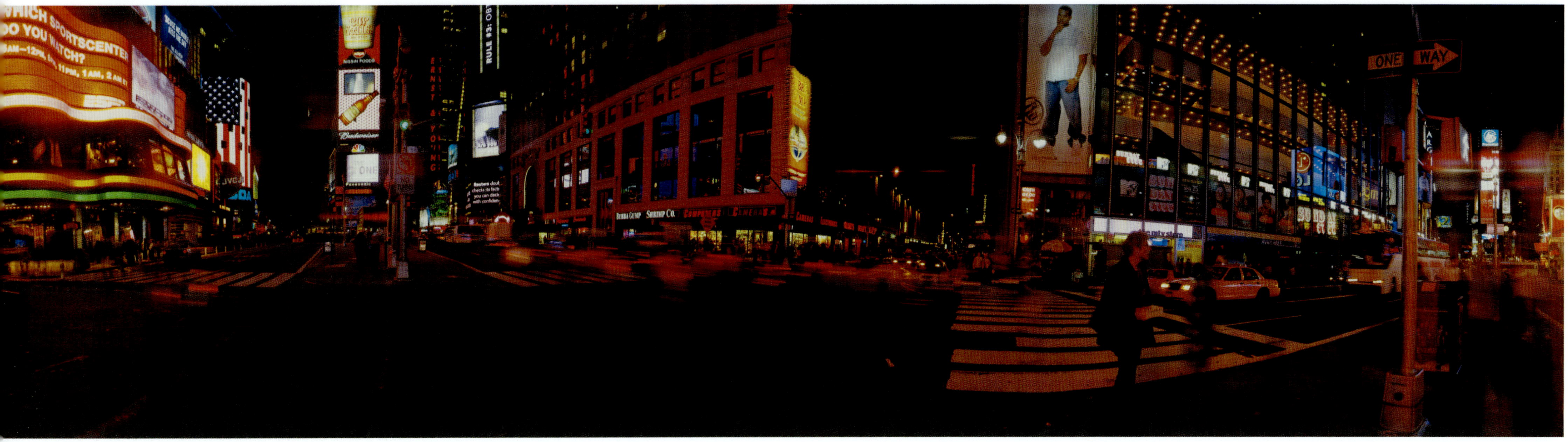

WHICH SPORTSCENTER DO YOU WATCH?
RULE #3:
Budweiser
BUBBA GUMP SHRIMP CO.
ONE WAY

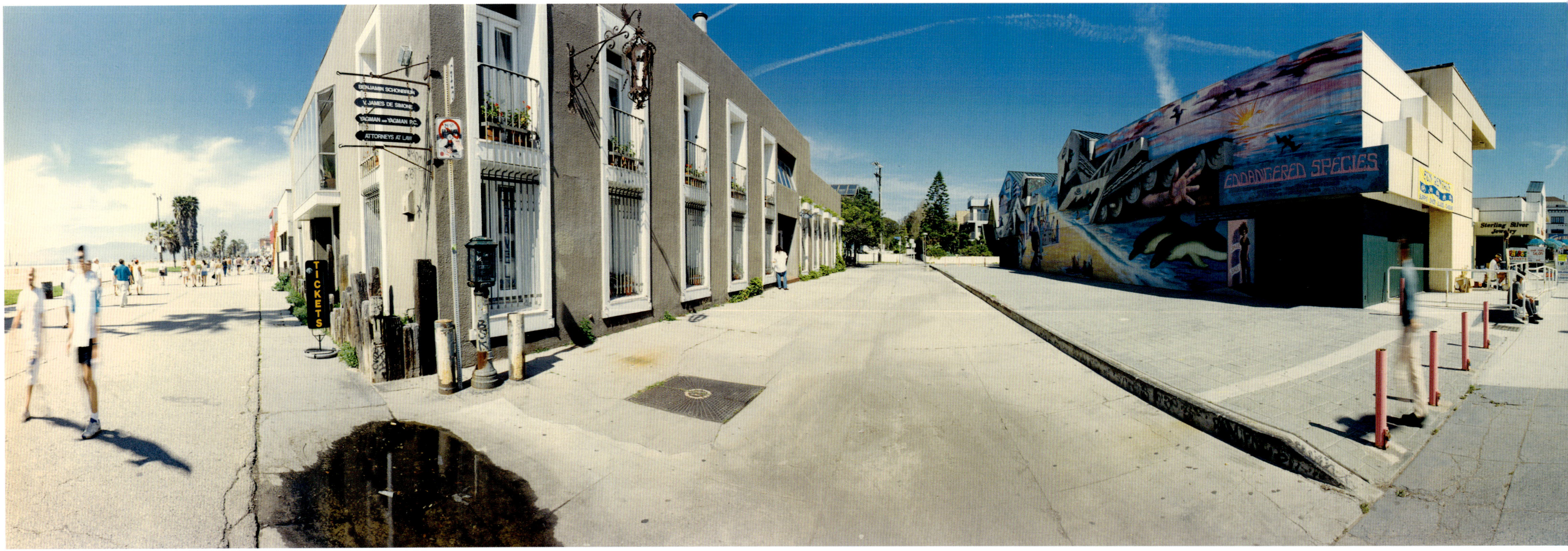
BENJAMIN SCHONBRUN
V. JAMES DE SIMONE
YAGMAN AND YAGMAN P.C.
ATTORNEYS AT LAW
TICKETS
ENDANGERED SPECIES
Sterling Silver

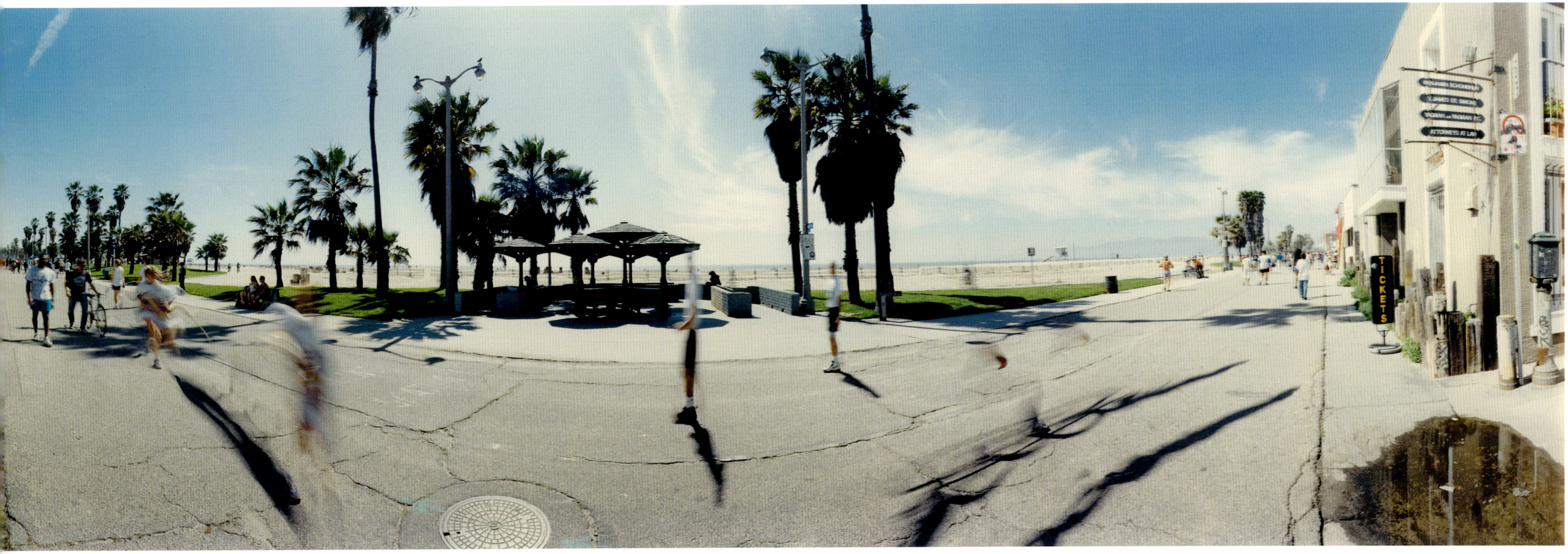

60 | TIME SWITCH, LOS ANGELES COUNTY, CALIFORNIA | 1995 | 428°

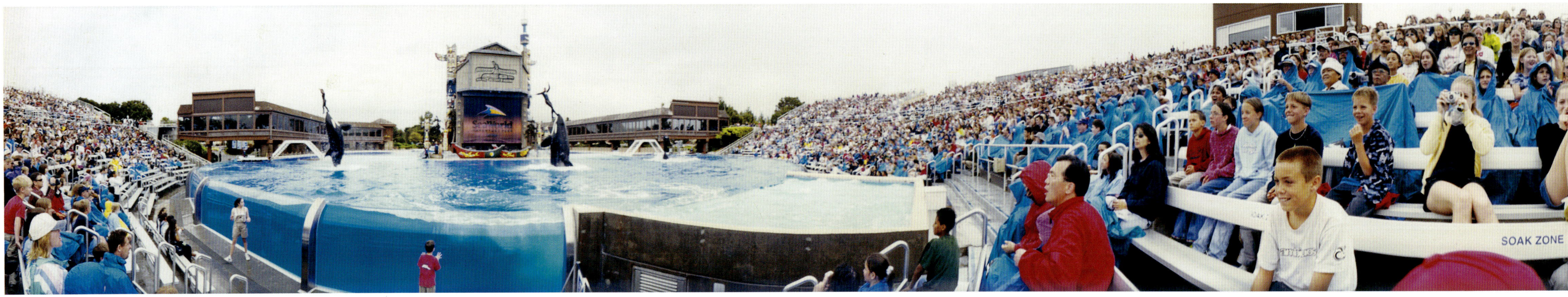
SOAK ZONE

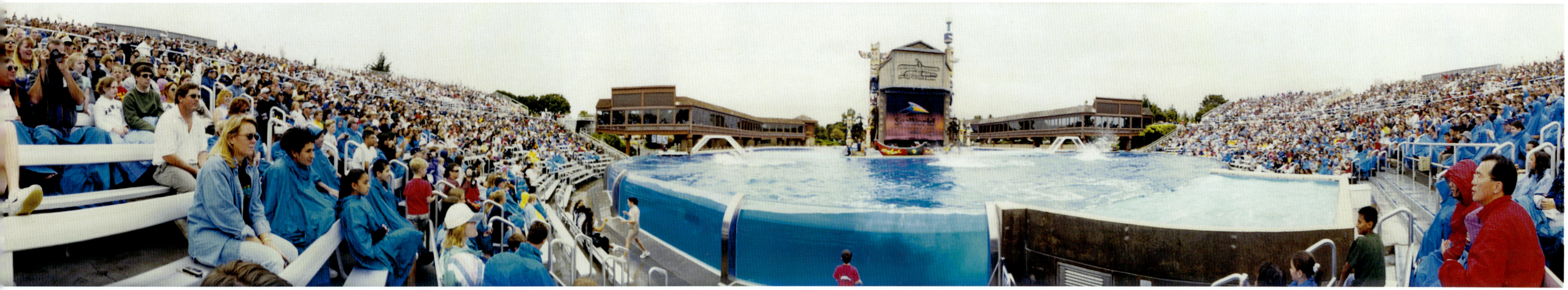

61 | TIME TO DISAPPEAR, SAN DIEGO COUNTY, CALIFORNIA | 2002 | 566°

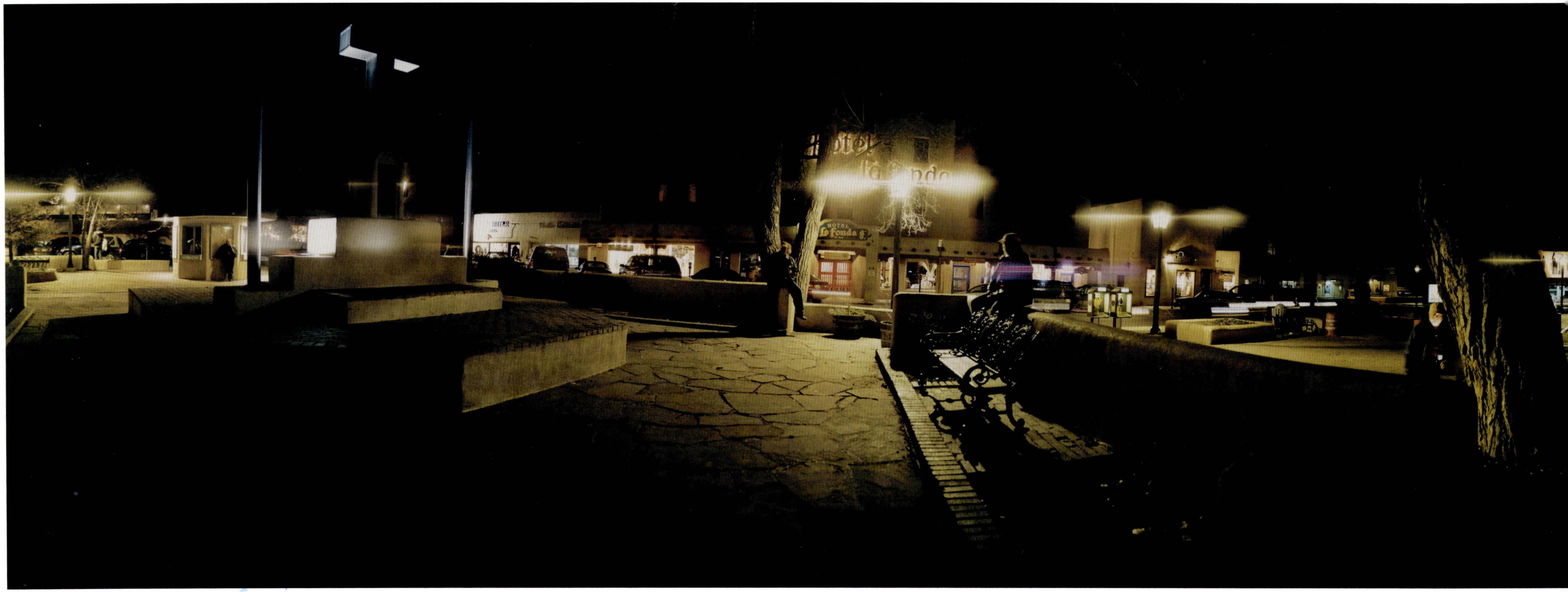
HOTEL
La fonda

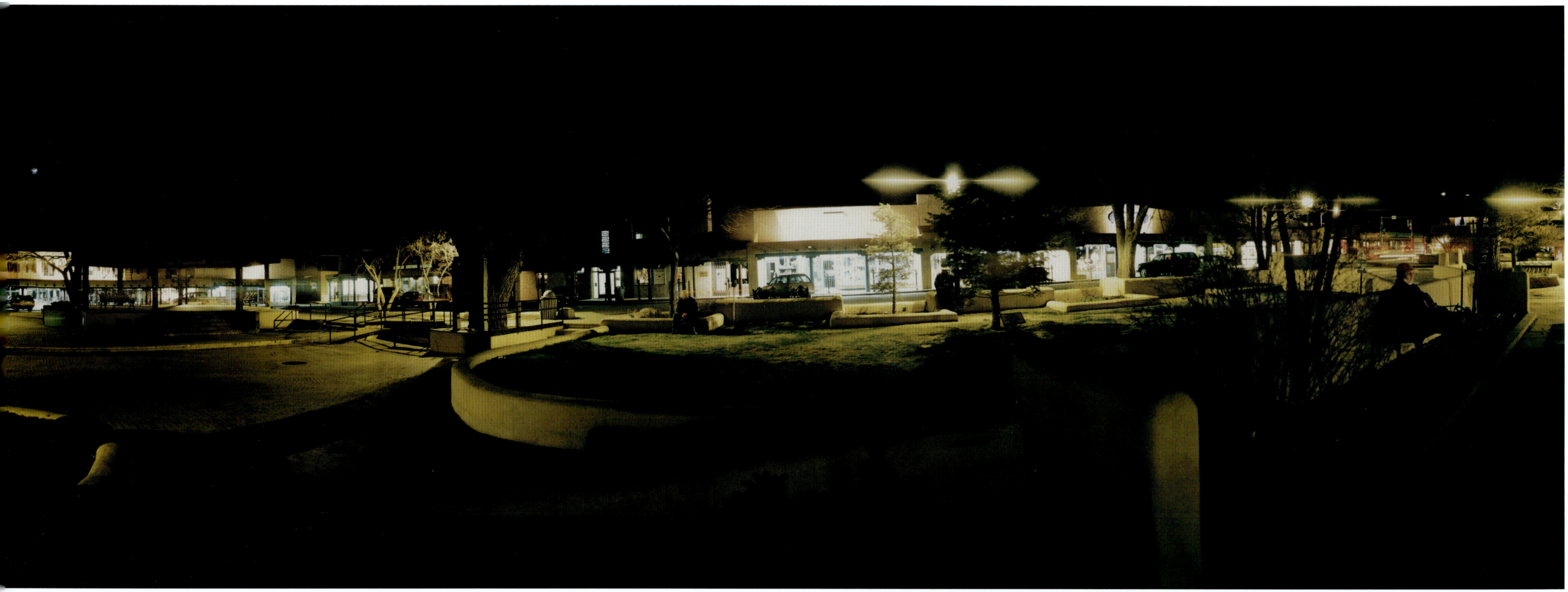

62 | PLAZA SELF-PORTRAITS, TAOS, NEW MEXICO | 2004 | 367°

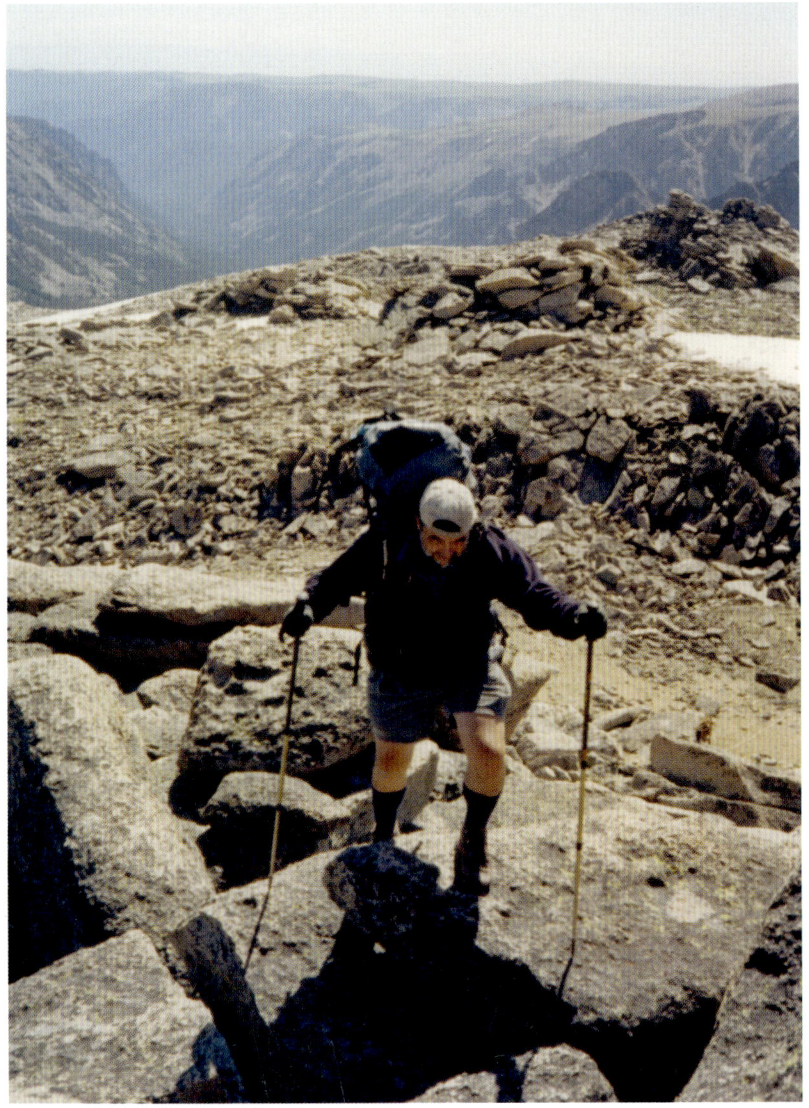

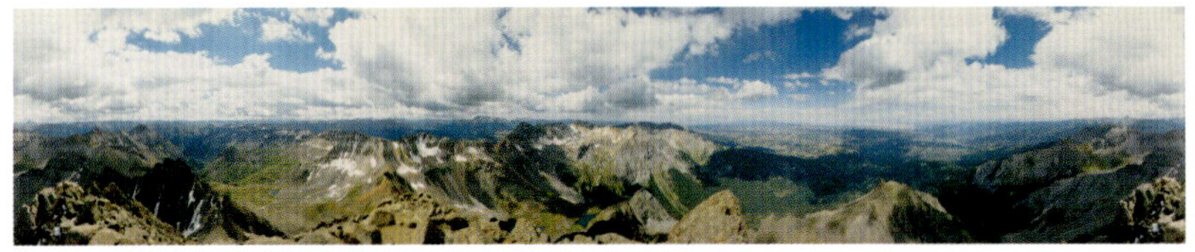

MOUNT SNEFFELS | In 1986, Tom Simons, my cousin, and I were standing on the 14,150-foot summit of Mount Sneffels in Colorado's San Juan Range. It was a beautiful midsummer day and we were admiring the view. There was a storm brewing well west of our position, and we were catching our breath before starting to disassemble the camera to pack it back down the mountain. All of a sudden, the hair on the back of my arms and on my head just stood straight up. It was an electrical charge emanating from the ground. Simons understood what was going on and said, "Run!" Since we were on a small summit, there was nowhere to run except downhill, so we went as quickly as we could down the rough terrain, going no more than a couple of hundred feet when the first raindrops hit. We dropped flat to the ground as the first lightning strike hit. There was a downpour and a half dozen more strikes in the next few minutes, and then it was done. It happened so fast that we hadn't even gotten the camera off the summit, a sixty-five-pound lightning rod. We watched the storm move past us, good weather resumed, we climbed back up, loaded the camera in our packs, and went on with our day.

On the trail, Absaroka Range, Montana, 1997. Photo by Roger Badash.

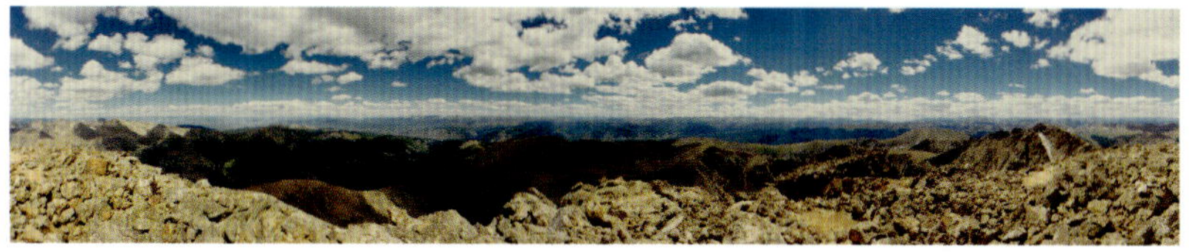

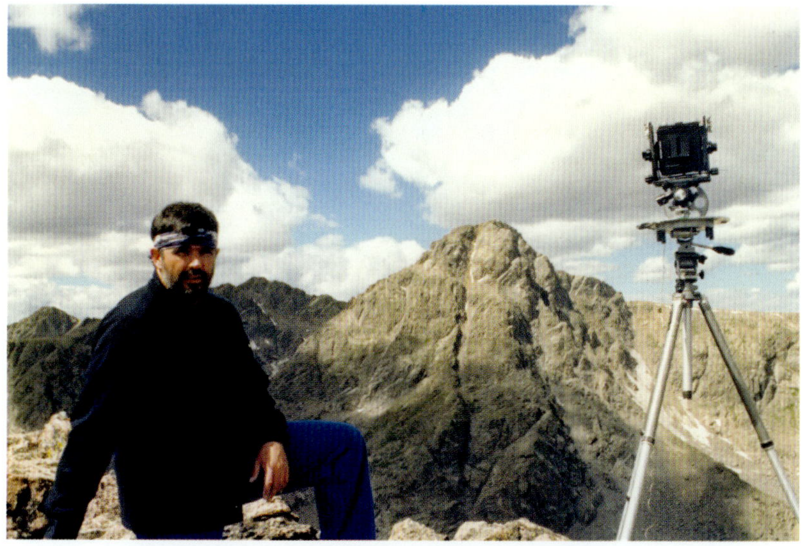

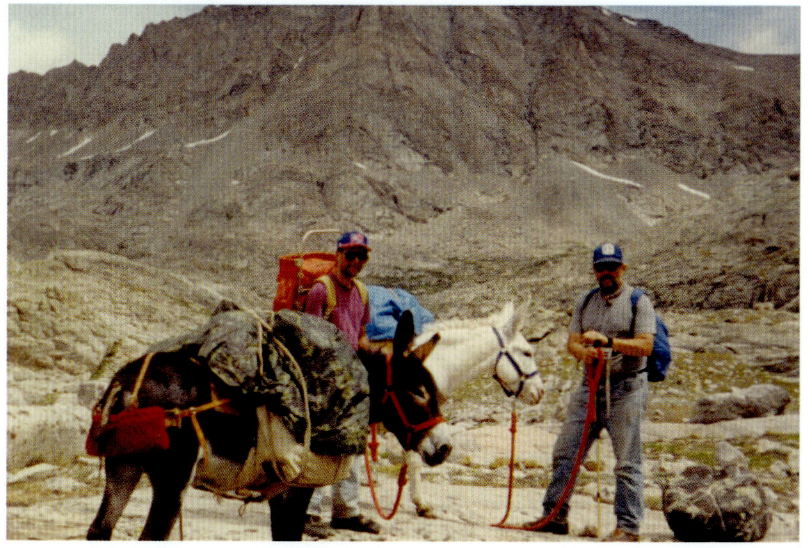

MOUNT OF THE HOLY CROSS | Located in the Sawatch Range in the central Rockies in Colorado, the Mount of the Holy Cross is one of the most famous 14,000-foot peaks. William Henry Jackson photographed the mountain from nearby Notch Mountain in the 1870s. His photo clearly shows a huge snow-filled cross shape on the side of the mountain, consisting of a long vertical chute and two horizontal ledges to complete the cross. (The cross is no longer visible, as the left branch of the cross was eroded out in an avalanche some years ago.) Jackson took his friend Thomas Moran to see this site. Moran later painted his great iconic landscape *Mount of the Holy Cross*, now in the Museum of the American West in Los Angeles. Getting to Holy Cross is difficult; it is 13 miles from the trailhead to the summit. My sister and I and another friend left at 4 a.m. to make the trip. We made the summit okay (one can clearly see the notch of Notch Mountain from there) and then started the return trip. The hardest part of the trip is that a couple of miles before getting back to the trailhead there is a place where you have to climb one thousand vertical feet to stay on the trail. That makes for a long day—26 miles round trip, 4,000 vertical feet up and back down, and an agonizing 1,000 feet vertical just before the finish line, which we reached after dark that same day, the longest single-day journey that I completed.

Top: *Mount of the Holy Cross from Notch Mountain, 1987, photo by Ruth Tobey;* Bottom: *Chico, Roger Badash, Sidney, and Gus in the Bridger Wilderness, 1994, photo by John Chamberlain.*

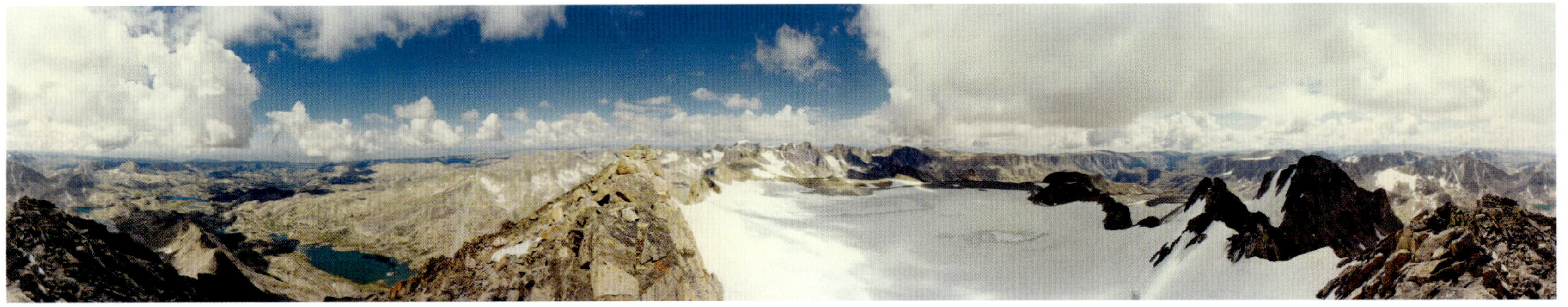

FREMONT PEAK | Fremont Peak, named after the early frontiersman John Fremont, is located in the Wind River Range of Wyoming. My party—Roger Badash, John Chamberlain, Jim Beckley, the burros Chico and Sidney, and I—started on the trailhead near Pinedale, Wyoming, for the three-day trek to the Titcomb Basin, where we would make our third-night camp and base camp for the climb the next day. The original intent was to climb Jackson Peak (named for one of my photographic heroes, William Henry Jackson), but recent snow had made that mountain unclimbable without ropes and technical gear, which we didn't have. So we decided to climb Fremont, which was an easier ascent, an adjacent and higher peak with a great view of Jackson Peak. This was all figured out from our fantastic third-night camp with amazing views of the Titcomb lakes and the huge mountains nearby. I made a panorama here, too. Ten years later I found a photo in a gallery that Jackson had taken of Fremont Peak, and going back through my own snapshots, I found a nearly identical image taken from our second-night camp at Seneca Lake. Climbing Fremont Peak was an arduous 6,000-foot vertical ascent culminating on the Continental Divide and one of the favorite trips of my life.

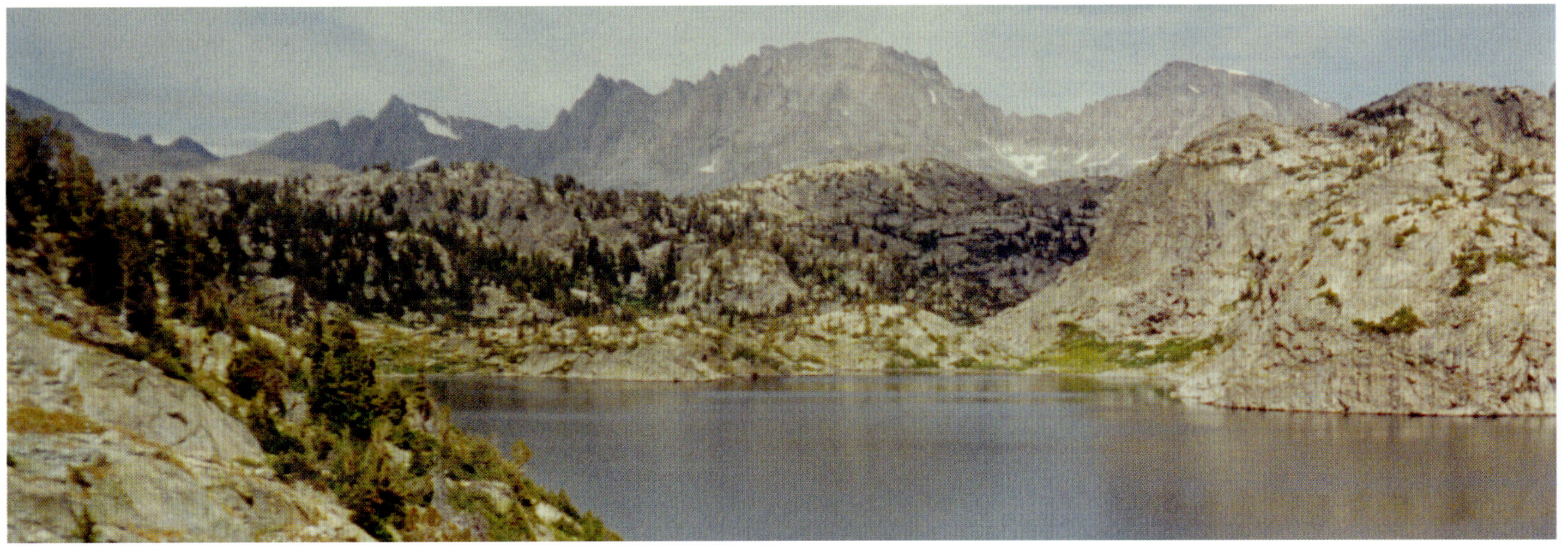

Above: *Second night camp by Seneca Lake, Wind River Range, Wyoming, 1994, photo by Gus Foster.*
Right: *William Henry Jackson, Fremont Peak (from Seneca Lake), albumen print, 1878, Foster Collection.*

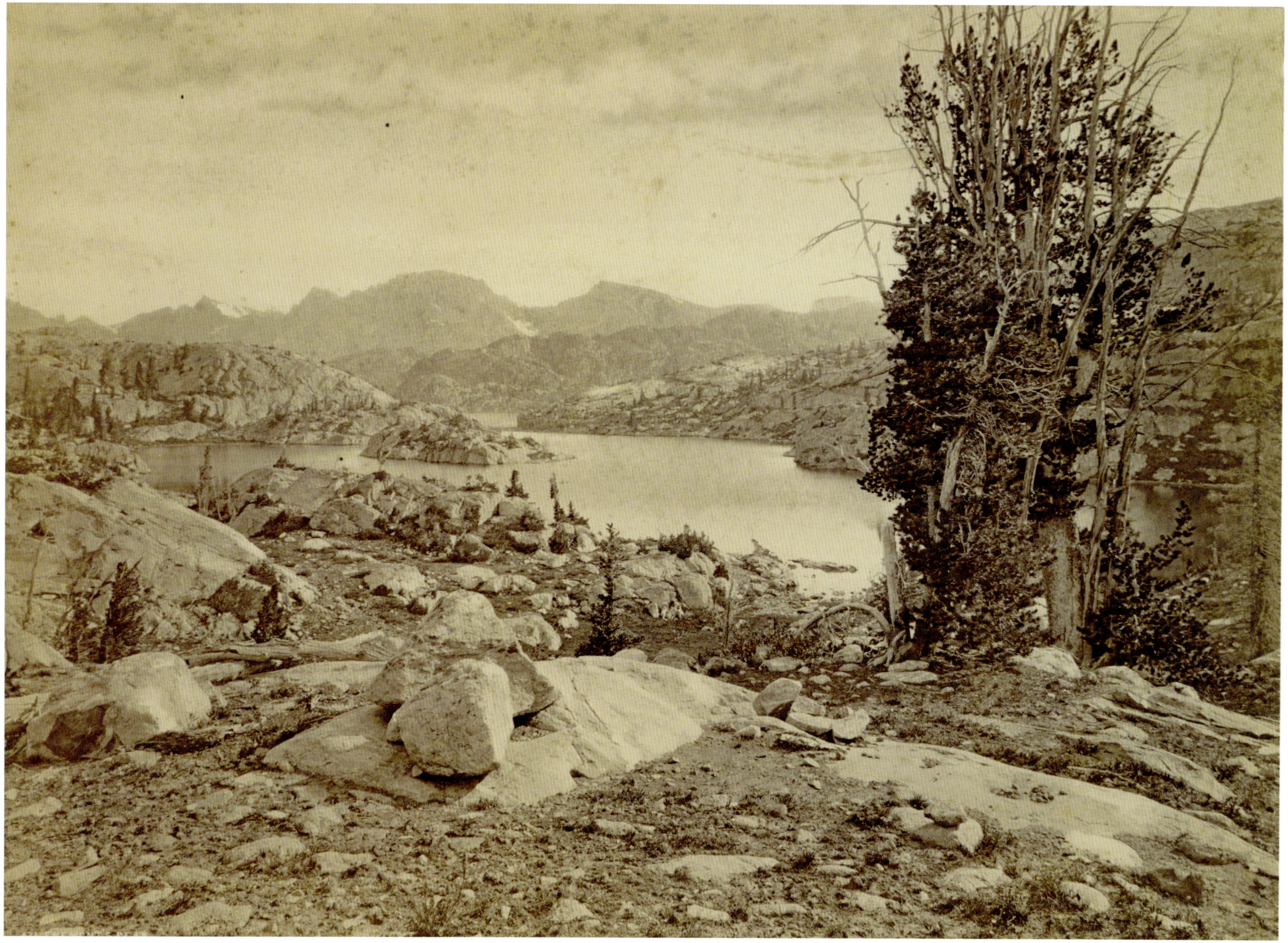

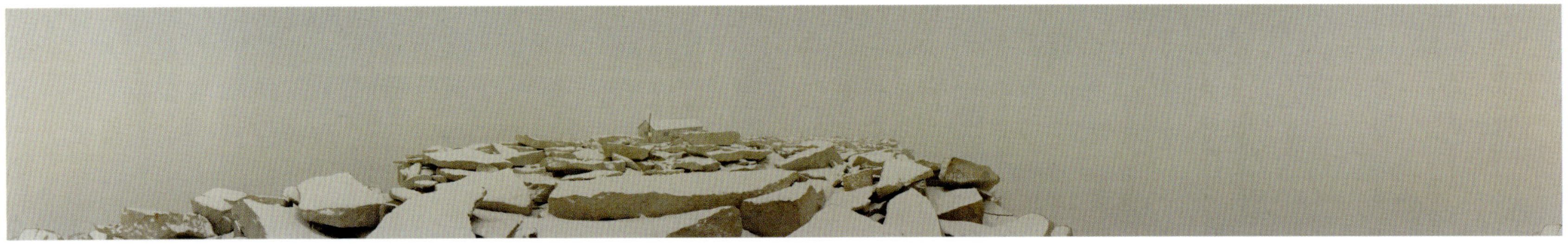

MOUNT WHITNEY | Mount Whitney is, at 14,505 feet, the highest point in the lower forty-eight states, and because of that it is very popular with climbers and tourists from all over. It is so popular that one needs a permit to climb it. In the year we went, six thousand permits were issued. Since I didn't want crowds of people visible in the photograph, my friend John Chamberlain and I opted for an early permit. We went in early June, not winter anywhere else but definitely so in the high Sierras. We drove from New Mexico, parked at a trailhead, then climbed for a day to a popular area for a base camp around 10,500 feet for those wishing to make the summit attempt. The third day, we started up this 3,000-foot slope to the ridge where you then go for maybe three miles to reach the summit. By the time we got on top of the ridge we were in a blizzard; you can only go up so you couldn't really get lost. Finally, we reached the summit, and it was a virtual whiteout. I walked over to the edge. According to the topo map, it was a couple of thousand feet straight down; I couldn't see a thing. I was upset as I had had this image in my head of a fantastic landscape view of endless vistas and in reality I couldn't see 200 feet. Determined not to go home empty-handed after this long trip, I set up the camera, took my consolation photograph, and we started back. Going back was different. You go down the ridge three miles, then descend the slope to your camp, correct? Well, there are no markers, and in a blizzard you can't see much. If you get it wrong, you end up in difficult straits, with no camp, no food, no way out. We sort of figured out where we might be based on elapsed time since leaving the summit. We glissaded down the slope 3,000 feet on our backs using the ice axes for brakes. We were a little off course but managed to make it back to base camp. When I saw the film, I was so happy I had made a shot because it was this very Zen-like image, pure black-and-white, that could have been taken many places—in the Japanese Alps or on the coast of Maine, so instead of disaster I got a winner.

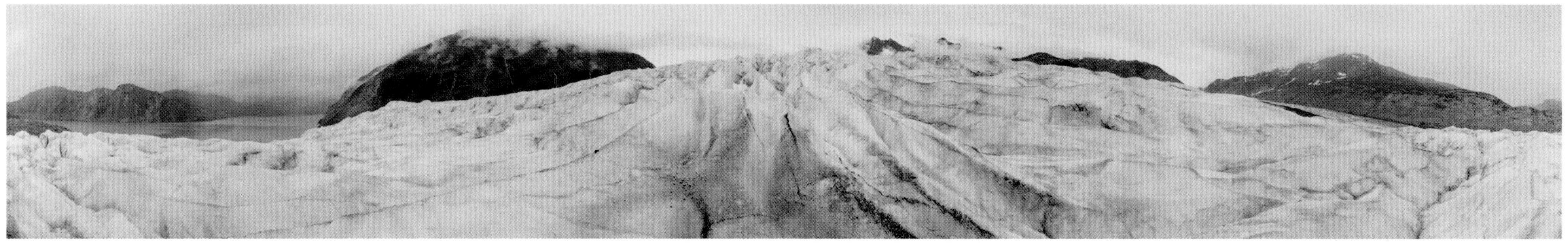

RIGGS GLACIER | Riggs Glacier is one of the glaciers terminating in Glacier Bay, Alaska. To get there I had to charter a small seaplane to deliver Robert Kjessel, me, and our gear into a tiny four-seat plane. Landing on water, the pilot said, "Be on this shore a week from now, don't be late, I'm not waiting and I'm not coming back." Thus began an adventure of ice climbing and camping on the ice. The weather didn't really cooperate: we never had more than a thousand feet visibility, and the temperature never rose above freezing. Setting out at daybreak, we started up the glacier with ropes, ice axes, and the camera. Eight hours later we hadn't gone more than a mile in and up. I looked up and saw this perfect vertical circular hole in the ice in front of me and took it as an omen that this was the perfect place for a photo. In the following days we did three more locations. Then on our last night, when we were in our tent at about 2 a.m., there was this tremendous crash followed by the sound of cascading ice all around us. We thought we had made camp on land, but it turned out to be on unstable black ice, and a huge chunk, ten feet wide by sixty feet long, had calved off not more than twenty feet from our tent's location. We were really lucky to escape unharmed.

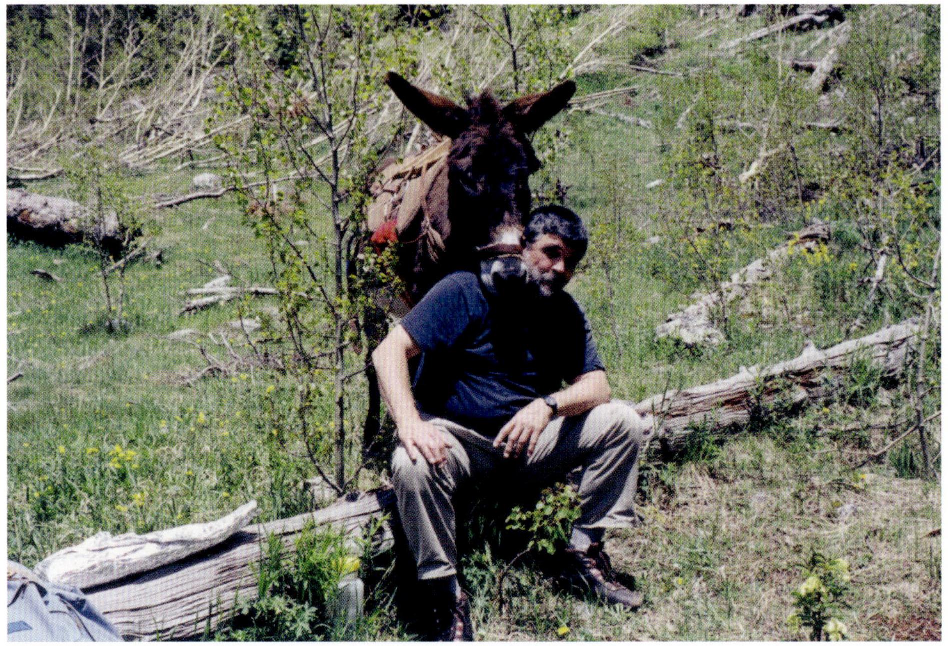
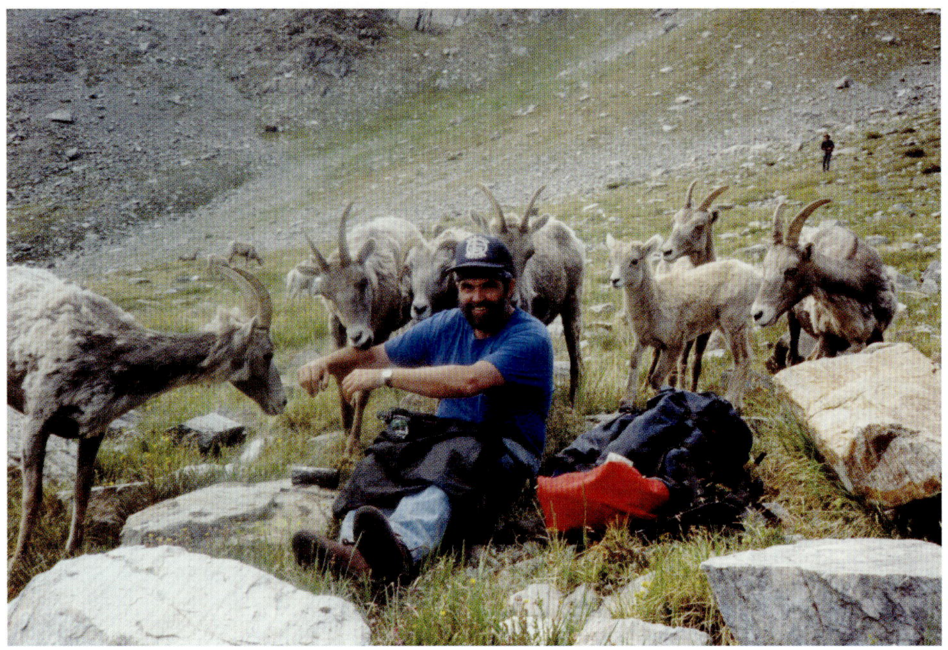
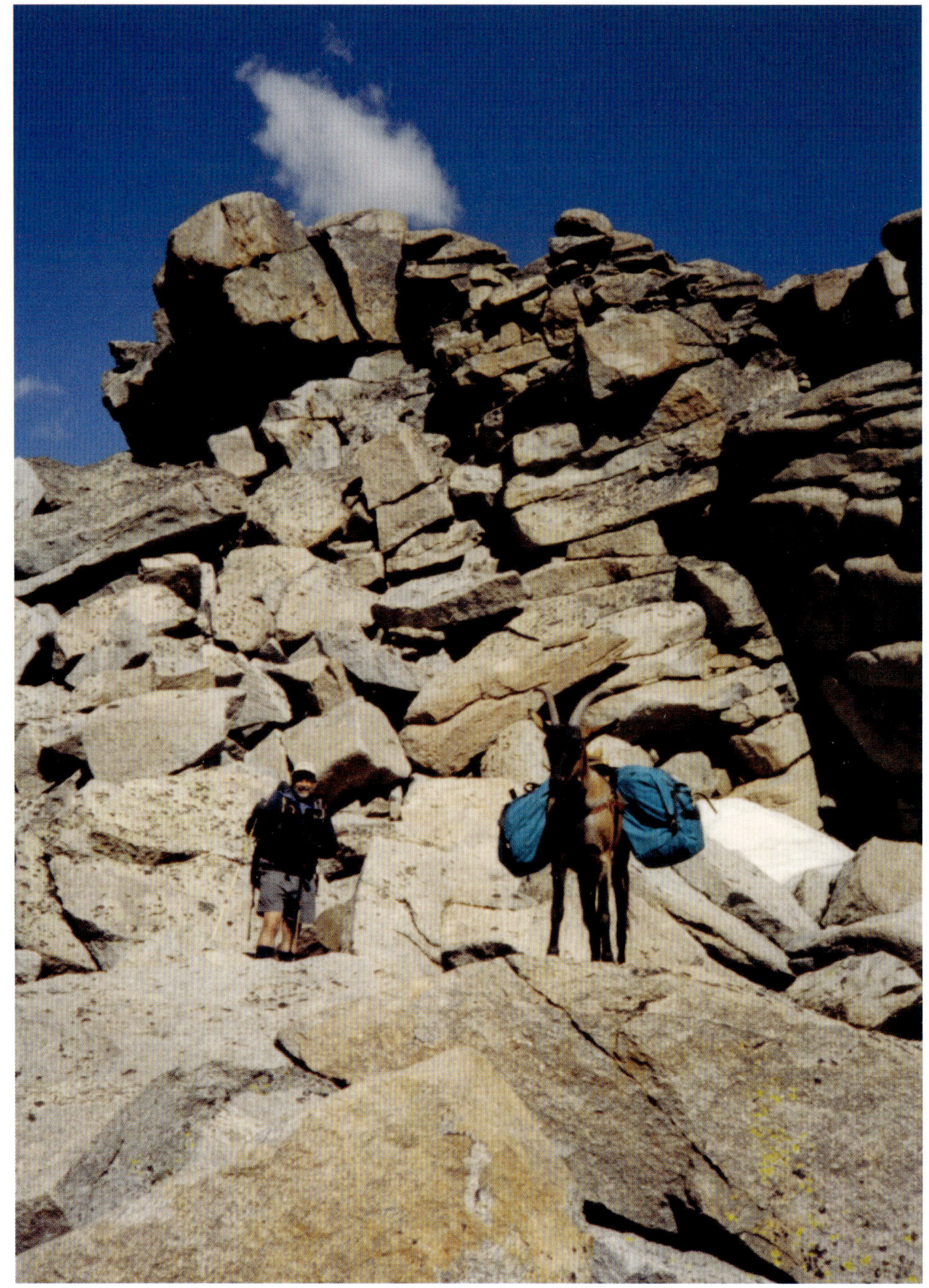

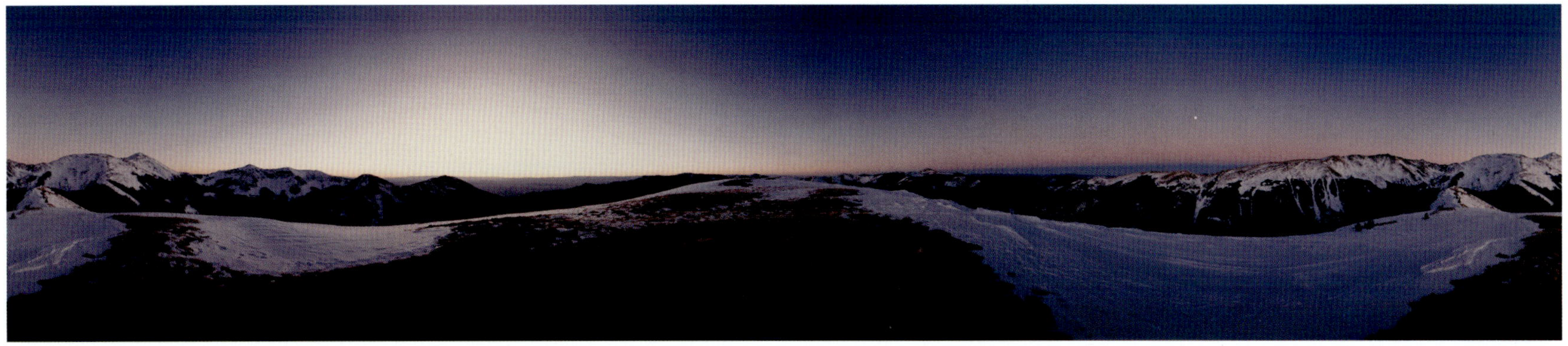

SUNSET, MOONRISE, HIGHLINE RIDGE | About twice a year, there is a time when the setting sun and the rising full moon occur within minutes of each other. I live near Taos Ski Valley and loved to ski there; I knew that the Highline Ridge at nearly twelve thousand feet had a great western view, so I arranged with one of my buddies who drove a snowcat (used to groom the slopes each night) to give me a ride to the base below the Highline Ridge. In ski boots and winter gear, the two of us climbed up eight hundred feet to the ridge with the camera pack and skis. It was something like six degrees below zero that February evening, and the winds were ferocious. We got set up just as the sun set and the rising full moon appeared, we got under the camera to keep it from being blown away, and managed to get one shot. Then my friend took the camera, climbed down the slope to his snowcat, and kept going with his job. I got the singular chance to ski from the ridge all the way down to the bottom of the mountain—no ski patrol, no crowds, nothing but moonlight. It was an unforgettable experience. Besides the special light of that evening, I had hoped for an abundance of snow. When I saw the film, I saw that the wind had stripped most of the snow off the ridge, and I was disappointed in the image, so only made one print of the photograph. It wasn't until thirty years later that I saw the photograph with new eyes and remembered how special the event was.

Left, clockwise from top: *Chico and Gus, Pecos Wilderness, 1988; Gus and William Henry in high country Montana, 1997; Gus and bighorn sheep, Pecos Wilderness, 1989. Photos by Roger Badash.*

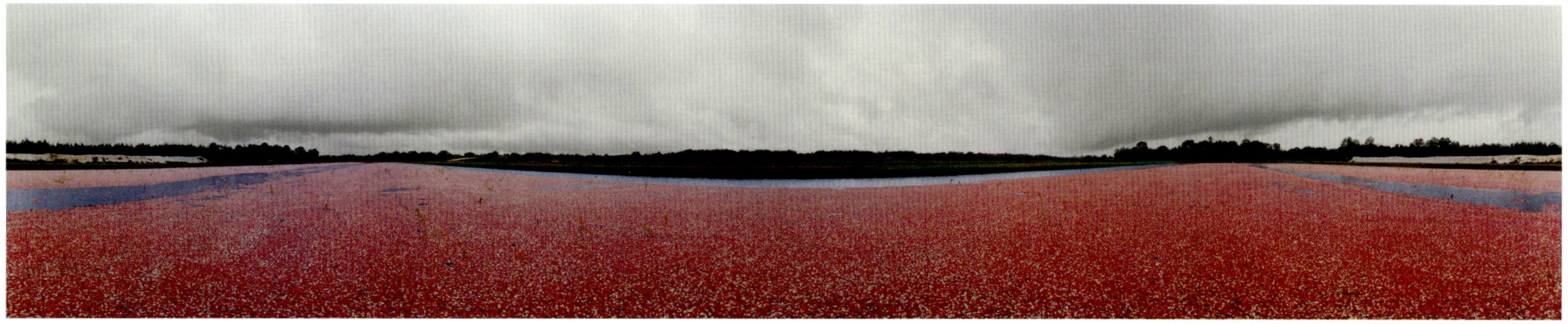

HARVESTING CRANBERRIES | When I was growing up in Wisconsin, wild cranberries grew in bogs in the northern part of the state and were hard to gather. Now they are a popular domesticated crop familiar to many holiday tables. I met a grower who allowed me to photograph the harvest. Cranberry bushes grow near water, but at harvest time the beds are flooded and the fruit, which floats, comes to the surface of the water. The fruit is then skimmed to one end of the growing area and loaded by conveyor belt onto trucks. I was using a brand-new prototype camera, the only one in existence, and had to wade out to the middle of this pond to get the picture. Everything had to be set up in advance as there was nothing but water and fruit out in the middle. The cranberry bushes, under the surface of the water, were a big hazard to me as they couldn't be seen, and one false step or tripping on a bush in my waders would have been the end of this one-of-a-kind camera. I was never happier to be back on dry land.

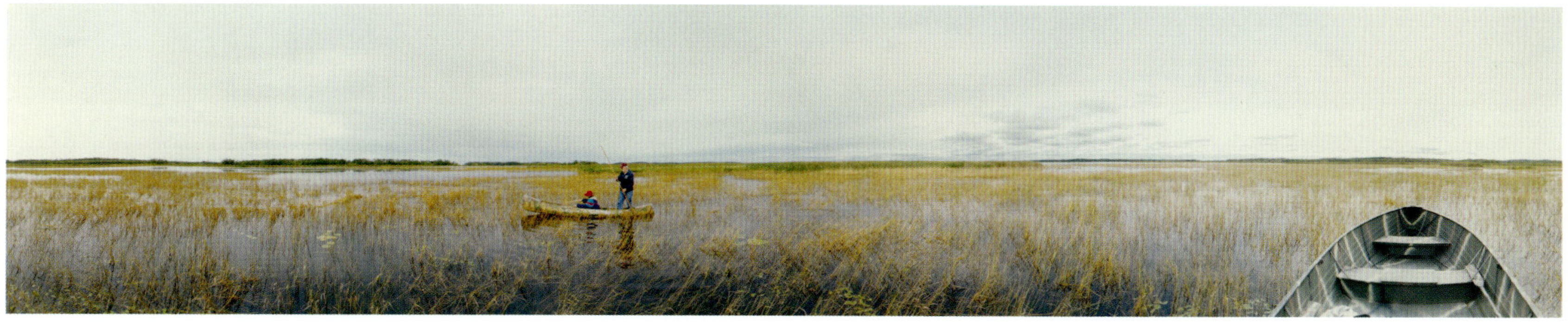

HARVESTING WILD RICE | Wild rice, in the United States, only grows in the northernmost regions of Minnesota and Wisconsin and in its wild natural form can only be harvested by Native Americans to whom it is sacred food. Ron Libertus, a friend from my old days in Minneapolis, was a member of the Anishinaabe or Chippewa Nation in northern Minnesota on Leech Lake. He got permission from the tribe for me to be able to photograph while he and his wife harvested the rice from a canoe just the way it has been done for hundreds of years. I was working on a project photographing food as it was grown around the United States as we approached the millennium, and was thinking about a food crop that existed and had been used a millennium before. I thought I would just go out, set my tripod on the lake bottom, do my shot, and be done with it. The water turned out to be twelve feet deep, so I ended up having to set up in an unsteady fishing boat some distance from the canoe. I got the photograph but it was not a 360-degree image without including the bow of the boat. Modern times intruded on my ancient scenario.

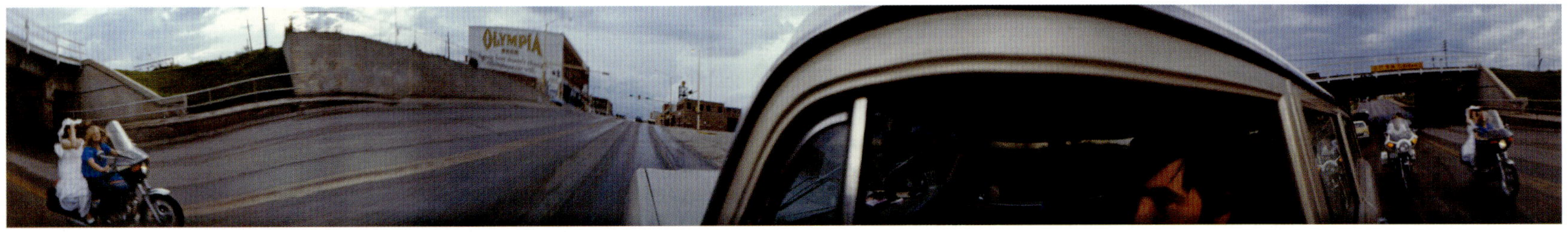

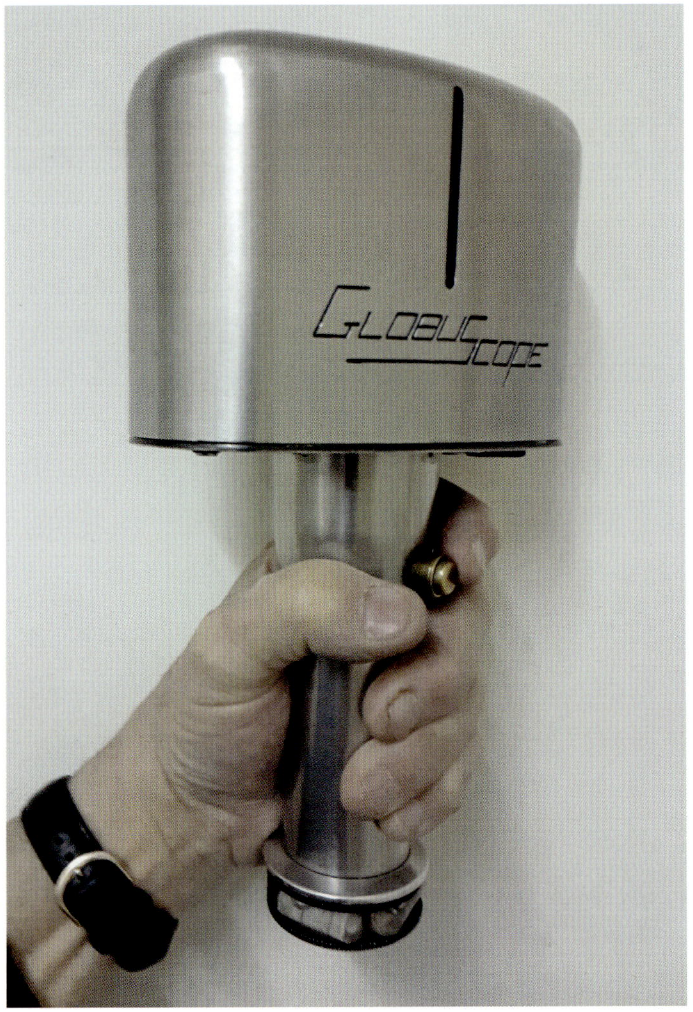

NEBRASKA WEDDING | I got my first 35mm Globuscope camera in 1982, a wonderful, lightweight (5 pound) handheld device invented by Ron Globus. It made a 360-degree revolution in 8/10ths of a second. I had only had the camera for about six weeks when, on a cross-country driving trip, I had the only Eureka moment of my life. I was driving through Hastings, Nebraska, when I saw a bride in full white gown on the back of a motorcycle. The scene struck my funny bone; I grabbed the camera, stuck it out the open window of the car I was driving, and managed to capture the bride on her way to the church twice as I passed her in my car. I realized immediately what the camera was capable of recording, and my Time Photographs began. The photograph was like a frozen movie, capable of telling a story about the passage of time. Unlike the Cirkut panoramic camera I had used, which took forty seconds to complete the circle, this device could do it in one second.

The Globuscope

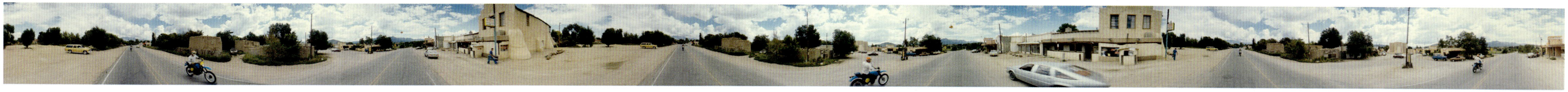

PASSING TIME IN RANCHOS | St. Francis of Assisi Church in Ranchos de Taos, New Mexico, is a landmark known for generations to visitors, painters, and photographers for its great adobe buttresses and architecture. O'Keeffe, Weston, Strand, and Stieglitz all painted or photographed this icon, and I wanted to do my version, too, so I asked Gene Dobos, another artist in town who owned a vintage World War II jeep that was open-top and had a short wheelbase, if he would drive me past the church while I stood behind him taking a picture with my Globuscope. We did this, driving down the road at the posted 35 mph speed limit. I started taking the picture when an impatient young guy on a motorcycle passed us on the double-yellow no passing line, and when he had completed his maneuver, he gave us the classic middle finger salute. Sadly, by that time the camera had run out of film, but I still got the story and the famous church, too, one of my favorite Time Photographs.

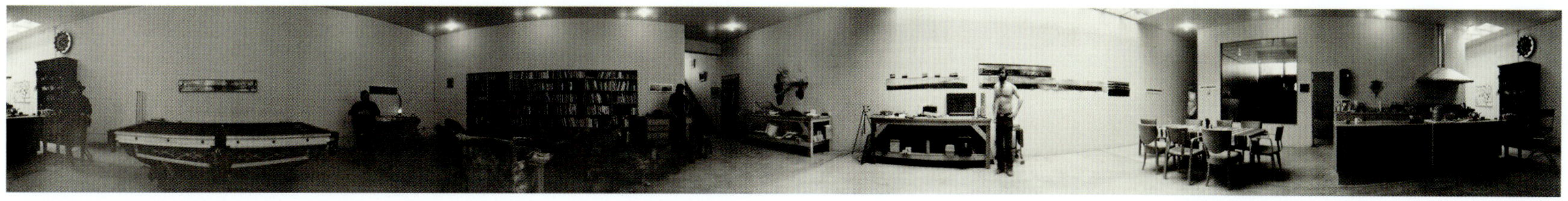

STUDIO SELF-PORTRAIT | One of the early uses of the panorama camera was to do group portraits of large military assemblies or graduating school classes. In the latter group, it was discovered that if a guy at one end of the shot got off the bleachers and ran like hell, he could get around the camera and get into the photograph from the other end of the line, thus being photographed twice. I always liked the joke, so one day I had the idea to do a version of that but with some differences. I started fully clothed under the big clock in the studio, then raced around counterclockwise to the direction of the lens, removing a piece of clothing each time I went around the camera. I had an English setter named Blue who thought this exercise was great fun so he started chasing me around the room, too. By the fifth time around, I was trying to take my pants off when I tripped on the dog, and thus was unable to get back to where I had started under the clock, preserving my modesty but leaving an empty chair under the clock when the circle was completed. In 2004, with a modern prototype of the camera, I did a version in the Taos Plaza, where I managed to get to seven different locations in the photograph (see plate 64).

EXHIBITIONS

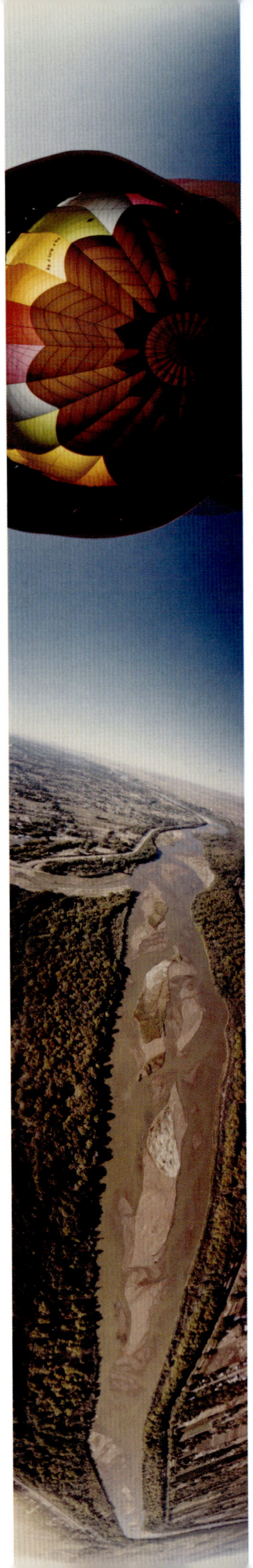

1978 *Artwords and Bookworks*, Los Angeles Institute of Contemporary Art, CA

1979 *Cooper, Foster, Hall*, Maggie Kress Gallery, Taos, NM

New Mexico Photographers, Santa Fe Festival of the Arts, NM

1981 *ARTlines: The First Eighteen Months*, Stables Art Center, Taos, NM

Group Exhibition, Taylor Gallery, Taos, NM

1982 Santa Fe Festival of the Arts, NM

Panoramic Photographs by Gus Foster, L.A. Louver Gallery, Venice, CA

Panoramic Photographs by Gus Foster, Marian Goodman Gallery, New York, NY

1983 *Around New Mexico*, DVS/Photographs, Taos, NM

Erotic Art, Advanced Art Gallery, Rinconada, NM

Six Seconds Real Time, Advanced Art Gallery, Rinconada, NM

Current Images, Unicorn Gallery, Aspen, CO

1984 *Christmas in Taos*, DVS/Photographs, Taos, NM

Gus Foster Panoramic Photographs, University of Michigan Art Museum, Ann Arbor

Panoramic Photographs by Gus Foster, Multiples/Goodman Gallery, New York, NY

Photographs in Color, DVS/Photographs, Taos, NM

Architecture of the Southwest, Stables Art Center, Taos, NM

The Animal Kingdom, Stables Art Center, Taos, NM

HOT AIR OVER RIO GRANDE, BERNALILLO COUNTY, NEW MEXICO | 1982 | 360°

1985 *Art in Embassies*, United States Department of State, Washington, DC
Photography from Northern New Mexico, Mission Gallery, Taos, NM
The Art Makers, Conlon Grenfell Gallery, San Diego, CA
On the Wall/Off the Wall, Center for Contemporary Art, Santa Fe, NM
Landscapes of the Southwest, Stables Art Center, Taos, NM
Embellished Calendars: An Illustrated History, Cooper Hewitt Museum, New York, NY

1986 *Road Show* (with R. Doen Tobey), San Juan College, Farmington, NM
Photography from Northern New Mexico, Mission Gallery, Taos, NM
Statements 86, Fine Arts Gallery, New Mexico State Fairgrounds, Albuquerque
Panoramic Photographs by Gus Foster, Bergstrom Mahler Museum, Neenah, WI
Panoramic Photographs by Gus Foster, Leigh Yawkey Woodson Museum, Wausau, WI
The Pueblos of New Mexico, Stables Art Center, Taos, NM
The New West, Colorado Springs Art Center, CO

1987 *Food for Thought*, Stables Art Center, Taos, NM
Earth Eyes/Sky Eyes, Two Photographers: Chappell, Foster, Wohlert Gallery/Nob Hill Café, Albuquerque, NM
Gus Foster: Panoramic Photographs, Lansing Community College, MI
Artists of Taos 1987, Stables Art Center, Taos, NM
Skyborn: Aerial Photography, North Dakota Museum of Art, Grand Forks, ND
Visions, Fine Arts Gallery, New Mexico State Fairgrounds, Albuquerque
Poetics of Space, New Mexico Museum of Fine Arts, Santa Fe

1988 *Vistas Buenas: Panoramas of Taos County*, Centinel Bank, Taos, NM
Photo Panoramas, Southern Alleghenies Museum of Art, Loretto, PA
Time Photographs, Jones Troyer Fitzpatrick Gallery, Washington, DC
Artists of Taos 1988, Stables Art Center, Taos, NM
Panoramic Photographs by Gus Foster, Kirby Arts Center, Lawrenceville, NJ
Time Photographs: Central Avenue, Hoshour Gallery, Albuquerque, NM
New Mexico Wilderness, Focus Series, Albuquerque Museum, NM

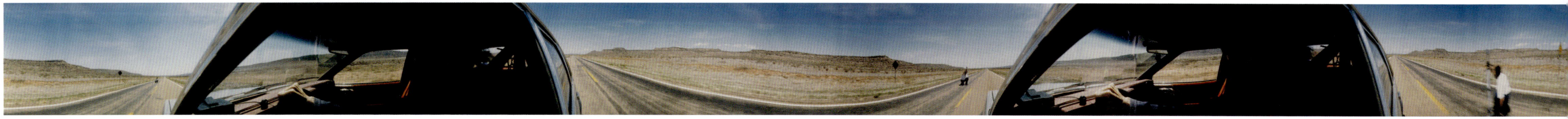

Visions, Fine Arts Gallery, New Mexico State Fairgrounds, Albuquerque

1989 *Contemporary Photography in New Mexico*, Stables Art Center, Taos, NM

1989 Invitational, Roswell Museum and Art Center, NM

Gus Foster Panoramic Photographs, Cirrus Gallery, Los Angeles, CA

American Hieroglyphics, Stewarts Fine Art Gallery, Taos, NM

150th Anniversary of Photography, Latvian Photo Art Society, Riga, Latvia, USSR

Time Photographs: 1989 World Alpine Championships, Village Hall, Beaver Creek, CO

Rendezvous: Bell, Cooper, Foster, West, Broschofsky Galleries, Ketchum, ID

High Country, New Mexico Museum of Natural History, Albuquerque

1990 *Corporate Art Wisconsin*, Wisconsin Manufacturers & Commerce, Madison

Night Moves, Millicent Rogers Museum, Taos, NM

Panoramic Photographs by Gus Foster, Albuquerque Museum, NM

Center for Contemporary Arts Invitational, CCA, Santa Fe, NM

Taos Up Close, Mission Gallery, Taos, NM

Gus Foster Panoramic Photographs, New Gallery, Houston, TX

1991 *21 Photographers from New Mexico*, Visions Gallery, San Francisco, CA

Gus Poster Panoramic Photographs, Thomson Gallery, Minneapolis, MN

Gus Foster Panoramic Photographs, CAFE Gallery, Albuquerque, NM

Contemporary Photographers, Ginny Williams Gallery, Denver, CO

Aspects of Landscape, Nutralite Products, Buena Park, CA

1992 *Gus Foster USA 360*, European Center for American Photography, Gallery Mlada Fronta, Prague, Czechoslovakia

Christmas at Taos Pueblo, Taos Inn, NM

Tokaido Road Panoramic Photographs, CAFE Gallery, Albuquerque, NM

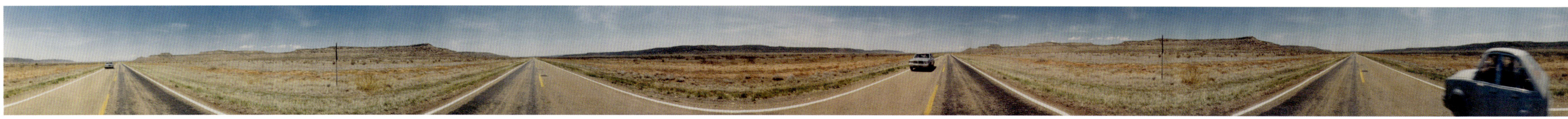

TOP: RELATIVITY ON THE ROAD, SAN MIGUEL COUNTY, NEW MEXICO | 1988 | 1404° (WITH RUTH TOBEY)

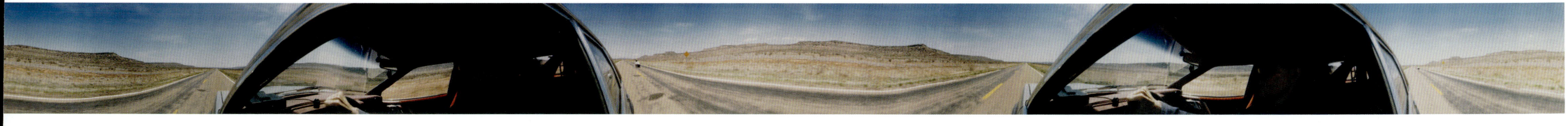

Tokaido Road Panoramic Photographs, Harwood Foundation Museum, Taos, NM
Landscapes of Northern New Mexico, Taos Inn, NM
Speaking with the Ancestors, Stables Art Center, Taos, NM
Between Home and Heaven, National Museum of American Art, Washington, DC
The New Romantics, Jones Troyer Fitzpatrick Gallery, Washington, DC

1993 *Contemporary Art Society V*, CAFE Gallery, Albuquerque, NM
Views of Kyoto, Cirrus Gallery, Los Angeles, CA
The Tokaido Road, Doizaki Gallery, Japanese American Cultural Center, Los Angeles, CA
Gus Foster Panoramic Photographs, Thomson Gallery, Minneapolis, MN
Gus Foster/Panoramic Photographs, Minneapolis Institute of Arts, MN
Above New Mexico Skies, Governor's Gallery, State Capitol, Santa Fe, NM

1994 *Panoramic Photographs*, Trading Post Cafe, Taos, NM
The Tokaido Road: Panoramic Photographs of the Fifty Three Stations, Sasakawa Peace Foundation USA, Washington, DC
Plains, Jones Troyer Fitzpatrick Gallery, Washington, DC
Time, Stables Art Center, Taos, NM
Quiet Skies, Bareiss Contemporary Exhibitions, Taos, NM

1995 *Wilderness Landscapes*, Nicholas/Alexander Gallery, New York, NY
New Work, New Directions Gallery, Taos, NM

1996 *Plain Pictures: Images of the American Prairie*, University of Iowa Museum of Art, Iowa City
Taos Invites Taos, Civic Plaza, Taos, NM
The Real West, Denver Art Museum, CO
Eye of the Camera, 3M, St. Paul, MN
New Mexico Landscape, Taos Inn Invitational, NM

1997 *Taos Invites Taos*, Civic Plaza, Taos, NM

1998 *Land and Water: The Artists' Point of View*, Colorado Springs Fine Arts Center, CO
Tokaido Road: Gus Foster and Ando Hiroshige, Minneapolis Institute of Arts, MN

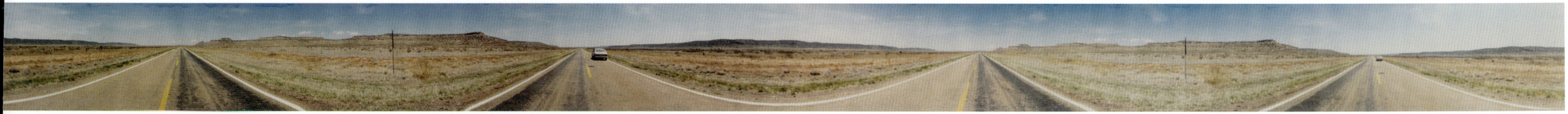

BOTTOM: RELATIVITY ON THE ROAD, SAN MIGUEL COUNTY, NEW MEXICO | 1998 | 1424°

New Works by Contemporary Artists,
Gerald Peters Gallery, Santa Fe, NM
Meet the Artist: Taos Inn Invitational, NM

1999 *The American Rockies: Photographs by Gus Foster*,
Albuquerque Museum, NM

2001 *Route 66: Panoramic Photographs by Gus Foster*,
University of New Mexico Art Museum, Albuquerque, NM
The American Rockies: Photographs by Gus Foster,
Colorado Springs Fine Arts Center, CO
The Great Wide Open: Panoramic Photographs and the American West, Huntington Library, San Marino, CA
In the Eye of the Beholder: Ten Photographers,
Health Science Center, University of New Mexico, Albuquerque, NM

2002 *Photographers, Writers, and the American Scene*,
Museum of Photographic Art, San Diego, CA

2003 *The Full Circle: Panoramic Photographs of the American West by Gus Foster*, Buffalo Bill Historic Center, Cody, WY
Large Format Photography in New Mexico,
516 Magnifico Artspace, Albuquerque, NM
Pilot Hill Collection of American Art,
Crocker Art Museum, Sacramento, CA
The Peaks and Plains of New Mexico: Panoramic Photographs by Gus Foster, Gerald Peters Gallery, Santa Fe, NM
Retrospectacle: 25 Years of Collecting Modern and Contemporary Art Photography, Denver Art Museum, CO
Art from the American Heartland, Art in Embassies Exhibition, US Embassy, Berlin, Germany

2004 *Creativity: Beyond the Norm*, Richard M. Ross Art Museum, Ohio Wesleyan University, Delaware, OH

2005 *Native Lands*, US Embassy, Tashkent, Uzbekistan
Gus Foster: The American Landscape Panorama,
Leigh Yawkey Art Museum, Wausau, WI

2006 *Yosemite: Art of an American Icon*, Autry Museum of the American West, Los Angeles, CA

2007 *Gus Foster and Ando Hiroshige: The Tokaido Road*,
Kalamazoo Institute of Arts, MI

2008 *Art in Embassies Exhibition*, US Embassy,
Nouakchott, Mauritania

2012 *Panoramic Photographs of the American West: Photographs by Gus Foster*, Gilcrease Museum, Tulsa, OK

2014 *New Art/New Mexico*, Richard M. Ross Art Museum,
Ohio Wesleyan University, Delaware, OH
Panorama: Gus Foster, Carlos Silva, Robert Vignoli,
333 Montezuma Gallery, Santa Fe, NM

WORKS IN PUBLIC COLLECTIONS

Albuquerque Museum, NM
The Art Institute of Chicago, IL
Autry Museum of the American West, Los Angeles, CA
Buffalo Bill Historic Center, Cody, WY
Center for Contemporary Art, Santa Fe, NM
Colorado Historical Society, Denver, CO
Colorado Springs Fine Arts Center, CO
Cooper-Hewitt, National Museum of Design, Smithsonian Institution, New York, NY
Davison Art Center, Wesleyan University, Middletown, CT
Denver Art Museum, CO
European Center for American Photography, Prague, Czech Republic
The Harwood Museum of Art, University of New Mexico, Taos, NM
High Museum of Art, Atlanta, GA
Joslyn Art Museum, Omaha, NE
Kirby Art Center, Lawrenceville, NJ
Latvian Photo Art Society, Riga, Latvia
Los Angeles Institute of Contemporary Art, CA
Mayo Clinic Art Collection, Rochester, MN
Millicent Rogers Museum of Northern New Mexico, Taos, NM
Minneapolis Institute of Art, MN
Museum of Decorative Art, Prague, Czech Republic
Museum of Fine Arts, Santa Fe, NM
National Museum of American Art, Washington, DC
Nelson Atkins Art Museum, Kansas City, MO
New Mexico Capitol Collection, directed by the Capitol Art Foundation, State Capitol, Santa Fe, NM
New Mexico Museum of Art, Santa Fe, NM
Phoenix Art Museum, AZ
Richard M. Ross Art Museum, Ohio Wesleyan University, Delaware, OH
San Juan College, Farmington, NM
Taos Public Library, NM
University of Michigan Museum of Art, Ann Arbor, MI
University of Missouri, Miller Nichols Library, Kansas City, MO
University of New Mexico Art Museum, Albuquerque, NM
US Embassy, Tashkent, Uzbekistan
Yale University Art Museum, New Haven, CT

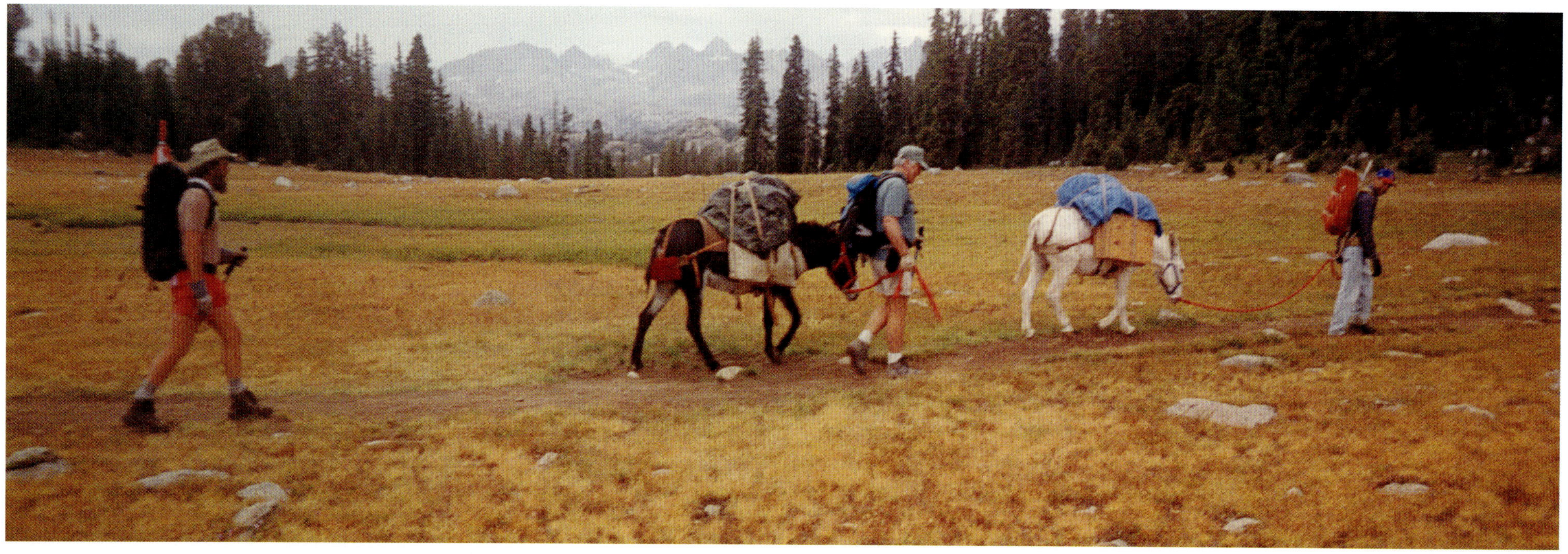
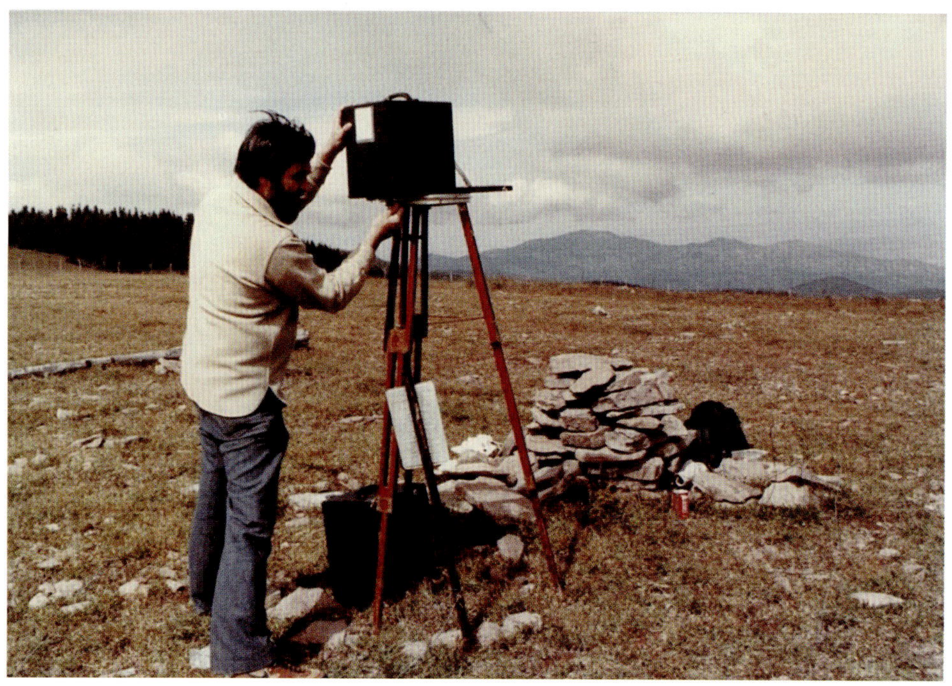
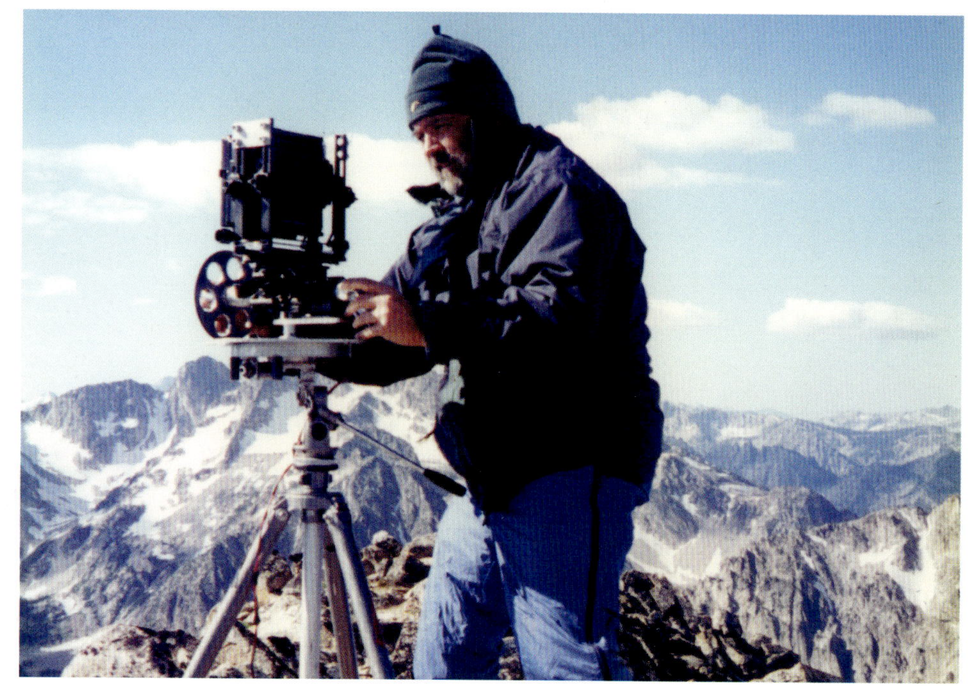

BIOGRAPHY

1940 Born October 22, in Wausau, WI

1952 First darkroom, Wausau, WI

1963 Graduated with BA in history of art from Yale University, New Haven, CT

1965–68 Assistant Curator of Prints and Drawings, Minneapolis Institute of Arts, MN

1968–72 Curator of Prints and Drawings, Minneapolis Institute of Arts, MN

1972 Moved to Los Angeles, CA
Darkrooms in Hollywood and Venice
Founded Sure Co. publishing, 1974–76

1974 Acquired Templeton Laundry property with artist Larry Bell, Taos, NM
Remodeled and constructed double studio with Larry Bell

1975 Acquired first panoramic camera, #8 Century Cirkut outfit

1976 Moved from Venice, CA, to Taos, NM, in November
Acquired #10 Cirkut camera
Built a black-and-white panoramic darkroom in studio

1979 First exhibition of panoramic photographs, Maggie Kress Gallery, Taos

1980 First use of Kodak 9½-inch color aerial film
Climbed first 14,000-foot summit, Handies Peak, CO

1982 Purchased 35mm Globuscope panoramic camera.

1982 First "Time Photographs"
First solo exhibitions: L.A. Louver Gallery, Venice, CA; Marian Goodman Gallery, New York, NY

1984 First color panoramas printed in Taos
First solo museum exhibition: University of Michigan Art Museum, Ann Arbor, MI

1985 Acquired Emil Bisttram studio, Taos, NM

1986 Acquired 5-inch Globus-Holway panoramic scanning camera
Designed and fabricated custom color enlarger for 5 x 25-inch negatives
Built first color darkroom studio

1991 Walked the Tokaido Road, Tokyo to Kyoto, Japan

1992 First solo exhibition in Europe, Prague, Czechoslovakia

1993 Exhibition and catalog *Gus Foster/Panoramic Photographs*, Minneapolis Institute of Arts, MN

1998 Remodeled and constructed current color lab and studio, Taos

1999 Exhibition and catalog *The American Rockies: Photographs by Gus Foster*, Albuquerque Museum, NM

2004 Cross Country I, 1,901-mile walk from Juárez, Mexico, to Sault Sainte Marie, Canada

2005 Cross Country II, 2,263-mile walk from Montana/Canada border to lands end, Gulf of Mexico, FL

Left, clockwise from top: *John, Chico, Jim, Sidney, Roger, Bridger Wilderness, Wyoming, 1994, photo by Gus Foster; Globus-Holway camera, Alpine Peak, The Sawtooths, Idaho, 1996, photo by Roger Badash; #10 Cirkut camera, Jicarita Peak, Pecos Wilderness, New Mexico, 1979, photo by Ruth Tobey.*

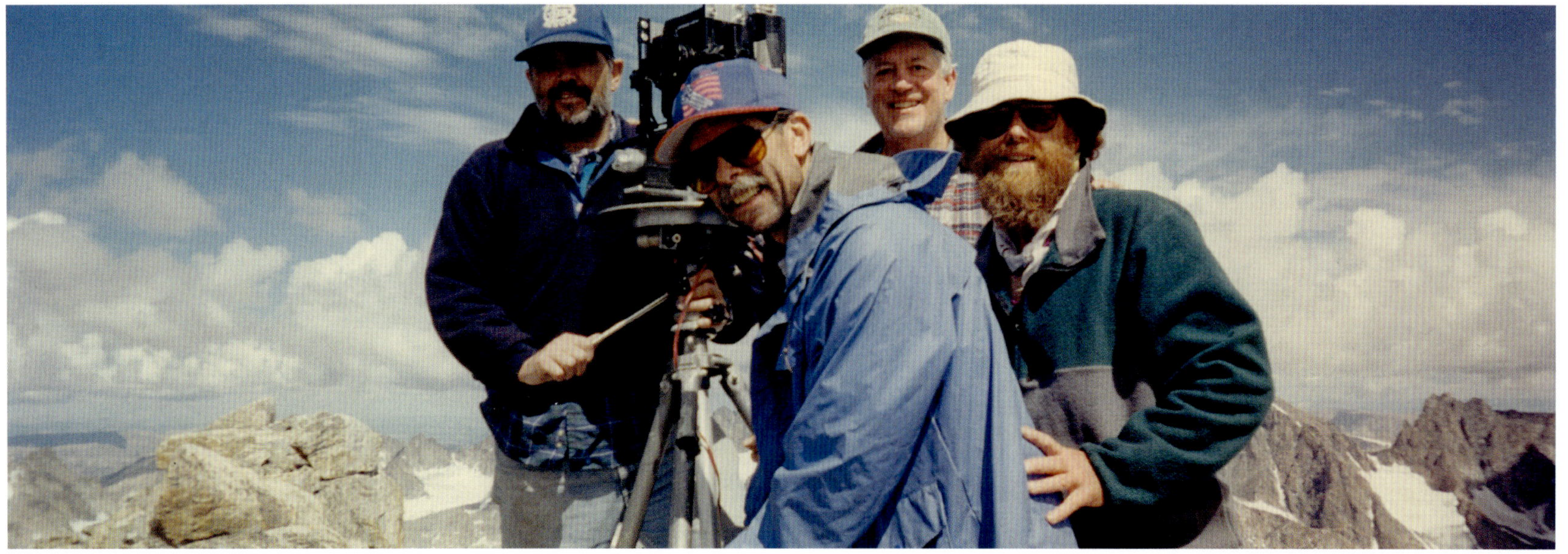

ACKNOWLEDGMENTS

To my family and friends: Alexandra Benjamin, Scott and Josie Foster, Larry Bell, Janet Webb, Desiree Manville

To my mountain partners: Tom Simons, Roger Badash, John Chamberlain, and the memories of the animals who made the journeys possible

To the authors: Evan Maurer, Jim Enyeart, and the late Ned Hall

To those who contributed to the book: Barry Norris and Sasha vom Dorp for the studio photography

To Michael Motley for the design, and Lucas Sharp and Chantra Malee for the typeface

To Jim and Lina Beckley and Sherman and Joyce Scott for their love and support

To Outward Bound and Taos Search and Rescue for my development and training in wilderness skills

To the artists who share their vision and the museums and galleries that show their work

Thank you all

Above: *Gus Foster, Roger Badash, Jim Beckley, and John Chamberlain, Fremont Peak, Wyoming, 1994*